Political Dramaturgies and Theatre Spectatorship

Methuen Drama Engage offers original reflections about key practitioners, movements and genres in the fields of modern theatre and performance. Each volume in the series seeks to challenge mainstream critical thought through original and interdisciplinary perspectives on the body of work under examination. By questioning existing critical paradigms, it is hoped that each volume will open up fresh approaches and suggest avenues for further exploration.

Series Editors
Mark Taylor-Batty
University of Leeds, UK

Enoch Brater
University of Michigan, USA

Titles
Adaptation in Contemporary Theatre
by Frances Babbage
ISBN 978-1-4725-3142-1

Authenticity in Contemporary Theatre and Performance
by Daniel Schulze
ISBN 978-1-3500-0096-4

Drama and Digital Arts Cultures
by David Cameron, Michael Anderson and Rebecca Wotzko
ISBN 978-1-472-59219-4

Social and Political Theatre in 21st-Century Britain: Staging Crisis
by Vicky Angelaki
ISBN 978-1-474-21316-5

Watching War on the Twenty-First-Century Stage: Spectacles of Conflict
by Clare Finburgh
ISBN 978-1-472-59866-0

Fiery Temporalities in Theatre and Performance: The Initiation of History
by Maurya Wickstrom
ISBN 978-1-4742-8169-0

Ecologies of Precarity in Twenty-First Century Theatre: Politics, Affect, Responsibility
by Marissia Fragkou
ISBN 978-1-4742-6714-4

Robert Lepage/Ex Machina: Revolutions in Theatrical Space
by James Reynolds

ISBN 978-1-4742-7609-2

Social Housing in Performance: The English Council Estate on and off Stage
by Katie Beswick
ISBN 978-1-4742-8521-6

Postdramatic Theatre and Form
Edited by Michael Shane Boyle, Matt Cornish and Brandon Woolf
ISBN 978-1-3500-4316-9

For a complete listing, please visit
https://www.bloomsbury.com/series/methuen-drama-engage/

Political Dramaturgies and Theatre Spectatorship

Provocations for Change

Liz Tomlin

Series Editors
Enoch Brater and Mark Taylor-Batty

methuen | drama

LONDON • NEW YORK • OXFORD • NEW DELHI • SYDNEY

METHUEN DRAMA
Bloomsbury Publishing Plc
50 Bedford Square, London, WC1B 3DP, UK
1385 Broadway, New York, NY 10018, USA

BLOOMSBURY, METHUEN DRAMA and the Methuen Drama
logo are trademarks of Bloomsbury Publishing Plc

First published in Great Britain 2019

Series design by Louise Dugdale
Cover image: From Andy Smith's *Summit* © Richard Lakos

A catalogue record for this book is available from the British Library.

Library of Congress Cataloging-in-Publication Data
Names: Tomlin, Liz, author.
Title: Political dramaturgies and theatre : spectatorship provocations for
change / Liz Tomlin.
Description: London, UK ; New York, NY : Bloomsbury Publishing Plc, 2019. |
Series: Methuen drama engage | Includes bibliographical references and index.
Identifiers: LCCN 2018056544| ISBN 9781474295604 (hb) | ISBN 9781474295628
(epdf) | ISBN 9781474295611 (eBook)
Subjects: LCSH: Theater–Political aspects. | Political plays. | Theater and society.
Classification: LCC PN2049 .T62 2019 | DDC 792–dc23 LC record available at
https://lccn.loc.gov/2018056544

ISBN: HB: 978-1-4742-9560-4
ePDF: 978-1-4742-9562-8
eBook: 978-1-4742-9561-1

Series: Methuen Drama Engage

Typeset by Integra Software Services Pvt. Ltd.
Printed and bound in Great Britain

To find out more about our authors and books visit www.bloomsbury.com
and sign up for our newsletters.

For my parents, Ted and Dorothy Tomlin, without whose lifelong love and support none of this would have been possible.

Contents

Acknowledgements

This book is the product of a number of years of reading, spectating and thinking together with friends, colleagues and students, and owes a debt of gratitude to far more people than I can acknowledge here by name. It would certainly not have happened without the periods of study leave that were generously afforded to me by the two institutions that have supported the project: the University of Birmingham where the project began and the University of Glasgow where it was completed. I have been lucky in both institutions to have been practically and intellectually supported by excellent and inspiring colleagues and students throughout.

My thinking on this project has also been immeasurably enriched by colleagues on the working groups in which I have participated during the time of writing: the Political Performances working group that is part of the International Federation of Theatre Research and the Performance, Community, Identity working group that forms part of the Theatre and Performance Research Association. Heartfelt thanks must also go to my colleagues in the Contemporary British Theatre Research Group in Barcelona who have informed and invigorated my thinking on notions of affect in particular, as well as providing wonderful retreats for reflection and collective research more broadly.

I would like to acknowledge Made in China, Common Wealth, Developing Artists and Andy Smith for access to unpublished work and for granting me permissions to cite from those sources here. I would also like to thank Tim Cowbury, Evie Manning, Andy Smith and Chris Thorpe for spending the time to share their own reflections on their practice with me, especially given that they may not always be in full agreement with the particular conclusions I have drawn. I would also like to extend thanks to Linda Taylor for inspiring conversations over the years, Caroline Radcliffe and Carl Lavery for very helpful readings of draft material, and particular thanks to Cristina Delgado-García who dedicated such generous time to helping me work through this project in its later and final stages.

Thanks to Mark Dudgeon, the team at Methuen Drama and the series editors for their patience with me while this book was being written in the midst of a move to a new job and country; to my parents for their unceasing support; and to Joseph, without whom this book would simply not have been possible.

Introduction

This book is concerned with how the address to the theorized spectator might be imagined by, or folded into, political dramaturgies that are designed for spectators who do not yet exist. It is concerned with invitations to meaning, possibilities of affect and calls to action. It is concerned with the artistic interpellation of the neoliberal subject and the strategic recognition and misrecognition of that subject in ways that might subvert hegemonic norms. It is concerned, above all, with the tension between the intentions of the theatre artist to provoke political change and the autonomy of the contemporary spectator to resist ideological steer.

The imagined, implicit or ideal spectator has always been vital to the design of political dramaturgies of theatre, and this study seeks to make the importance of such a figure explicit. Central to this book's argument is the proposal that the changing discursive conceptions of the mode of political in play, throughout recent European theatre history and across different models of performance, have pivoted around the degree to which the dramaturgy aims to elicit desired political responses from the spectator or prioritizes the spectator's autonomy to produce their own interpretation. Critically, I argue that it is the latter imperative that has been in the ascendency since the advent of poststructuralism, an ascendency that has been more recently accelerated by significant and influential interventions such as Hans-Thies Lehmann's postdramatic politics of perception (2006: 185), Jacques Rancière's emancipated spectator (2009) and the broader cultural turn to theories of affect.

I term this the rise of the autonomous spectator, a figure that is named to align with the ascendency of the logic of autonomy within the post-Marxist project of radical democracy proposed by Ernesto Laclau and Chantal Mouffe ([1985] 2014). Laclau and Mouffe's thesis, fully explored in Chapter 4, argues that, with the advent of poststructuralism, a logic of autonomy was introduced into the discourse of left-wing radicalism, which sought to liberate the individual from ideological conformity and insist on the pluralism, contingency and endless irreconcilability of diverse and multiple relations of inequality. From this point on, the logic of autonomy was to exist in continual tension with the Marxist project's hitherto singular logic of equivalence that sought to address all inequality through a sole class antagonism and insist on the possibility of a collectivist resolution and a consensual Utopia to come.

Laclau and Mouffe's logic of equivalence is reconfigured in this study as the logic of egalitarianism that dominates the ideological steer of the historical Marxist project. This study proposes that an understanding of the necessary tension between the logics of autonomy and egalitarianism can provide a useful axis around which the intended spectatorship of contemporary political dramaturgies can be understood to revolve. I further argue that such a project is critical to undertake in the contemporary moment, where the ascendency of the logic of autonomy and the sustained scepticism around ideological steer stand in need of critical re-examination in specific relation to, what I will term, the spectator-subject of twenty-first-century neoliberal capitalism.

A brief history

The tension between a political that seeks to offer ideological steer to the spectator and a political that seeks to resist the transmission of knowledge has historically been located as a tension between models of theatre; most often a realist, socialist dramatic theatre has been pitted against subsequent iterations of avant-garde performance that seek to evade, as Maggie Gale identifies in the context of Dada and Surrealism, 'the rational, the intellectual, the logical' (2016: 171). Sarah Grochala identifies George Bernard Shaw as one of the first Marxist-inspired dramatists who sought to induce 'a dialectical thought process in the audience's mind' (2017: 38) in order that they might 'question their own assumptions and reconsider the validity of the ideals that society has constructed for them' (38). While Grochala is clear that Shaw's dialectic is 'an open one' (36), posing questions rather than asserting answers, the 'serious drama' (18) that she tracks from Shaw through to contemporary playwrights such as David Edgar is clearly driven by ideological steer and is repeatedly placed in opposition, as I have discussed in a previous study, to modes of the political that trace an alternative trajectory through the twentieth and twenty-first centuries in their attempts to evade Marxist (or any) dialectics (Tomlin 2013).

The historical avant-garde movements, such as Dada and Surrealism, seeded the modernist conception of a countercultural political that rejected dialectical narratives underpinned by socialist ideas and rather sought to shock audiences out of their habitual modes of perception with theatres that were disturbing, strange and sometimes incomprehensible. This mode of the political was to reappear in different aesthetic models and under different terms throughout the twentieth and twenty-first centuries and was repeatedly posited in opposition to a predominantly dramatic dialectical theatre that continued to thrive and develop, not least through the work and influence of Bertolt Brecht.

Carl Lavery points to an infamous moment of such tension in 1958 when theatre critic Kenneth Tynan, upholding the political currency of playwrights such as Brecht, John Osborne and Jean-Paul Sartre, condemned the 'escape from realism' in the work of Eugène Ionesco (Tynan 1958 in Lavery 2016a: 551), to which Ionesco responded that 'a work of art has nothing to do with doctrine' (Ionesco in Lavery 2016a: 551). Lavery proposes that, contrary to the Marxist dialectics preferred by Tynan, the works of so-called absurdist playwrights such as Samuel Beckett, Ionesco and Jean Genet are underpinned by the 'negative dialectics' advocated by Theodor Adorno which foreshadow the political ideas of poststructuralist philosophers such as Jacques Derrida, Jean-François Lyotard, Gilles Deleuze and Félix Guattari through a shared emphasis on 'undecidability (*différence*), impossibility and respect for otherness' (Lavery 2016a: 551). The importance of contingency and *différence* to the poststructuralist logic of autonomy that this book intends to interrogate can thus be seen to be already gathering pace by the mid-twentieth century. This mode of the political had migrated from the enclaves of the historical avant-gardes to the mainstream stages on which both the absurdist theatre and the new wave of social realism emerged in the 1950s. It subsequently traversed through the neo-avant-gardes and postmodernist performance aesthetics of the 1980s and 1990s, ultimately taking up a dominant role on the twenty-first-century, predominantly postdramatic, European touring circuit.

By the 1970s and 1980s, the emergence and consolidation of poststructuralist discourse and the influence of postmodernist aesthetics had consolidated the cultural interest in open texts that resisted prescribed or intended readings and highlighted, as Roland Barthes's *Death of the Author,* first published in 1967, most famously proposed, the authority of the reader and their right to autonomous interpretation (Barthes 1977). Although theatres that were underpinned by a Marxist, or post-Marxist, call for ideological response and political action never disappeared, the preservation of the autonomy of the spectator has been in the ascendency in practices described as political since the earliest shoots of poststructuralist thinking. Since the turn of the century, as noted above, this long-standing trend has been further accelerated by significant and influential interventions such as Hans-Thies Lehmann's postdramatic politics of perception (2006: 185), Jacques Rancière's emancipated spectator (2009) and the broader cultural turn to theories of affect.

The rise and rise of the autonomous spectator has cemented the now long-standing resistance to the historical understanding of a political theatre that seeks to offer ideological steer with the intention of eliciting a collective ideological response and political effect beyond the theatre. As Rebecca Hillman contends, contemporary echoes of such a tradition are too often dismissed as polemic, outdated, ideological or hectoring, as a throwback to a tradition of agitprop that has itself been substantively rewritten to erase any aesthetic or political value that existed. Hillman argues that theatre categorized not only as agitprop but under terms such as '"Marxist", "socialist", "alternative", "community", or "popular" theatre' has commonly been 'perceived in recent discourse as naive, unrealistic, simplistic or hectoring; falling short of artistic merit and therefore political potential' (2015: 384). Not only was the critical and aesthetic potential of the agitprop form itself conclusively written out of mainstream theatre analysis, as Hillman's article argues, but theatres of all stripes in which ideological steer was discernible were then discredited by the inaccurately pejorative appellation of 'agitprop', thus consolidating the resistance that reached its zenith in the 1990s against theatres that explicitly sought social and political effect. Since the 1990s this has culminated, in theatre scholarship, in a discourse in which the 'old political' is always aligned to the intention of ideological steer, and is dismissed and discredited for the naivety of its alleged imposition of fixed interpretations or concrete solutions to the political challenges of our time, a charge that, even in Shaw's work as noted above, is rarely wholly justified. Conversely, the radical claims made on behalf of the 'new' notions of the political that arise in opposition to the 'old' are too often reasserted without due interrogation.

Despite the proliferation, within theatre studies, of different conceptions of the political since the poststructuralist fracturing of the singular ideological steer of the historical Marxist-leaning model, there persists a lack of specificity when defining the ideological logics of the various 'politicals' that are in play across dramatic and postdramatic forms of theatre, as well as within dramaturgies that transcend or problematize the limitations of this binary. Rather than a detailed analysis of the 'what' of the political, which has commonly been assumed across all models to be broadly radical or oppositional in some way to the neoliberal status quo, the debate has rather focused on *where* any given 'political' might be located: Are the politics to be found in the form or the content; the reception or the intention; the performance or the process? There is thus an absence, which this study is hoping to redress, of an analytical framework that might allow a more detailed interrogation of what mode of political is operating in any given instance and across the whole spectrum of theatrical models.

The project

It is the intention of this book to interrogate and correct the sometimes overly enthusiastic embrace of the logic of autonomy that has threatened, in recent discourses of political theatre, to suppress, or discredit, its twin logic of egalitarianism. This interrogation will primarily be undertaken by an examination of the radical potential of ideological steer in this contemporary moment, with a particular focus on the British situation as located in the wider context of Europe. Although the dominance of the autonomous spectator within theoretical discourse has been, if anything, strengthened in recent years, it may yet be challenged by the renewed interest in politically driven and ideologically charged dramaturgical practice in European theatres and scholarship that emerged in the early years of the twenty-first century to be acutely accelerated by the financial crisis of 2008. The decade since 2008 might be characterized, most notably but not exclusively, by the ongoing threat of global recession following the financial crisis of 2008, the decimation of Syria by warring factions and the subsequent refugee crisis, the rise of ISIS as an occupying force in the Middle East and as active and proliferating terrorist cells on the European continent, the multiple financial and political crises within many countries of the European Union, increasingly oppressive and volatile political regimes in the United States, Russia, Turkey and Spain, and the rise of the far right across European publics and political parties in Austria, France, Germany, Italy and Greece, among others. In response there has been an acceleration of explicitly resistant political engagement within European mainstream and emergent theatre practices, dramatic and postdramatic models of theatre, live art, activist and community-orientated projects, often reflecting the significant turn towards revised notions of Marxism and collectivism that have been apparent in the growing influence of socialism, as opposed to social democracy, within European mainstream politics in countries such as Greece, Spain and the UK over the same period.

Scholarly publications addressing the politics of European theatre in the past decade have proliferated accordingly. Studies by Jenny Hughes (2011), Julia Boll (2013) and Clare Finburgh (2017) have focused on the staging of war, terror and conflict. Alison Jeffers (2012), Charlotte McIvor (2016) and S.E. Wilmer (2018) have explored the intensification of theatre's engagement with the refugee crisis and the European response. Political engagement within British new writing has been examined by Vicky Angelaki (2017) and Sarah Grochala (2017) and within international postdramatic and participatory forms of performance, respectively, by Karen Jürs-Munby et al. (2013) and Andy Lavender (2016). Key edited volumes appearing in the same period would include *Performance, Politics and Activism* (Lichtenfels and Rouse 2013), *Performances of Capitalism, Crises and Resistance* (Zaroulia and Hager 2015), *The Grammar of Politics and Performance* (Rai and Reinelt 2016) and *Performing Antagonism: Theatre Performance and Radical Democracy* (Fisher and Katsouraki 2017). This list, of texts in English alone, is by no means comprehensive but is sufficient to evidence a significant re-engagement with the explicitly – and increasingly post-Marxist – political, on the part of both theatre makers and the scholars who examine their work.

This re-engagement, evidenced across a wide spectrum of dramaturgical frameworks in the previous decade, has not, however, led to any significant revisions of the insistence on the autonomy of the spectator to forge their own interpretation nor any notable revision to the discursive aversion within the contemporary moment to the concept of ideological steer, political intention or desire for concrete effect beyond the theatre. In a highly significant keynote address to delegates at the 2014 annual conference of the International Federation of Theatre Research, Janelle Reinelt mounted a rare resistance to the recent tide of scholarly opinion that 'politics and theatre should be uncoupled' (2015: 241) in the ways that the work of theorists such as Alan Read, Nicholas Ridout, Hans-Thies Lehmann and Jacques Rancière might suggest. The sustained and persistent influence of the political discourses that Reinelt questioned has, I believe, made this study, which was influenced in its early stages by Reinelt's thinking, both timely and necessary.

In his introduction to *Performing Antagonism*, Tony Fisher confirms the dominance of this discursive trend that he terms 'the "efficacy argument"', which rejects the metaphysics of causality that underpins the assumptions of those who hold that theatre is primarily a form of communication that produces "predictable" rhetorical effects on its audience' (2017: 16). Fisher does urge caution, warning 'die-in-the-wool "effect-deniers"' that 'we should not substitute one form of complacency for another by equating scepticism over theatre's political efficacy with outright denial of its capacity to produce effects' (16). Nevertheless, Fisher, in common with the majority of theorists in this field, holds the political operations of contemporary practice at a clear distance from a denigrated political theatre of the past, asking, 'what kind of theatre exists today that can respond to such events, and *while resisting the peremptory assumptions and expectations of a moribund "political theatre"* exploit the power of theatre to bring this new politics to the stage' (2017: 4, my emphasis).

It is my intention in this book to refute the latest manifestation of the new versus moribund binary indicated by Fisher and to resist advocating for any one notion of 'the political' over any other. Furthermore, I will reject the dominant tendency within theatre studies that claims that given models of theatre can ever be seamlessly folded into one category or the other. I will rather suggest that the two key political logics of autonomy and egalitarian ideological steer are, and always have been, in tension and at play throughout all left-leaning, politically engaged models of theatre practice, notwithstanding the possibility that a clear dominance of one or the other within particular practices or historical periods may be apparent. Through a close, and material, analysis of how this tension between the two logics manifests in specific performances that I have attended, I aim, on the one hand, to test and interrogate the radical politics that are claimed to be in operation under the auspices of autonomy and, on the other, to investigate what political potential might still remain in the mostly discredited dramaturgical strategies that seek to steer spectators towards Marxist or post-Marxist ideological interpretations or actions. This will be undertaken, firstly, in Part One, by configuring the theorized spectator of neoliberalism to whom the dramaturgical invitations are designed to be addressed and, secondly, in Part Two, by a rigorous political analysis of the modes of interpellation, invitation and provocation adopted by the dramaturgies in question.

My theorized figuration of the contemporary spectator-subject as precarious, individualized and ironic is drawn from common features that have been attributed to the neoliberal subject across the fields of psychology, sociology and economics: namely, that the precarity of her condition, also traceable back to the emergence of the rise of autonomy, leads to a reduction in her capacity for empathy, agency and ability to imagine better futures. This, in turn, leads to a predilection for ironic response to injustice that is driven by a concern for the feelings of the subject-self, rather than concern for the suffering other. These characteristics are argued to shape even those towards the left of the political spectrum who might be validly assumed to make up the most part of the audiences under examination in this study.

I have intentionally omitted dramaturgies of participation from this exploration, not least given the wealth of recent scholarship focusing precisely on the shift from spectator to participant as noted in Chapter 2, but principally due to the centrality to this study of Jacques Rancière's theories of emancipated spectatorship that address the autonomy of the critical interpretation of the spectator, not the autonomy of the material contribution of the participant. I have likewise restricted my focus to dramaturgies of theatre or performance occurring in the professional context of the theatre industry, given that activist performance demands the explicit transmission of meaning and intent from interlocutor to audience. Whether such activism comes in the polemic form of banners and chants of protestors or aesthetically rich performances such as Liberate Tate's anti-BP installations, the intention for a desired political effect on its audience is the raison d' être of the artistic act and cannot logically be divorced from it, however much the degree of desired efficacy attained remains open to question. This places such work beyond the tension induced by the demand for autonomous spectatorship on which this study is focused.

Given the significant increase in books concerned with British political theatres and performance in recent years, not least in this series, this book does not seek primarily to expand that field nor does it claim to offer any kind of representative overview or taxonomy of British political theatre practice. I am rather interested in digging deeper into the theoretical premises of the field itself in order to critically and robustly interrogate the tension between artistic political intention and autonomous spectatorship at this point in theatre history. Thus, practice exists variously, in this study, as a mechanism through which theory can be exemplified, articulated and examined and, on occasion, as a mechanism through which theory can be challenged, expanded or produced. When I began writing the book I intended to draw on theatres from across Europe, but given the centrality of the spectator to my dramaturgical analysis, I have chosen to draw only on those practices I have personally attended that are best placed to operate in dialogue with the theoretical framework I am proposing. It may, or may not, be an accident that of the performances I have seen over the past four years, it is those produced by British artists, albeit artists working within and influenced by wider European networks, that have been the most productive dialogue partners with the pan-European theoretical debates with which this study engages.

There is also a deliberate absence within my analytical framework of any sustained dialogue with notions of Hans-Thies Lehmann's notion of the postdramatic. Given the influence of Lehmann's work within contemporary discussions of the political, this seems worthy of a brief explanation. As noted above, Lehmann's work on the postdramatic at the turn of the century was influential in the trend to decouple theatre from explicitly ideological content and political intention or effect. Yet, as Reinelt also notes in her keynote address, Lehmann did begin to advocate a necessary re-engagement of theatre and the political in the later 2000s. In his more recent publications (2013, 2016) Lehmann has explored the idea of a contemporary political theatre being inescapably harnessed to the idea of a contemporary, and postdramatic, tragic form that he terms 'a theatre of situation' (2013: 89). Such a theatre seeks modes of 'direct intervention in the public sphere' (87) and lies in a 'twilight zone between political activism and aesthetic practice' (87). Key, for Lehmann, is the necessity, within such a theatre, for the aesthetic practice it offers to be interrupted or broken apart by the 'intervention of social reality' (108) in some way or another. It is no longer, it seems, sufficient for the postdramatic to merely offer a deconstruction of the dramatic; to be both political and tragic the postdramatic is now required to offer a fissure in the aesthetics of the theatre event in its entirety.

I have written extensively on Lehmann's early conceptualization of the postdramatic and contested his conflation, at that point, of politics with aesthetic form (Tomlin 2013: 44–76). Examining his new paradigm of the political which I find guilty of the same conflation, I continue to feel insufficiently secure in his analysis to draw on it in any depth in the new vocabularies of the political I am proposing in this study. As exemplified in the final chapter of *Tragedy and Dramatic Theatre*, there is still, for me, an unexplained contradiction between Lehmann's insistence that the tragic-political must enact a rupture of the aesthetic framework of the theatre event and his citing of Kane's later written texts for theatre as seminal postdramatic tragic-political works. Kane has regularly been offered by Lehmann as a postdramatic playwright, but her playtexts do not, regardless of their openness to critical interpretation, undertake the type of explicitly interruptive activity within the theatrical event that Lehmann's own more recent theories would seem to explicitly require them to do.

The terms 'dramatic' and 'postdramatic' remain, for me, both unclear and unproductive as descriptors that can help to advance or elucidate the alternative theoretical framework I am proposing in this study. Indeed, most of the theatre that I examine here could probably be described as either dramatic or postdramatic through applying a selective range of criteria from an ever-widening net of reference. It is only left to note that there is adamantly no proposal here that whatever finds itself named as postdramatic – despite Lehmann's early insistence on autonomy of interpretation – will inherently lead towards the logic of autonomy; and, likewise, no suggestion that whatever finds itself named as dramatic will necessarily favour the egalitarian logic. I thus continue to refute Lehmann's conflation of form and politics, and this study explicitly seeks to offer an alternative framework in which the politics of contemporary performance can be identified and interrogated outside of a fixed ideological reading of the model or form of theatre in which they momentarily, and often differently, appear.

I will leave it to the reader, and my own future research, to further investigate how the theoretical framework proposed here might operate productively, or differently, within broader geographical contexts. Certainly, the dramaturgical strategies of irony and empathy and the dramaturgical models of theatres of real people and verbatim are not confined to the British context, but such practice may well read differently in diverse political situations. In a time of such global political complexity, the specificity of a single cultural location has productively enabled a more precise focus on the material context that inflects the spectator-subjects who attend and under which the political dramaturgies are bound to operate. My own first-hand analysis of the potential political efficacy, or limitations, of selected dramaturgical strategies operating in particular contexts is, of course, subjective and open to debate. The book does not lay claim to any kind of definitive political analysis of such strategies, or the work under discussion, but rather seeks to challenge existing and limiting orthodoxies, offers revised and reinvigorated critical definitions and frameworks through which ideological analysis can be better articulated, contested and debated, and ultimately expands the dramaturgical palette and analytical vocabularies of artists and theorists of contemporary political theatres in Europe and beyond.

Reading the book

The book is divided into two parts, the first part offering a series of shorter chapters that will set up my theoretical configuration of the spectator-subject of neoliberalism that will feature in the subsequent analysis of contemporary political dramaturgies to be examined in Part Two.

The book builds its thesis from chapter to chapter and will be most productively enjoyed if read in the same way. However, for those who have a particular interest in specific chapters or themes, I have offered a brief summary of previous conclusions at the beginning of each chapter to more easily situate that chapter's contribution to the thesis as a whole. I would, however, suggest that Chapter 4 serves as an important introduction to all subsequent chapters and that Chapters 2 and 6, and Chapters 7 and 8, work particularly well in dialogue. To further assist the more selective reader, I will now map out the key argumentation of the book in the remainder of this Introduction through summaries of each of the chapters.

Part One: Configuring the spectator-subject

Chapter 1 will begin by locating my theorizing of an imagined spectator in the context of the recent turn towards empirical research into the analysis of real, non-expert theatre spectators. While acknowledging and highlighting many of the valuable insights such work has produced, I will contest the suggestion that such a methodology is less theorized or speculative than the combination of materialist analysis and auto-ethnography I propose to undertake. Furthermore, I will argue that the turn to empirical audience research can risk bolstering the reconfiguration of spectator into consumer that is central to the activity of neoliberal cultural institutions and might thus be seen as a potential threat to the project of politically engaged theatre practice.

This book is not only swimming against the tide of empirical audience research but also seeking to challenge the prevailing narrative that, in the context of professional theatre practice, political dramaturgies holding ideological intention, or seeking political interpretations or effect beyond the theatre, are without significant currency at this point in history. Chapter 2 examines the rise of the autonomous spectator who is central to this rejection of ideological steer. Here, I propose that, subsequent to the emergence of poststructuralist thought and postmodern aesthetics, the discourse of postdramatic theatre, trends in immersive and participatory theatre practice and the turn to affect theory all serve to consolidate the dominance of the assertion of the individual's right to subjective and autonomous interpretation. This, I suggest, raises the risk that the autonomous spectator, like the 'real' spectator of Chapter 1, might be as easily aligned with the neoliberal consumer as the critical, emancipated spectator that is more often envisaged by the theorists concerned, a tension that will be pursued and examined throughout the book.

This chapter is the first of two to focus on the work of Jacques Rancière (2009) and functions to introduce his thesis of the emancipated spectator that has been so influential in advocating for the logic of autonomy that is interrogated throughout this study. His thesis rests on a particular understanding of the political that, for Rancière, lies in the assertion of equality: the spectator is liberated from her role of recipient of meaning or intended interpretation and is rather empowered to assert her equality with the artist through the creation of her own meaning from the work that is placed before her. Consequently, as Rancière concludes, 'the very same thing that makes the aesthetic "political" stands in the way of all strategies for "politicizing art"' (2009: 74), as the artist's intention to provoke a particular political response, in my terms ideological steer, is discredited under his political rubric.

In this chapter, I briefly examine Rancière's notion of emancipation in the context of applied theatre to propose that, for those at the sharp edge of neoliberal capitalism, the attempt of the artist to suspend her desire for any particular effect or outcome can indeed be understood as progressively political in the way Rancière intends, given that it constitutes a redistribution of pleasurable affective and emotional capital to those for whom it is most often limited in range and supply. However, I question to what degree an unfettered logic of autonomous response can be understood as progressively political when removed from the contexts of cultural and economic deprivation and relocated in the professional touring circuit that is this book's field of study. In such a context, I argue, when divorced from any ideological steer, the impact on the spectator might more accurately be described as therapeutic, or indeed pertains to a libertarian political logic, rather than an egalitarian one.[1] This is a thread I pick up again in Chapter 6, but I conclude my introduction to Rancière with a further caution that reverberates throughout this study: a spectator's response may be autonomous from the artist's intention, but no response can be wholly autonomous from the influence of the ideological structures of neoliberalism by which the spectator, to a greater or lesser degree, might be said to be shaped.

In Chapter 3, I give this caution full consideration. While I am certainly not arguing, after Louis Althusser ([1971] 2008), that the dominant ideological structures of contemporary neoliberalism are monolithic or inescapable, I will suggest that they should, at the very least, be taken into account in any theoretical prefiguration of the contemporary spectator-subject, notwithstanding the individuality of constituent audience members or the importance of divergent factors of socio-economic background, ideological affiliation, cultural or national identity, race, gender, age or sexual orientation. This pre-configuration will enable the analysis of political dramaturgies in the second part of this book to be undertaken with regard to the human subject of neoliberalism who constitutes the broad outlines of the theorized spectator of the contemporary aesthetic invitation.

This human subject has been variously considered as individualized (Bauman 2001), precarious (Bourdieu 1997; Standing 2011) and ironic (Chouliaraki 2012) and is commonly located as emerging during the most recent wave of global capitalism that is characterized by the ascendency of the logic of autonomy and the consequent acceleration and intensification of neoliberalism around the beginning of the 1990s. The characteristics of precarity, individualization and irony will thus directly inform the theorized spectator-subject who is central to my subsequent analysis of the efficacy of contemporary political dramaturgies that are operating around the axis that counterbalances autonomy and egalitarian ideological steer.

Part Two: Contemporary political dramaturgies

In the short introductory chapter to the second part of the book, I will map out the theoretical framework through which I am going to undertake the subsequent dramaturgical analyses. Sidestepping Lehmann's dramatic/

---

[1] My thinking on the libertarian implications of Rancière's politics when divorced from contexts of deprivation and the counterpoint of the egalitarian logic was set in train by the concern voiced by Andy Lavender that Rancière's understanding of equality was 'in some respects a model for individual libertarianism within a communal (shared) context' (2016: 138).

postdramatic analysis and rejecting the commonly inferred binary between 'old/moribund' and 'new' political models of theatre, I will repurpose an existing axis of post-Marxist political theory to propose that the twin logics of autonomy and egalitarian ideological steer are to be found in productive tension, if in differing degrees of dominance, across a diversity of contemporary political dramaturgies.

This chapter draws direct parallels between the post-Marxist project of Laclau and Mouffe and the ascendency of the logic of autonomy in the discourse of political dramaturgies since the poststructuralist critique of Marxism emerged. For Marxist theatre makers such as Bertolt Brecht, wholly driven by ideological imperatives of egalitarianism, it was only through increased equality that freedom was possible. On the contrary, for those dramaturgies influenced by poststructuralist demands for autonomy, it was only through individual freedom that equality could be assured. However, the logics of freedom and equality, the bedrocks of liberal democratic thought, continue to exist in tension in post-Marxist political and artistic projects, as Mouffe's later work on agonism further contends. This chapter examines how political philosophy has responded to the advent of the logic of autonomy and proposes that an understanding of the necessary tension between the logics of autonomy and egalitarianism can provide a useful axis around which the intended spectatorship of contemporary political dramaturgies can be understood to revolve.

I have selected the productions I wished to analyse, in Part Two, in response to the questions raised by the thesis of this study as it developed. An initial examination of ironic dramaturgies, in Chapter 5, seemed a pertinent way to ascertain if the long-standing critical tradition of political theatre, to which ironic dramaturgies belong, could retain the political purchase of the ironic invitation when addressed to the spectator-subject who is, herself, constituted as precarious, individualized and ironic. In this chapter, I trace the concept of ideological interpellation back to Louis Althusser and draw on Judith Butler's influential interrogation of Althusser to highlight, through an analysis of Made In China's *Gym Party* (2013), the common dramaturgical strategy of ironic, or provocative, interpellation. Here, spectators are ironically configured as faithful neoliberal subjects in order to instil reflection on, and ultimately rejection of, their complicity in neoliberal structures, thus gesturing to the possibilities of resistance and revolt. However, I caution that such a strategy is, nonetheless, vulnerable to the necessity of an over-reliance on the egalitarian logic that would anticipate a collective horizon of ideological expectation from its audience. Conversely, I argue that the hail might be guaranteed to land provocatively on some spectators while risking alienating others.

In the chapter's subsequent analysis of Martin Crimp's *In the Republic of Happiness* (2012), I argue that a sustained tension between the logics of autonomy and egalitarianism counters a potentially absurdist and nihilistic ironic instability with an ideological steer that invites its audience to consider a more egalitarian politics through sustained reflection on a grotesque mirror image of their own individualization and its horrific consequences. Nonetheless, I highlight remaining three challenges for all ironic dramaturgies operating in the contemporary moment, given that their invitations are addressed to a spectator-subject of neoliberalism who is, herself, always-already precarious and ironic. Firstly, that the focus on the potentially narcissistic self-reflection and emotional response of the spectator-subject who enjoys a privileged cultural role within neoliberalism threatens to occlude less privileged others from any consideration. Secondly, that the spectator-subject, who is also characterized by their precarity and reduced capacity for agency in the neoliberal moment, is not signposted to any secure response or course of action and is thus required to take individual responsibility for systemic injustice and oppression, much as they are required to do under the neoliberal structures that are the subject of critique. Finally, I note Jacques Rancière's argument that the incapacitated, ironic or precarious spectator-subject is not a given around which political dramaturgies need to be shaped but has been precisely created and sustained by those who require such a figure to justify the efficacy and political intention of such dramaturgical structures. This is the basis of his scepticism of the critical machine that 'unveils the impotence of the imbeciles' (2009: 48) and his outright rejection of ironic structures on the grounds that 'where one searches for the hidden beneath the apparent, a position of mastery is established' (2004: 46). Rancière rather proposes that the critical tradition, and its assumption of incapacity, is discarded, and a new approach forged: 'an egalitarian or anarchist theoretical position that does not presuppose this vertical relationship of top to bottom' (2004: 46).

The identification of these three limitations of the ironic dramaturgies of the critical tradition, when addressed to the precarious, ironic spectator of the neoliberal moment, sets the parameters for my choice of productions to engage with in the subsequent chapters of the study.

Rancière's rejection of the mastery implicit in the egalitarian logic inherited from the Marxist critical tradition, and his influence in establishing a new topography of the political driven almost entirely by the logic of autonomy, necessitates a close engagement in Chapter 6 with his proposal for a politics of unintended aesthetic affect. This chapter examines how Rancière attempts to extricate the individual subject from its sovereign, bourgeois history where it stands as the enemy of the collective and relocates it as autonomous, vulnerable, contingent and partial, only achieving meaning through difference from, and in relation to, others. This reconfiguration of the sovereign individual of historical capitalism and the neoliberal moment, to serve as an autonomous agent within the contemporary communist imaginary, is vital both to Rancière's own political project and to the radical narrative of the autonomous spectator I interrogate throughout this study. It underpins the politics of the turn to affect that has been influenced by Rancière's thinking and presents the autonomous spectator as a radically oppositional figure to that of the collective audience or certain community, which are rather located as ideologically regressive throwbacks to the authoritarian consequences of the State-Communism that evolved in the USSR.

While there has been fascinating work to come out of the auspices of such thinking, in theatre studies and beyond, I highlight some existing concerns with the limitations of Rancière's framework, and I offer my own thoughts on how the application of his thinking within certain material contexts of theatre practice raises still further questions about the alleged radicalism of the logic of autonomy when severed from the ideological steer of the logic of egalitarianism altogether. In such instances I propose that the politics that are operational within the space may more accurately be described as libertarian, as I argued in Chapter 2, than communist. Ultimately, this chapter argues for the importance of a material analysis of the context in which dissensus takes place, a re-harnessing of affect within the theatre to effect beyond it, and the necessity for the logic of autonomy to remain counterbalanced by a logic of egalitarianism that connects the individual response with a wider collective responsibility.

Following my engagement with the political project that Rancière proposes, I have chosen to offer Kieran Hurley's *Heads Up* (2016) as a lucid example of theatre that explores the current thinking on autonomous affect in both form and content, but in which the political charge, while enhanced by the affective experience of the form, is driven by the egalitarian logic of the narrative content. I then enter into a more sustained conversation with the theory and practice of Andy Smith, drawing on *Commonwealth* (2012) and *Summit* ([2017] 2018) in particular. I have selected Smith's work here to demonstrate how practice can seek *affective* impact and operate consciously within the logic of autonomy as advocated by Rancière, but which can nevertheless seek political *effect* outside of the theatre through attempts to bridge the divide between the material and microcosmic event of the performance and the inegalitarian injustices in the world beyond it. Thus, while the autonomy of individual response is upheld, the individual spectator is explicitly located within, and invited to take responsibility for, a wider collective. I will suggest that through employing a gentle and sincere counter-hegemonic interpellation of the spectator-subject as an already-radical agent of change, Smith's work is also able, through the imaginative employment of egalitarian ideological steer, to actively counter the potential limitations of a precarious and ironic spectator-subject always-already imbricated in neoliberalism and primed to respond from that ideological position.

In the subsequent chapters I turn my attention to contemporary political dramaturgies in which the egalitarian logic might be said to dominate. Where Rancière critiqued ironic dramaturgies for their assumption of mastery, my key contention was the risk that they occluded 'the other' from both the stage and the critical consideration of the spectator. Recent trends in practice that seek to explicitly address this occlusion are verbatim performance and theatres of real people, whereby space is made on the stage for the autobiographical stories of testifiers or non-professional performers who are most often presumed to be other to the imagined spectator-subjects who are predicted to attend the production (Gaarde and Mumford 2016: 5).

In Chapter 7, I turn to a seminal example of such practice, *Queens of Syria* (2016), a piece of theatre featuring Syrian refugees performing for audiences in mainstream theatres across the UK. This analysis enables me to introduce and interrogate contemporary employment of the empathy operation, whereby the spectator is required to engage with those who are considered 'other' to them, a strategy that might be expected to address the limitations of the ironic dramaturgies of the critical tradition. Given the identification of the precarious neoliberal subject as individualized, ironic and lacking in the capacity for empathy, the need for dramaturgies that can support or encourage empathetic engagement with different others would appear to be vital at this historical moment and perhaps underlies the resurgent popularity, post-2008, of verbatim strategies and theatres staging non-professional performers to this end.

This chapter will explore, in particular, the ways in which the empathy operation has been notably reconfigured, for its contemporary employment, by the poststructuralist logic of autonomy that has been discussed throughout this study, despite the explicitly egalitarian steer of *Queens of Syria* and much comparable practice. The tension between the two logics thus enables an invitation for empathetic response to operate as politically vital in the neoliberal moment. Most importantly, I will examine how the political operation of empathy is now most commonly located in the other's resistance to being understood, thus insisting on a two-way dialogic operation that refuses to permit any easy colonization of the other. This resistance, I will argue, opens up a critical field for agonistic debate in which the complexity of the political context beyond the plight of the suffering individual might be addressed. In my analysis of *Queens of Syria*, I will explore the ways in which many of its dramaturgical choices draw on such reconfigured frameworks.

However, I will also examine how the dramaturgy of real people closes down the potential for two-way dialogic engagement between spectator and performer due to the absence of character that eliminates the critical field on which such engagement might be possible. By so doing, such practice can evade the agonistic debate that is required to accommodate the complexities of the political situation in question. Here, I will suggest that the potential of the egalitarian logic is hampered by the disavowal of the pluralist antagonisms insisted upon by the poststructuralist logic of autonomy and the subsequent drive to political consensus between egalitarian-leaning spectators and refugee performers. In conclusion, I will argue that the production risked raising a potentially dangerous antagonism between the consensus in the theatre and the spectres of the 'other others' who do not welcome refugees or subscribe to the cosmopolitan liberalism of the audience and who, furthermore, are unlikely to be in the auditorium to engage in dialogue or to defend themselves from the implied accusation made in their absence.

This, I will argue, drawing on Mouffe and Sara Ahmed, is one of the fundamental problems with the utopian, cosmopolitan consensus shared by many liberal theatre makers and spectators in the West. The cosmopolitan valorization of difference that is central to the poststructuralist logic of autonomy constructs its own 'other other' of those who perceive the acceptance of difference as a threat to their own survival. When such 'other others' are cast outside the legitimate terms of debate then the agonistic tensions of democratic politics are most at risk of becoming violent and obscene.

I will continue this thread in Chapter 8, beginning with an analysis of Chris Thorpe and Rachel Chavkin's verbatim-driven production, *Confirmation* (2014). In light of the previous chapter, this production might be seen as an exercise in pushing the demands of dialogic empathy to its limits. Thorpe's solo performance draws predominantly on his encounters with an 'other' who is his ideological and antagonistic 'enemy', a white supremacist neo-Nazi he calls 'Glen'. Much of the theory explored in the previous chapter in relation to the reconfiguration of empathy, as is common across the field of theatre studies, locates empathy with the other as an ethical aim and tends to avoid the more difficult question of how this might continue to apply, or not, when confronted with an 'other' who is, himself, antithetical to the egalitarian, democratic project in its entirety. *Confirmation*, I will argue, thus extends through its own fieldwork and reflection, the thorny questions of empathy and engagement addressed in the previous chapter, with Thorpe ultimately rejecting the ethical call for an endless, mutual dialogue of unknowable difference with his 'other'.

This conclusion sets up the second part of this final chapter which questions whether Thorpe's decision to relinquish his attempts to empathize with the other in order to hold onto his own sense of self might have traction as an alternative ethical or political position beyond its rationalization, in this instance, as a necessary defence against fascism. I engage with this question through an analysis of Common Wealth Theatre's *The Deal Versus the People* (2015), directed by Evie Manning and devised with non-professional performers with experience of unemployment and economic hardship. This production was driven by the egalitarian logic, with an explicit and specific political task for its actors and spectators to undertake together: opposition to the proposed Transatlantic Trade and Investment Partnership between the United States and the EU. Through placing this performance in dialogue with Slavoj Žižek, Judith Butler and Athena Athanasiou, I will argue that the affective *feeling* of the security of the illusion of selfhood, as clung to by Thorpe, may offer agency to those subjects who are most denied agency under neoliberalism, and thus might hold further political potential that is underexplored in a historical moment that remains dominated by the poststructuralist insistence, driven by the logic of autonomy, on acknowledging one's own subjectivity as fragmented, contingent and ultimately illusory.

Not least, I argue in conclusion to this study, the poststructuralist conviction, shared by Butler and Rancière, that no mode of interpellation can be secured, nor any artist's desired response to their invitation be determined, will always safeguard the autonomy of the spectator-subject regardless of any ideological steer that may be offered. This study ultimately proposes that there is thus nothing to fear from a strategic, counter-hegemonic hail to the spectator that may, on the contrary, hold significant potential to counteract the neoliberal imbrication of the precarious spectator-subject and offers specific means by which the neoliberal project can be discredited or derailed. In an age of precarity, an invitation to step onto firmer ground in which subjecthood and future actions take on concrete form may, in certain dramaturgies and in certain material contexts, be precisely what is most needed.

In the Epilogue I close this critical study with a creative stepping-off point and invite the reader to share one of the key starting points for this project, a piece of spoken-word performance I developed as a testing ground for many of the ideas that run throughout this study. I hope that the book as a whole can inspire theatre makers to construct multiple new manifestations of dramaturgical practice that refuse the limitations of a binary that stipulates the superiority of one political logic over the other, and encourage a consideration of how the tension between the two might best be managed and manipulated in relation to specific material contexts of production. I also hope that the new political vocabularies I propose can enable scholars to further develop and refine the discursive analysis of political theatres of the future.

Part One

Configuring the
Spectator-Subject

1

Real and Imagined Spectators

A trend of revitalized interest in the spectator can be seen to emerge towards the end of the 2000s, heralded by Bruce McConachie's *Engaging Audiences: A Cognitive Approach to Spectating in the Theatre* (2008), Helen Freshwater's *theatre & audience* (2009), Helena Grehan's *Performance, Ethics and Spectatorship in a Global Age* (2009) and Josephine Machon's *(Syn)aesthetics: Redefining Visceral Performance* (2009). These texts are commonly seen as vanguards for the subsequent decade's interest, respectively, in cognitive, ethnographic, ethico-political and participatory modes of spectatorship. This flurry of interest is notable given that it had been almost two decades since the first publication of Susan Bennett's *Theatre Audiences: A Theory of Production and Reception* (1990) and Herbert Blau's *The Audience* (1990), only significantly preceded by Jill Dolan's *The Feminist Spectator as Critic* (1988) and Daphna Ben Chaim's *Distance in the Theatre: The Aesthetics of Audience Response* (1984).

The nascent field of audience research that emerged in 2008–9 was rapidly accelerated and broadened by a swathe of subsequent publications,[1] but McConachie and Freshwater have been particularly influential in their advocation for empirical, if distinctly different, approaches to spectator analysis, both sharing a scepticism of the kind of theoretical study of spectators that is the focus of this book. In this chapter, I thus begin by addressing the challenge that is mounted by both cognitive analysis and audience research to the theoretical tradition of analysis that this study pursues. I will argue that, despite claims to the contrary, no mode of analysis transcends theorization and, furthermore, that modes of audience research are particularly vulnerable to assimilation within the neoliberal obsession with the spectator-consumer. In conclusion, I will thus argue for the potency and potential of a theorized, or imagined, spectator as a necessary figure in the design of political dramaturgies of all models.

---

[1] Examples would include *The Audience Experience* (Radbourne et al. 2013), *The Feminist Spectator in Action: Feminist Criticism for the Stage and Screen* (Dolan 2013), *Audience as Performer: The Changing Role of Theatre Audiences in the Twenty-First Century* (Heim 2015), *Locating the Audience: How People Found Value in National Theatre Wales* (Sedgman 2016), *Audience Revolution: Dispatches from the Field* (Svitch 2016), *Unfolding Spectatorship: Shifting Political, Ethical and Intermedial Positions* (Stalpaert et al. 2018).

Real spectators

Bruce McConachie's vanguard call to the discipline dismisses proponents of theorized audience research from psychoanalysts to poststructuralists for trying 'to place their ideas beyond the protocols of empirical evidence and falsifiability' (2008: 11). Materialist criticism is afforded only marginally more credibility before it too falls under the umbrella of 'many of our current theories in theatre and performance studies' that 'cannot be falsified or supported with reliable evidence' and are consequently charged with offering conclusions that are 'potentially built upon sand' (13). Yet, as McConachie himself acknowledges, 'scientists themselves do not agree on what I have called (with intentional blandness) "a fair reading of the available evidence"' (15), thus scientific *theories* are admitted to being precisely that. McConachie argues that the ongoing theoretical debates between scientists offer theatre and performance scholars an opportunity to further scientific research with their own insights and investigations, but he himself confesses to only drawing on 'theories about culture, history, and audiences from anthropology, phenomenology, communications, and cultural studies' with the intention 'to supplement the insights of cognitive science' (14), thus asserting a clear hierarchy of knowledge that is all, nonetheless, equally theoretical.

Conversely, I would argue that insights drawn from cognitive research as often serve to reinforce understandings of spectatorship and reception that have long been arrived at via theorized calculation. For example, cognitive research into mirror neurons (McConachie 2008: 18–19) that suggests how a spectator may internally replicate the actions performed by the actor reinforces, rather than challenges, historical theories of empathy that propose the spectator can vicariously experience the 'fear', in Aristotelian terms, of the protagonist. Thus, science, in some key instances, gives us different ways of talking about operations that have long been familiar to scholars within the discipline. This should give us confidence in current informed and theorized speculation that might, in the future, also prove to be ahead of the scientific 'evidence'.

Further challenges to the kind of theoretical analysis that this study will propose have been mounted by scholars such as Freshwater and Kirsty Sedgman, who both demand that greater attention is paid to empirical methods of audience research, long-standing in film and television criticism but virtually absent, until recent years, in theatre studies. In *theatre & audience*, Helen Freshwater asks why theatre scholars 'appear to prefer discussing their own responses, or relaying the opinions of reviewers, to asking "ordinary" theatre-goers – with no professional stake in the theatre – what they make of a performance?' (2009: 4). Unlike the long tradition of empirical audience research in the fields of film and television, Freshwater argues, theatre scholars have tended to speculatively theorize audiences rather than asking real audiences what they think, thus limiting, she suggests, the scope and potential of disciplinary enquiry. Kirsty Sedgman likewise argues:

> The field of theatre studies has sometimes seemed on the verge of moving from 'rhetorical' work, understanding audiences by dismantling texts for their capacity to produce responses, via 'high theory' about how hypothetical audiences do or should respond to things, to conducting cognitive experiments on them, without actually stopping to *talk to audiences* on the way. (2016: 10, original emphasis)

Both Freshwater and Sedgman offer a number of reasons why this might be the case, from the methodological complexities noted by Christopher Balme (Balme 2008: 34 in Freshwater 2009: 36–7), to the time-consuming nature of empirical enquiry (Freshwater 2009: 37), to a long-held suspicion that audiences can't be trusted (Freshwater 2009: 38–55), to a full-blown sense of protectionism over the 'ineffable' nature of the art object and the desire to hold onto the expertise of the professional critic or scholar who alone is qualified to appreciate it (Bourdieu 1996: xvi–xvii in Sedgman 2016: 25).

Implicit within the allegations of unwelcome expertise that are levelled at the critic or scholar is the underlying assumption that these are somehow less valuable, and perhaps less authentic, than the responses of 'real' audience members who are without professional or vested interest. The trend in audience research also plays to the broader movement that is the focus of this study: the logic of autonomy that valorizes the subjective and individual response (that in audience research can be evidenced and authorized after the fact) over any speculative prediction of collective interpretation. Yet, the reservations voiced by Kim Schröder et al. in the context of ethnographic media research would also hold here. Schröder et al. argue that when real-life responses, such as interviews, are assumed to be of 'a higher quality than, say, textual analyses or surveys [s]uch an insistence easily slides into an academic fundamentalism that has no methodological or theoretical grounding' (Schröder et al. 2003: 85). The claims that would validate qualitative interviews over quantitative surveys or textual analysis are ultimately derailed by the fact that, as with all personal testimony, the respondent's narrative is never an unmediated truth. It is shaped firstly by the questionnaire itself which, as Reinelt et al. caution, 'does not always capture ordinary experiences of theatre spectatorship but may model a new kind of theatre spectatorship' (2014: 52). Secondly, it is mediated by the respondent themselves, aware of the context of the interview, the status of the interviewer and the narrative of self they are presenting. Sedgman's comparative analysis of respondents who feel they hold more or less cultural authority is telling, and her work highlights that ways of articulating value are intrinsically bound up in 'Who Feels They Have the Right to Say What, and on What Grounds' (2016: 115). Finally, and inevitably, the research is shaped by the researcher. For it to go beyond an unmediated cacophony of testimony that may be more or less distorted by issues of cultural confidence, 'contradictions' that arise within individual transcripts (Reinelt et al. 2014: 32) and, *pace* Erving Goffman (1959), particular presentations of self, the discourse that emerges requires the authority of the analyst to construct a metanarrative that finds commonalities and patterns that enable the research to offer something of cultural significance. Without this metanarrative, as Schröder et al. contend, 'we may trace the meanderings of contemporary mediated meaning-making in their depth and richness, but we cannot hope to simultaneously chart the full breadth of these processes – let alone predict how they will proceed' (Schröder et al. 2003: 85). Thus, despite its evident capacity to offer additional, and sometimes valuable, insights, the idea that empirical audience research can somehow evade the limitations of subjective expert theorization is not, I would argue, a sustainable one.

The 'real' spectator's 'authentic' response is, rather, doubly mediated: firstly, by the spectator herself, who is constructing a response that is congruent with the narrative of self she wishes to sustain and promote; and secondly, by the researcher, who is then required to select, edit and position the response in a way that supports the shape of the particular theoretical narratives that she wishes to sustain and promote. The first mediation is particularly notable in its absence from most accounts of contemporary audience research, possibly because it continues to give credence to 'the behaviourist "effects" model' which followed Theodor Adorno's critiques of the mass media and which was subsequently dismissed by Herbert Blumer and empiricists after him (Staiger 2005: 44). This model suggested, as Janet Staiger observes, that the responses of participants were unreliable: 'If mass media necessarily produced a psychological regression for audiences, open-ended questionnaires and other sorts of empirical questioning of individuals made no sense' as the answers given were not to be trusted (Staiger 2005: 30). Subsequent trends in criticism have sought to challenge the assumed passivity and vulnerability to media manipulation that the behaviourist effects model proposed, but beyond Adorno's Marxist argument, philosophers from Jacques Derrida to Slavoj Žižek have also problematized the degree to which any subject is able to represent herself or her opinions in isolation from cultural ideological conditioning. In Derridean terms, ideology apart, the 'thing itself' – in this case the authentic response – slips from our grasp the moment it becomes subject to its own representation – in this case its articulation through speech or writing. As Derrida contests, 'contrary to what our desire cannot fail to be tempted into believing, the thing itself always escapes' (1973: 104). In this sense, the 'real' spectator's 'authentic' response, while a perfectly valid object of research, is no more authentic or reliable than the predicted response of the theorized spectator who is the subject of this study. Furthermore, as I will argue at length in the following two chapters, no response can entirely escape the effects of the ideological conditions in which it is conceived, thus necessitating some level of materialist analysis to productively interpret each 'authentic' response in its wider context.

Spectator-consumers

The enthusiasm for audience research, in the context of political dramaturgies, carries additional risks in the contemporary neoliberal moment in which the sovereignty of the individual consumer is paramount. Like the immersive and interactive models of performance, discussed in the following chapter, that have also risen to prominence in the first two decades of the twenty-first century, qualitative audience research prioritizes the subjective, individual and affective response that is central to phenomenological modes of analysis. In the report *Critical Mass: Theatre Spectatorship and Value Attribution* (2014), undertaken by the British Theatre Consortium, Janelle Reinelt et al. are clear that within the broad parameters of the empirical field, 'the phenomenology of actual experience' (2) is the methodology at the heart of their research. In a real sense both *Critical Mass* and Sedgman's empirical research in *Locating the Audience* (2016) broaden the opportunity for each individual spectator to engage in the kind of phenomenological analysis that underpins the performative writing of scholar Peggy Phelan. As Helen Freshwater notes,

> At its best this approach can show how fully our responses to performance are generated by individual preoccupations and experiences, as well as allowing the writer to explore – and thus validate – emotional and physiological aspects of response which will never be captured by statistical analysis and which have not been considered 'proper' subjects for academic analysis in the past. (2009: 24)

Freshwater's identification of the potential of phenomenological research to unlock responses that are both specific to the individual and emotional or physiological in nature demonstrates the necessary synergy between new models of practice that seek to explore the emotional and physical affects of theatre through a range of immersive strategies, the individualization of experience through trends such as one-to-one theatre and the new methods of analysis required for these kinds of audience experience. The potential of widening opportunities for phenomenological analysis within empirical models might be understood as democratizing the scholarly tradition which Phelan's work exemplifies – a tradition that Sedgman notes is too often 'embedded within a set of "expert" discourses inflected by the position of its author, and so is unable to map the existence of different kinds of responses from varying subject positions' (2016: 9). Yet, an over-reliance on phenomenology within an empirical framework, regardless of the expertise or otherwise on the part of the reflexive analyst, necessitates the insistence on the autonomy and subjectivity of response that this book is seeking to interrogate. Following work by Jen Harvie (2013) and Adam Alston (2016) in relation to the spectator-participant of, respectively, social art and immersive theatre, I will now suggest that the turn to audience research also holds the risk of substantiating the reification of the neoliberal, individualized consumer operating within the auspices of contemporary global capitalism.

It is significant that the projects undertaken by Reinelt et al. and Sedgman were conducted in the context of (in the first instance in explicit collaboration with) specific theatre institutions and both placed the question of if, and how, particular theatre productions were 'valued' by their audiences at the heart of the research. Helen Freshwater notes that the common distinction between audience research undertaken by the theatre industry and that undertaken by scholars is that the latter 'for the most part, [are] interested in how audiences interpret what they have seen, whereas the industry is concerned with ensuring the profitability of its investment and is consequently more interested in why a production appeals and in generalising about patterns of consumption' (2009: 30). Freshwater's caution about the distinctly economic interest of the industry's investment, while clearly logical from a venue's perspective, does underline, for me, an uneasy alignment of recent academic interest in what the 'real' spectator thinks and the neoliberal concern with the customer being given exactly what it is that they think they want. In response to Sedgman's research, for example, John E. McGrath, then artistic director of National Theatre Wales, acknowledged that the challenge for him was how to use the outcomes to 'usefully inform the new production' (Sedgman 2016: 165). Although McGrath was clear that 'understanding audiences' responses does not necessarily mean doing everything differently' (165) and that 'to make shows that absolutely everyone will like, all the time, is simply impossible' (165), I'm not as confident as Sedgman in her conclusion that 'finding out more about audiences does not therefore have to lead to fewer risks' (165).

For some time now, in the UK theatre ecology, venues have gone further than the extrapolation of data from audience evaluations of previous shows to inform the selection, or production, of new ones. Helen Freshwater notes that 'the desire to engage with audiences and their responses has resulted in the emergence of a new category of work in the United Kingdom in recent years, as venues have begun to host "scratch nights," where unfinished work is presented and artists have an opportunity to gather feedback from audiences' (2009: 73). My view on scratch nights, while acknowledging the many productive aspects of them, is more critical than Freshwater's, and I have elsewhere expressed wider concerns about some of the implications of the proliferation of scratch nights on the new work ecology (Tomlin 2015: 277–9). Scratch nights are, as Freshwater observes, marketed to audiences with a strong emphasis on the opportunity to see future work at an early stage of development, and to input directly into a work in progress, whether through post-show discussions or questionnaires, or both. When I was first making work in the early 2000s, such responses were predominantly for the company to consider and could be extremely helpful in gaining disinterested perspectives on a piece of work in progress. However, as the decade advanced, it became increasingly common for venues interested in potential future production of the work to utilize these as guidance for the artist, with companies being asked to follow certain directions indicated by their scratch night spectators as a condition of further support.[2] Here, for me, we return precisely to that uneasy alignment between audience analysis and customer satisfaction where the art is at risk of being led by what the consumer thinks they want. This holds serious consequences for the type of work that is made which inevitably rests on how work comes to be valued and, ultimately, funded. By 2018 Arts Council England was set to re-tender for the latest version of the discredited Quality Metrics Framework, rebranded, rather terrifyingly, as the Consumer Insight Toolkit (Hill 2018). Like its discarded predecessor this would establish a standardized evaluation system to be used across (initially) the larger National Portfolio Organizations, so that a set of predetermined quality metrics, largely drawing on consumer satisfaction, could be used to measure and benchmark the quality of each organization's

---

[2] This knowledge is based on informal conversations with artists that are not possible to publicly evidence given the precarity of relationships between artists and the venues on which they rely.

artistic output against their own objectives and the corresponding statistics of their competitors.

Lewis, Inthorn and Wahl-Jorgensen argue that the market ideal of the consumer is now subsuming the agency of the human subject, no longer 'actively engaged in the shaping of society and the making of history' but rather consigned to 'simply choose between the products on display' (Lewis et al. 2005: 5–6). In the discourse of political theatres, the danger of such a reconfiguration is hugely counterproductive. Locating not the active citizen but the consumer at the heart of the theatre experience is to relocate the artistic work as a commodity that is designed to please consumers who already know what they like and what they want to buy. The implications extend further as the rules of the marketplace then seek artistic products that will sell the best and satisfy the widest range of spectators. At this point, art becomes an exercise in giving audiences more of what they have already enjoyed and abandoning the risk factor – and the possibility of changing existing aesthetic preferences or political perspectives – altogether.

This, of course, is precisely the kind of commodification of art that Theodor Adorno and Max Horkheimer (1997) identified in their seminal critique of the cultural industries and that practitioners of politically engaged theatre have historically been intent on resisting. The figure of the consumer can be seen to stand, throughout the range of political philosophy drawn on in this study, for the spectator-subject who has accepted the terms of the ideological norms of their society and their own role and complicity within neoliberalism. The consumer within the economic and political order happily accepts the compensations on offer from that economic and political order and does not question the structural apparatus, with all its inequalities and unethical practices, that enables them to continue to consume. Conversely, the spectator-subject who holds the potential of becoming the active citizen is most productively confronted with something unexpected, or in Bertolt Brecht's terms, something that should be familiar but is made to appear strange, to enable them to recognize and critically challenge such structures and their own role within them. In the next section I will argue that this makes a critical consideration of the imagined spectator as central to the political call-and-response operation as it is to consumerist modes of production, albeit in the service of very different ends. In the latter case, the artist or producer wishes to imagine the spectator well so that they can be given what they want; in the design of political dramaturgies, the artist or producer needs to imagine the spectator well so that their existing horizons of expectation can be targeted precisely before the work proceeds to subject them to challenge, or deconstruction.

Horizons of expectation

There is, of course, a healthy and entirely productive suspicion on the part of artists to an overemphasis on who it is that might be the future spectator of their work. As theatre maker Chris Goode lucidly describes, 'our attitude to "the audience" is so often a kind of benign paternalism ... that it causes us to target our operations at a kind of bogus Joe Public figure, a regular user of whatever it is that's replaced the Clapham Omnibus as our yardstick for averageness' (2011: 468). As Sedgman notes, 'this is one of the complaints levelled at audience researchers more generally: that artists do not want to know what audiences want because then they might try to give it to them, and what will that produce? Perhaps something slightly less than art' (2016: 164). Yet, such valid concerns notwithstanding, the political danger of entirely disregarding the future spectator of the address is that, as Jill Dolan identified in the late 1980s, a default spectator is always nevertheless implicitly addressed during the making process. In Dolan's argument, such a spectator was always 'assumed to be white, middle-class, heterosexual and male ... carved in the likeness of the dominant culture whose ideology he represents' (1988: 1). In the decades that have followed Dolan's work such a spectator might be hoped to have diversified somewhat, given the social progress that has been made, but it remains the case that where the spectator is not imagined, the default spectator is likely to take a shape not unlike that of the artist. This can sometimes provoke readings from spectators who feel themselves to have been misrecognized that might politically undermine the invitation that has been offered. As a spectator at Chris Goode's *Men in the Cities* (2014), for example, I left the performance with a female friend who shared my feeling of unease in being part of an audience in which we were directly addressed, yet unintentionally, it seemed, entirely alienated. Given the title, it wasn't a surprise to encounter a narrative that was wholly focused on men and boys, from the fictional characters to the murder of Drummer Lee Rigby, the role of the writer himself, his father and the friends Goode met down the pub, but the absence of flesh-and-blood females throughout unnervingly highlighted the sole representation: Prissy, the black doll who had belonged to a man's dead wife, was brutally mutilated by the man before he tries to write PROSTITUTE on her crumpled body. That the absence of women, or their figurative replacements, featured in the narrative principally to underline the emotional trauma of the male protagonists made it very difficult to feel that the piece was speaking to women at all, or if it was, what it was saying to them. When Goode looks directly into the eyes of his spectators at a critical point and echoes the words he has just spoken to his father, 'Can we not just put it all down. Aren't you tired of it all. Aren't you just tired' (Goode 2014: 72), my internal response was to wonder why he was talking to me as if I had ever been part of his narrative or complicit with it in any way. The book cover of the published script likewise promises a 'radically humane portrait of how *we* live now' (my emphasis), as if the whole of human experience had been accounted for here.

My examination of the artist's interpellation of the spectator, introduced in Chapter 5 and drawn on throughout this study, demonstrates that it is when spectators are misrecognized, or badly imagined, that the political aims of the dramaturgies in question are most likely to fail. Furthermore, it is not just artists who seek to advance specific ideological goals that might be advised to consider their audiences carefully. Avant-garde artists who merely intend to shock their audience out of their assumed habitual complacency by overturning the conventions or protocols of theatrical form or acceptable content will find their intentions thwarted if the audience in question is well-versed in the shock tactics being used and, indeed, has arrived at the performance in the very expectation and anticipation of their employment. Such tactics are, of course, particularly vulnerable to repeated use in front of returning audiences. Here, they soon become accepted conventions that no longer perform the original purpose of disruption or critical reflection, as Dennis Kennedy notes in his analysis of the spectators' gleeful complicity in riots at Futurist performances in the early twentieth century (2011: 57–9).

In such instances, I would argue, there are unforeseen problems between the encoding of the work with the intention of transgression and the decoding of the work as now-familiar and recognizable conventions. Thus, it is not just in the context of the political theatres that are the focus of this study that the speculative configuration of audience has a role to play. Whether it is Brecht's configuration of his audience as diners of a 'culinary' theatre that drives his Marxist-inspired aesthetic (Brecht 2015: 63) or the Futurists' configuration of a passive bourgeoisie who needed to be shocked into action, in both cases the ideological efficacy of their respective artistic intentions necessitates that the existing horizons of expectation held by their audiences are well-conceived.[3] The efficacy of Baz Kershaw's ideological transaction, to be discussed in the following chapter, relies precisely on the artist's speculative identification of the audience's existing ideological location in order to engage with them from within that horizon, before issuing them the invitation to think beyond their comfort zone. Political theatres that seek to offer new knowledges to their audiences would also be advised to make a reasonable guess as to what particular audiences might already know. Even Hans-Thies Lehmann's

---

[3] See Bennett 1990: 51–2 for the emergence of the concept of 'horizon of expectation' in literary history, emerging from the work of Hans Robert Jauss.

politics of perception, which underpins much work that would disavow Kershaw's validation of ideological intention, also relies for its affect – if not efficacy – on the shock that catapults the seemingly familiar into the momentarily strange, resulting in a shift of perception, as further discussed in the following chapter. This also requires a reasonable prediction of what the seemingly familiar, and indeed the potentially strange, to the audience in question might be.

Insights from recent empirical studies of audiences are, in fact, able to evidence the importance of the spectator's (in this case individual rather than collective) horizons of expectation in relation to the meanings each spectator takes from the performance, and the affects and effects that the performance has produced for that spectator. The first significant research into spectators' structures of investment, what subsequently became known as the user and gratifications (U+G) approach, evolved in mid-twentieth-century mass media audience research in opposition to the then prevailing reliance on the classic transmission communications model (or the 'behaviourist "effects" model'), noted above, of the 'vacant individual conditioned by individual media messages' (Staiger 2005: 44). The U+G approach proposed the analysis of audience response from the perspective and intentions of the proactive individual spectator *towards* the media, rather than the effect of the media *on* the allegedly passive spectator. The U+G approach was subsequently challenged in turn, Kim Schröder et al. argue, by reception research, which defined itself

> in dual opposition: on the one hand, to humanistic textual analysis, with its implied position that media meanings and ideologies are imposed on passive minds and may be brought to light by textual analysis alone; on the other hand, to the survey-based uses and gratifications (U+G) approach, whose analysis of media gratifications ignores the meanings that create these gratifications. Reception research is critical of both for neglecting to explore the everyday contexts in which meanings and uses arise in the first place. (2003: 122)

The continuing importance and deepening of reception, or audience, research to establish what is brought by the individual spectator to the performance (be that mass media or live theatre) is evidenced by Martin Barker's insistence that 'investment' is 'one variable which research has consistently shown to be crucial within audiences' responses' (2012: 191):

> By 'investment' I refer to the multifaceted ways in which, and degrees to which, audiences *become involved* in cultural forms and activities. ...

> Put simply, the different ways that audiences *care about* their media and
> cultural engagements, and how they *matter* to them, play radical roles in
> what they notice and attend to in them, their strategies for making sense
> of, assessing, critiquing, storing and cataloguing them as 'memories'
> (additions to self). (Barker 2012: 191)

In *Locating the Audience,* Kirsty Sedgman highlights the different structures
of investment spectators might hold in relation to 'Barmouth', 'theatre' and
'the relationship between Barmouth and theatre' in the context of a site-
specific show staged around Barmouth that purported to explore the history
of the town (2016: 101). In all cases the expectations and investments that
spectators brought with them to the performance are shown by Sedgman to be
an active agent in shaping each spectator's subsequent reception of the work.
In her further analysis of audiences attending two productions by National
Theatre Wales, she focuses in detail on audience expectation, constructing,
from collating individual responses, three orientations she defines as
'evaluative' (2016: 78), 'curious' (78) and 'critical' (110) which set up particular
frameworks of response. For the 'evaluative' spectator, the performance is
assessed in relation to a particular expectation of what was anticipated; its
value is measured by the degree to which it lived up to (or not) what was
anticipated. The 'critical' spectator had particular expectations that were
defined by previous, often more expert, knowledge of the field and how well this
particular performance might be measured against those criteria. The 'curious'
spectator came without particular expectations and was quite happy to be
surprised by what they found and to evaluate the experience on its own terms,
without reference to prior expectations, or specialist criteria. The structures
of investment for individual spectators can clearly not be predetermined
by the artist, but Sedgman's research demonstrates, by its narrative shaping
of individual responses into three broad categories, that collectively shared
structures of investment can be productively identified and, I would argue,
be productively predicted. For politically engaged theatres a consideration
of the likely horizons of expectation and structures of investment that their
spectators might hold in common would seem to be a vital component in their
dramaturgical design, as this study will go on to argue.

   Clearly, in case it needs stating, this study is not proposing that political
effect can ever be calculated, or assured, from any piece of art; conversely,
political effect can also be realized without, or in spite of, any intention on the
part of the artist. As Joe Kelleher states,

> Theatre remains unpredictable in its effects, given that its effects reside
> largely not in the theatrical spectacle itself but in the spectators and

what they are capable of making of it ... there is no guarantee that [a production's] effects will 'work' in the way they are supposed to or that its carefully constructed political messages will be understood in the ways they are supposed to be understood. (2009: 24)

As Stuart Hall also argues, the encoder 'cannot determine or guarantee ... which decoding codes will be employed. Otherwise communication would be a perfectly equivalent circuit, and every message would be an instance of "perfectly transparent communication"' (1980: 136). Nevertheless, he also counters, 'the vast range must contain *some* degree of reciprocity between encoding and decoding moments, otherwise we could not speak of an effective communicative exchange at all' (136).

Gareth White's (2013) notion of the invitation that is made to the spectator, and the importance of the aesthetic design of the invitation to its ultimate efficacy, will be appropriated from the context of participatory theatre which is his focus, to serve here as a useful lens through which intention and efficacy in the projects of political theatres might be examined. Like the 'procedural author', a term White borrows from Jan Murray (White 2013: 31), the political artist can design their invitation in ways that are more or less likely to affect the spectator, more or less likely to inspire the spectator to take up the invitation to play their part, however small, in furthering political change. The dramaturgical strategies of such invitations will be examined in Part Two of this study, following the deeper investigation undertaken in the subsequent two chapters into the configuration of the contemporary spectator to whom such invitations are addressed.

Conclusion

In this chapter, I have argued that, despite the assertions sometimes made by advocates of this approach, empirical audience research is no less theorized, no more reliable or authentic a model of analysis than the theorized approach this study intends to take. I also highlighted the risk that empirical research was furthering the neoliberal project of consumer satisfaction in the theatre industry, in the UK at least, and noted the dangers this posed for contemporary models of politically engaged theatre practice. Nevertheless, important findings from the field of empirical audience research supported the key premise of this study that artists making theatre of all kinds might be advised to think through, in advance, who their imagined spectators might be and to consider how existing horizons of audience expectation might impact on any intended outcomes of the work.

2

The Autonomous Spectator

In the previous chapter, I examined the growing trend in theatre studies, since the publication of Helen Freshwater's *theatre & audience* (2009), for empirical research into 'real' spectators. In this chapter, I turn my attention to a more deeply entrenched trend in the analysis of the spectator that reaches well back into the twentieth century but has been significantly consolidated since the 1990s. I term this the rise of the autonomous spectator, a figure that is named to align with the increasing emphasis on the logic of autonomy both within the contemporary phase of global capitalism and within a post-Marxist discourse, as I will further explore in the two subsequent chapters. Given the political duality of such a logic, the 'autonomous' spectator, I will argue, treads a thin line between the figure of the radical and active subject required by political theatres and the individualized consumer of neoliberal capitalism.

In this chapter, I will focus on the discursive insistence on the radical autonomy of the spectator of theatre to make or experience their own meaning, an insistence that proliferated during the emergence of postmodernism and poststructuralism and that has, since the turn of the century, been reaffirmed by significant and influential interventions such as Hans-Thies Lehmann's postdramatic politics of perception (2006: 185), Jacques Rancière's emancipated spectator (2009) and the broader cultural turn to theories of affect. The chapter is the first of two to focus on Rancière's influential analysis which is further explored in Chapter 6. Following a brief history of the rise of the autonomous spectator, I will offer an introduction to Rancière's understanding of the political, and the ways in which his theories of emancipated spectatorship have shored up the narrative of the autonomous spectator and the rejection of artistic intention and ideological steer in theatre and performance analysis.

Dramaturgies of spectatorship

The emergence of revitalized interest in the spectator towards the end of the 2010s was noted in the previous chapter. During the same period, the proliferation of immersive, interactive and participatory models of performance further shaped and accelerated the growing scholarly engagement with spectatorship, given that the spectator is not only central to discourses of reception within such practice but an integral aesthetic component of the work. The interest in the spectator-participant is reflected in the number of full-length studies and edited collections that have been published on this trend in a comparatively short space of time, including Josephine Machon's *Immersive Theatres: Intimacy and Immediacy in Contemporary Performance* (2013), Gareth White's *Audience Participation in Theatre: Aesthetics of the Invitation* (2013), Leslie Hill and Helen Paris's *Performing Proximity: Curious Intimacies* (2014), Adam Alston's *Beyond Immersive Theatre: Aesthetics, Politics and Productive Participation* (2016), James Frieze's *Reframing Immersive Theatre: The Politics and Pragmatics of Participatory Performance* (2016), Rose Biggin's *Immersive Theatre and Audience Experience: Space, Game and Story in the Work of Punchdrunk* (2017) and Josh Machamer's *Immersive Theatre: Engaging the Audience* (2018).

The notable emphasis on the primacy of individualized response in the field of immersive and participatory theatre is unsurprising, given that such models of practice are characterized by their efforts to locate each spectator in unique relation to the work, often through the lens of phenomenological analysis that is necessarily individualized, as noted in the previous chapter. The autonomy of the individual spectator has not, however, been so commonly foregrounded as desirable in the diachronic narrative of politically driven dramaturgies that is the subject of this book. In *The Politics of Performance*, published in 1992, Baz Kershaw undertook an examination of the 'ideological transaction' (1992: 16) that takes place in the reception of a politically engaged theatre event, arguing that the first act to ensure the efficacy of political performance must be to 'connect with that audience's ideology or ideologies' before subjecting the ideology – which underpinned the shared identity of the audience – to challenge (1992: 21). By so doing, Kershaw argued, the artist could provoke a 'crisis' in those ideological beliefs that might instigate a change of perspective in the audience that could be carried forwards into the world beyond the theatre (1992: 27). Kershaw thus dismissed Martin Esslin's assertion that 'meaning must be different for each individual member of the audience' (Esslin 1987: 21 in Kershaw 1992: 35), a claim that was exposed by Kershaw as 'an ideology of individualism which assumes that a society can function through discourses that do not produce common meanings' and which had 'profound ideological ramifications' (Kershaw 1992: 35). The 'ideology of individualism', rightly identified by Kershaw as a risk to the collectivist transactional model of political effect, was, of course, at the very heart of the postmodern project that was to characterize the mainstream of theatrical innovation throughout subsequent decades.

Sceptical of the grand narrative of Marxism that had underpinned the political theatres of the 1960s and 1970s, the 1980s saw leading avant-garde artists, such as the UK's Forced Entertainment, eschew not only explicitly ideological narratives but the very idea of a transaction between artist and audience in favour of fragmentation and plurality of meaning that would resist consensual or collective interpretation. The politics of the exchange between artist and spectator, in postmodern discourse, was framed in terms of a shift from consumer to critical spectator, with Florian Malzacher arguing that in the work of Forced Entertainment 'the spectator thus becomes a witness – the counter model to the idea of a passive being in Guy Debord's *The Society of the Spectacle*' (2004: 124).

The publication of Hans-Thies Lehmann's *Postdramatic Theatre*, in German in 1999, translated into English in 2006, was to offer theatre studies a discipline-specific lens through which to analyse the aesthetics that had often been branded as postmodern and had been in the ascendency for some time. Lehmann's work, which I discuss at length in a previous study, has been pivotal to the dismissal of ideological steer through his insistence that the radical political credentials of the postdramatic rested on the autonomy of spectator response (Tomlin 2013: 44–76). For Lehmann, the political work of theatre, what he terms 'a politics of perception' (2006: 185), is not undertaken with a collective audience or discernible ideological project in mind but operates through the invitation to each individual spectator to think critically and self-reflexively about what they are shown, and to be open to unanticipated affective impact that might disorientate their habitual response. In Lehmann's later work he insists on 'an *interruption* and caesura of the sphere of aesthetic representation. Then and only then is it possible to experience a shaking or destabilising of the basic grounds of our cultural existence, even a blurring of the boundaries of the self, of conceptual understanding as such' (2013: 98–9). For Lehmann, it is only through transgressions that overstep the accepted framework of theatrical representation that the spectator can be shocked out of their habitual mode of perception and regain the capacity to become critically active and alert to their own customary practices of engaging with the world around them.

Following the spectator's reconfiguration as a post-Brechtian witness, advocated by both postdramatic and documentary forms, came, in the 2000s, the rise of participatory, immersive and interactive performance and, as a consequence, the demand for increasing degrees of participation from the spectator. This spectator-participant was also mostly configured as a radical figure, supported by parallels with sociopolitically charged participatory practice such as that of Augusto Boal, and too often placed in false opposition, as I have argued elsewhere, to the figure of the so-called passive spectator (Tomlin 2013: 171–5). Claims for the radical political potential of interactive and immersive performance were, however, thoughtfully explored, if still much contested, via artists and scholars who drew on the relational aesthetics of Nicolas Bourriaud, who was interested in the context of visual arts, in how 'inventing ways of being together' might offer a shift in subjectivity and relation (2002: 60).

Given the emphasis – both within the marketing of immersive theatre and the scholarly analysis surrounding it – on the unique experience of the individual spectator, some critics have noted the more uncomfortable political parallels with the experience economy offered to the consumer by neoliberal capitalism (see Wickstrom 2006; Harvie 2013; Tomlin 2013: 171–206; Alston 2016). Such cautions notwithstanding, the emphasis on the spectator's sensory and somatic experience within immersive and interactive performance has predominantly strengthened the radical claims of autonomous spectatorship and accelerated the marginalization of intended *effect* by foregrounding examination of the *affective* impact on the individual spectator – one that might encompass emotional, phenomenological and multisensory responses. Although, as Erin Hurley (2010) clearly outlines in *theatre & feeling*, 'questions of feeling have always been central to theatre' (2), phenomenological concerns about liveness, embodiment and the felt experience in the real space and time of the event have clearly been in the ascendency in the making and analysis of contemporary theatre practice. Recent scholarly publications such as *Between Us: Audiences, Affect and the In-Between* (Whalley and Miller 2017), *Performance, Feminism and Affect in Neoliberal Times* (Diamond, Varney and Amich 2017) and *Ecologies of Precarity in Twenty-First Century Theatre: Politics, Affect, Responsibility* (Fragkou 2018) not only attest to the revitalized interest in affect in theatre studies but importantly gesture consistently to its political potential. This interest in affect within the discourse of political theatres marks a significant break with the Brechtian scepticism of theatres that sought an overly affective response. For scholars such as Carl Lavery, the politics at play in a medium such as theatre that is predominantly 'embodied, ephemeral and affective' (2016b: 230) are most productively conceptualized, not through 'what the theatre text means but rather … what the theatre medium "does"; in how, that is, its dramaturgical distribution of organic and inorganic bodies in actual time and space creates sensations and experiences in the here and now' (2016b: 230).

The contemporary emphasis on the political potential of autonomy, relationality and affective response, while offering rich contributions to the discipline, has less productively served to somewhat undermine the historical notions of political theatre, as Janelle Reinelt argued in her keynote address to the 2014 meeting of the International Federation of Theatre Research. Reinelt highlighted in her keynote, and in a subsequently published article (2015), many of the scholars I will engage with throughout this study, including the seminal influence of Jacques Rancière, and I must acknowledge a debt to her thinking which touched an important nerve within my own research in the early stages of writing this book. The historical political theatre against which the tide, as Reinelt noted, had turned was one that, in the words here of Alan Read (2008), was 'operative through efficacy, commitment and opposition' (22). Read summarily dismisses a theatre which is characterized by 'the desire for political resolution, through an expedient rhetorics of *solution*' (22), along with a theatre which 'announces its political purpose' (28), attempts 'to *solve* the social question "by offering some prosthesis for political action"' (Latour 2005: 160 in Read 2008: 51) or seeks to 'construe political outcomes' (74). Lavery, while 'reluctant … to dismiss theatre's social impact out of hand' (2016b: 229), nevertheless advocates an 'indirect and "negative"' pedagogy 'that hesitates to prescribe a "strong meaning" and which willingly opens itself to further interpretation and dialogue … to trouble notions of mastery and intentionality, to remain hypothetical and suspensive' (2016b: 230). In *Passionate Amateurs: Theatre, Communism and Love* (2013) Nicholas Ridout explicitly aligns his project with Rancière's rejection of mastery and intention, arguing that the politics of theatre should not be understood in terms of theatre's sociopolitical agency, that is as something that takes place within the theatre that *then* has a political effect on the world beyond it, but as affective labour taking place in the very real world of the theatre: 'a real place, where real people go to work, and where their work takes the form of "conversation"' (124). For Ridout, 'the act of dedicating oneself to acting and speaking together … is, in and of itself, a political act' (16).

I will return in Chapter 6 to this discursive trend that Tony Fisher terms the 'efficacy argument' (16), a discourse that 'rejects the metaphysics of causality that underpins the assumptions of those who hold that theatre is primarily a form of communication that produces "predictable" rhetorical effects on its audience … what Rancière dismisses as the "pedagogical model" of political theatre' (16). Read, Ridout and Fisher all draw on the theories of Jacques Rancière who, throughout his extensive body of work, has consistently questioned the validity, good faith or possibility of what he variously terms politicized art, critical art and committed art practices. As Simon Bayly confirms, Rancière, in common with many of his contemporaries, 'suspend[s] a belief in the earlier promise of performance from the 1960s and 1970s as a means of direct political transformation, but acknowledge[s] …

that the politics of theatre can now only be entrusted to the possibility of heterogeneous and incalculable imaginings by individual spectators' (2009: 26). Bayly is speaking here of the politics of theatre in its broadest sense, pertinently noting that the usefulness of theatre as a metaphor for political dissensus seems to clearly supersede, in Rancière's own writings, the potential of literal manifestations of theatre itself to perform the politics he requires. The difficulties Rancière seems to encounter when approaching any political analysis of contemporary models of theatre practice are also noted by Hans-Thies Lehmann (2013: 100–4), yet despite Rancière's preference for, in Bayly's words, the 'no-nonsense contemplation of an image or screen' (2009: 25) over participation in the messy apparatus of the theatre event, Rancière's influence on the discipline of theatre and performance – mainly via his notions of the emancipated spectator – has been quite phenomenal, thus necessitating the following in-depth interrogation of his philosophy.

The politics of dissensus

Drawing on and deepening the now-familiar postmodern and postdramatic theories of reception, Rancière proposes, in place of political efficacy, an 'aesthetic efficacy … a paradoxical kind of efficacy that is produced by the very rupturing of any determinate link between cause and effect' (2009: 63). He thus explicitly relocates the political in the assertion of the spectator's *non-anticipated* and entirely individual response to an aesthetic experience. Of artistic practices, he explicitly acknowledges that their capacity to shift our affective attention

> can open up new passages towards new forms of political subjectivation. *But none of them can avoid the aesthetic cut that separates outcomes from intentions and precludes any direct path towards an 'other side' of words and images.* (2009: 82, my emphasis)

Rancière's highly influential treatise of the emancipated spectator thus conclusively rejects any notion of a political theatre that relies on the transmission of meaning by the artist that is intended to be received and acted upon by the spectator to political effect or outcome. When Rancière states that the performance 'is the third thing that is owned by no one, whose meaning is owned by no one, but which subsists between them, excluding any uniform transmission, any identity of cause and effect' (2009: 15), he is not speaking here simply of the contemporary distrust of the explicit political message inherited from the postmodern turn.

Rancière would also deny the more modest desire of an artist to elicit even 'a form of consciousness, an intensity of feeling, an energy for action' (14), if this was understood as something that could in any way be determined by the artist's intention. His treatise of the emancipated spectator thus rests on a particular understanding of the political that, for Rancière, underpins the assertion of equality: the insistence on the spectator's equality with the artist through her subsequent act of creation, composing 'her own poem with the elements of the poem before her' (13). Consequently, as Rancière concludes, 'the very same thing that makes the aesthetic "political" stands in the way of all strategies for "politicizing art"' (74), as the artist's intention to provoke a particular political response is denied under the political operations of aesthetic efficacy.

Rancière conceptualizes *the political* as the field of encounter between emancipatory politics (the insistence on the equality of each individual) and the governing policies of the state that dictate the given (and unequal) order of things (1992: 58–9). Such an order comes to be perceived as the accepted distribution of the sensible (*partition du sensible*) – the 'divisions and boundaries that define, among other things, what is visible and audible within a particular aesthetico-political regime' (Rockhill 2004a: xii). The political is first and foremost dissensual in its operation to create 'a fissure in the sensible order by confronting the established framework of perception, thought, and action with the "inadmissible"' (Rockhill 2004b: 88–9).

Critically for the dialogue I will undertake, in this chapter, with Rancière's notion of the political, his conceptualization of the dissensus it operates is understood as democratic in its insistence on the admittance of those who would otherwise be, or who have been, excluded from the given distribution of the sensible. The excluded are understood by Rancière as the 'supplementary part of every account of the population', often termed the 'no parts', '[t]hose who have no name, who remain invisible and inaudible' (Rockhill 2004a: xiv), as opposed to the 'parts' who are already accounted for within the existing coordinates of the sensible. Thus, dissensus, as will become central to the argument of this chapter, is egalitarian and democratic in so far as it constitutes a disruption of 'the distribution of the sensible *by supplementing it with those who have no part in the perceptual coordinates of the community*, thereby modifying the very aesthetico-political field of possibility' (Rockhill 2004a: xiv, emphasis mine). This modification of the coordinates of a non-egalitarian distribution of the sensible is undertaken, Rancière argues, 'by implementing the universal presupposition of politics: we are all equal' (Rockhill 2004a: xiv). Thus, equality, for Rancière, is not an aspiration, but an assertion that, in itself, constitutes the political potential of dissensus. Rancière's political 'is the terrain upon which the verification of

equality confronts the established order of identification and classification'
(Rockhill 2004b: 93–4).

Rancière traces the etymological roots of 'emancipation' to the notion
of 'emergence from a state of minority' (2009: 42), and it is the inequalities
that are upheld by the self-validating distribution of the sensible, which is
the fundamental target of Rancière's notion of dissensus through which all
are imbued with the equal capacity to speak and to interpret. In the broader
sense of the aesthetic realm, that for Rancière comes before any discussion of
artistic practices, the politics of the distribution of the sensible thus 'revolves
around what is seen and what can be said about it, around who has the
ability to see and the talent to speak, around the properties of spaces and
the possibilities of time' (2004: 8). Through and beyond the allegorical dyads
of schoolmaster/student and artist/spectator that are well known to theatre
scholars, Rancière exemplifies the operation of dissensus with reference to
situations that arise from an explicitly materialist divide between those who
are granted the capacity and privilege to know/see/speak and those who are
not. He argues, for example, of the political potency of a worker's account
written during the French Revolution whereby his labour was interrupted
when his gaze was distracted towards an appreciation of a picturesque
view. Here, the 'aesthetic rupture' produced an 'appropriation of the place
of work and exploitation as the site of a free gaze' (Rancière 2009: 71), and
other similar ruptures that dislocate the accepted terms of unequal material
contexts abound throughout Rancière's writings. As Slavoj Žižek notes in his
afterword to Rancière's *The Politics of Aesthetics*, 'Rancière endeavours again
and again to elaborate the contours of those magic, violently poetic moments
of political subjectivization in which the excluded ... put forward their claim
to speak for themselves, to effectuate a change in the global perception of
social space, so that their claims would have a legitimate place in it' (Žižek
2004: 65).

As Rancière's political seeks to disrupt the non-egalitarian 'global
perception of social space' through an assertion of equality, so does the
same conception of the political, within the context of the dramaturgies of
theatre that are the object of this study, seek to disrupt the given coordinates
of the historical understanding of critical art that allocate to the artist the
role of steering the reception of the work and to the spectator the role of
receiving the message, or lesson, or meaning, in accordance with the artist's
intention. Rancière has termed this disruption 'the aesthetic break' which he
characterizes as 'a break with the regime of representation or the mimetic
regime' (2009: 60). For Rancière, such a regime constitutes 'concordance
between sense and sense' (60), the conviction that the actions on the stage
are accurate reflections of the real world.

The aesthetic break with such a regime, for Rancière, is firstly enacted in the requirement for the artwork itself to reject the mimetic vocabulary that would propose a straightforward correspondence between the 'sensory signs' of the artwork and the 'natural signs' of a world beyond it, and thus prevent the subsequent conviction that intended ethical effects, pertaining to both, would logically follow (60). The second enactment incorporates a break not only with the mimetic representations of naturalism but also with the Brechtian *Verfremdungseffekt* of demystification. Here, the break enacts a dismantling of the correspondence between the way in which the work is constructed to be received and the way in which it is, in fact, received. Aesthetics, as Rancière concludes, is 'the rupture of the harmony that enabled correspondence between the texture of the work and its efficacy' (62).

Thus, as seen from the operations outlined above, Rancière understands the politics of aesthetic efficacy to be embedded in the assertion of equality that constitutes, in this context, the insistence on the individual's autonomy from the artist's intention to construct their own meaning. This challenges Kershaw's conception of political efficacy due to the reliance of the ideological transaction on a cause-and-effect model. Such a model, Rancière would argue, upholds the relation of mastery that is implicitly assumed by the transference of knowledge from one whose role is to know and to speak to one who is excluded from artistic capacity and designated only to learn and to listen. Conversely, the political currency of aesthetic efficacy, Rancière argues, lies precisely in the capacity of art forms to disrupt the allocations of those roles within the received distribution of the sensible and assert the equality of the spectator (arguably, as I'll return to, a 'no part' within the configuration of the given coordinates of artistic creation) to, herself, create through the insistence on an autonomous response or interpretation that may be far from that the artist intended.

So just as the 'emancipated proletarian is a dis-identified worker' (2009: 73), free to be more than their allocated social role, so the emancipated spectator becomes conceptualized as a dis-identified recipient of transmitted knowledge, of what she is intended to see, think or feel. Thus, the emancipatory, and radical, potential of Rancière's newly configured relationship between artist and recipient is drawn from the wider political potential of the aesthetic cut that can disrupt the social givens of who is empowered to speak and who must listen; who is empowered to teach and who must learn; those who have a part to play and those 'parts with no part' who exist as politically fertile contradictions in the current hegemonic order. The political charge of dissensus is thus inextricably bound to the disruption of a given distribution of the sensible that is structured by material inequality, and this, I will now argue, needs to be more fully considered than is often the case when Rancière's aesthetic break is recontextualized within specific material artistic practices.

The politics of affect

It is a mark of Rancière's influence within theatre and performance studies that his work has impacted significantly even in the fields of applied theatre and theatre for development, historically those practices tethered most securely to the notion of artistic intention designed to be followed by specific, and sometimes quantifiable, political impact beyond the work itself. In her analysis of theatre for development in a neoliberal context, Maurya Wickstrom (2012) draws directly on Rancière to argue that the political effects required or predetermined by the humanitarian development agencies are too often designed to further secure the ideological divide that such agencies uphold – the divide that separates those whose knowledge is superior (the developers) and those who are designated as lacking (the recipients). In Rancière's terms, this divide replicates the neoliberal distribution of the sensible that consigns certain roles to certain subjects and maintains the authority of the designated over those who have been ideologically constructed as incapable (i.e. the 'parts' and the 'parts with no part'). For Wickstrom, following Rancière, 'emancipation begins ... when the desire or demand for efficacy ceases, as efficacy implies structures of who says and who does not say, who knows and who does not' (Wickstrom 2012: 104). The potentially radical impact of this suspension of intended political effect features significantly in Rony Brauman's reconception of humanitarianism which Wickstrom strongly advocates. In Brauman's account the purpose of humanitarian aid is to support individual recovery without steering the direction of travel; thus, whether the individual who has been supported finds the strength and motivation to become a suicide bomber, an illegal migrant or a successful businessman is irrelevant to an evaluation of the 'success' or 'failure' of the humanitarian agency involved (Wickstrom 2012: 119). As Wickstrom notes, Brauman's refusal of the divide between those who are assigned the capacity to know best and those who are assigned the capacity to learn and respond as intended enables unknown and unintended effects to take place which have the capacity to disrupt the existing distribution of the sensible in ways that have not been foreseen.

James Thompson is also explicit about the change of direction he is advocating for applied theatre as pronounced in the title of his book: *Performance Affects: Applied Theatre and the End of Effect* (2009). Although Thompson is clear that this provocation is not to be taken as 'a death knell

announcing the untimely demise of the term' (2009: 3), but in the spirit of
enquiry or 'boundary testing' (3), he too critiques, with a nod to Rancière,
the potential of applied theatre practitioners to slip into relations of mastery
(134) towards the communities in which they work and is among the first to
explicitly advocate the introduction of 'an *affective register*' (7) into applied
practice. The understanding and analysis of affect within the discourse of
political dramaturgies takes many varied forms, and I will return to different
political readings of affect in Chapter 6. In Thompson's work, however, his
call for attention to affect constitutes a proposal for a greater emphasis, within
applied theatre practice, on modes of feeling, sensation and emotion, rather
than the existing focus on specific social or political outcomes, or effects.
This aligns with the broader rejection of the intentionalism of 'politicized
art' that is advocated by Rancière; and Thompson's field of study, theatre in
war zones, is a useful one to demonstrate how unintended affect, as opposed
to ideologically steered meaning, can secure the democratic or egalitarian
potential of the aesthetic break in the context of an unequal aesthetic
economy. Through this lens it can be seen how the negation of an *intended*
political effect, as advocated by Lavery, Read and Ridout above, can indeed
remain aligned to an egalitarian discourse of theatre that operates in sites of
explicit inequality as Thompson and Wickstrom propose.

Thompson is clear that his turn to affective outcomes is not a rejection of
'effect', but rather 'an augmentation of what should be understood, hoped for
and considered in relation to any experience' (2009: 120) that might counter
the tendency for practitioners to understand their work 'solely in the realm
of effect, where performance communicates messages or concentrates on
identifiable social or educational impact' (7) – a concentration resulting,
Thompson argues, on a weakened or restricted practice which fails to
'recognise affect – bodily responses, sensations and aesthetic pleasure' (7).
Thompson (2009: 7) draws on Jill Dolan's (2005: 5) 'exquisite moments' of
utopian performances to construct a 'terrain of sensation: of the aesthetic
concerns for beauty, joy, pleasure, awe and astonishment' (Thompson 2009:
117) that can counter an exclusive focus on political effects within applied
performance practice. Moreover, Thompson argues, 'the fact that, in and of
itself, affect has no point is its critical point of departure' (128), as it offers
individuals the opportunity to take precisely what they want from those
exquisite moments rather than merely receive what those on the other side of
the divide deem is productive in order to maintain the existing distribution
of the sensible.

Unintended affective response holds radical potential under the rubric
of Rancière's aesthetic efficacy, both through its pointlessness (the absence
of intention) and through what might be understood as its redistributive

potential in a context of deprivation. Within what we might call, *pace* Bourdieu (1993), a redistributive aesthetic economy, the potential for resistance might indeed be said to lie in a rebalancing of the aesthetic or emotional capital that is globally weighted against the disenfranchised, or parts with no part, to the same degree that economic capital is recognized to be. In this context, as Thompson also persuasively argues, aesthetic pleasure can transcend its capacity for respite to become instead an act of 'resistance *and* redistribution' when it occurs in 'a world of inequality, social injustice and endemic violence' (2009: 11). Nigel Thrift's influential analysis of affect also advocates the benefits of 'receptive practices' which 'are not reliant on an implicit or explicit promise to satisfy some request' (2004: 70), arguing that broadening our palette of affective capacity will enable us to be moved by more and moved differently. Thus, the capacity of the spectator-subject to respond fully to Rancière's aesthetic rupture is increased, enabling a potentially more radical reconfiguration of 'what presents itself to sense experience' (Rancière 2004: 8).

Silvija Jestrovic's account of aesthetic activity within the siege of Sarajevo corroborates the validity of Thompson's analysis, stating that 'all the examples of cultural production … could be read as forms of resistance' to an acceptance of the inhabitants' otherwise reduced capacity from citizens with agency to mere 'naked life' (2015: 85). As Judith Butler confirms, 'though neither the image nor the poetry can free anyone from prison, or stop a bomb or, indeed, reverse the course of the war, they nevertheless do provide the conditions for breaking out of the quotidian acceptance of war' (Butler 2009:11). In an increasingly precarious Europe, the 'world of inequality, social injustice and endemic violence' (Thompson 2009: 11) that Thompson locates at distance would appear to be somewhat closer to home in the reality which many European citizens, and the millions who arrive here fleeing devastation in their home countries, are now experiencing. The closer the continent slides towards a critical state of collapse, and the more of its inhabitants who find themselves living on the precipice of what might meaningfully constitute a citizenship with agency, the more we might want to acknowledge the potential of artistic activity without specific political intention to, in Thompson's account, transcend respite.

But Dolan's 'exquisite moments' (2005: 5) and Thompson's affects of 'beauty, joy, pleasure, awe and astonishment' (2009: 117) can only perform the politics of dissensus in material contexts of inequality that reflect those highlighted in Rancière's own work. Beyond such contexts, affective responses can indeed, in Thrift's words, be 'a means of celebrating the joyous, even transcendent, confusion of life itself' (2008: 15), but while such moments of celebration may well be therapeutic and vitally necessary for all spectator-subjects they cannot perform the politics of dissensus in contexts that leave the wider, and inegalitarian, distribution of the sensible undisturbed. To do so would be to argue for a conceptualization of dissensus that knows no distinction between the provision of exquisite moments for the spectator who is being held in a refugee camp, the spectator who sleeps in the doorways of European cities living on food banks and handouts, and the theatre scholar, to use myself as an example, who watches *The Magic Flute* with delight from a £70 seat in the Edinburgh Opera House. In the first two instances, the spectators would be emancipated from their capacities as 'naked life' or 'no-parts' and, consequently, their empowerment to engage in and interpret aesthetic activity would indeed be one of dissensus. In the third instance, the spectator would be fulfilling her allocated capacity to continue being enriched by the affective aesthetics that were a cultural given of her location within the current distribution of the sensible. To argue that the 'equality' presumed on the part of all three spectators to take what affects or effects they desired from their aesthetic experience was in and of itself political in an egalitarian sense would be to ignore Rancière's own insistence that 'equality is not, to begin with, political in itself' but 'only generates politics when it is implemented in the specific form of a particular case of dissensus' (2004: 48–9). The equality of the third spectator can be insisted on in terms of the egalitarian right to autonomous response, but this declaration of equality does not enact the same political movement towards egalitarian aims more broadly. Here, the sensations of 'beauty, joy, pleasure, awe and astonishment' (Thompson 2009: 117) can thus be seen as therapeutic, rather than politically dissensual, operations in a context in which the non-egalitarian distribution of the sensible and the spectator's privileged role within it is upheld, regardless of how 'emancipated' the spectator might be from the role of 'recipient of meaning' in the micro-sphere of a particular artistic event. This is an important caution to consider given that the political dramaturgies that are the focus of this study operate for paying audiences, rather than in an applied context.

In such instances, as I will further explore in Chapter 6, the political operation of the logic of autonomy – if not held in tension with dramaturgical strategies that seek to address the wider context of inequality beyond the theatre – might more accurately be characterized as libertarian in its freedom from any responsibility beyond the protection of individual sovereignty of interpretation (see footnote p. 12). A logic of libertarianism liberates the spectator-subject not only from the determination of the artist (as libertarian politics demand freedom from the determination of the state) but also from any obligation to those who are 'other' to the spectator-subject's sense of individual or collective identity (an operation libertarian politics also enacts). If the logic of autonomy is entirely severed from the inegalitarian contexts discussed above, and without other means of potentially disrupting the wider inegalitarian distribution of the sensible beyond the theatre, then I would argue that the practice in question is libertarian in its politics and cannot productively be considered to be aligned with the post-Marxist project of radical democracy, however else it may be justly valued for its aesthetic, philosophical or therapeutic benefits.

The limits of autonomy

The contemporary emphasis on the political potential of the spectator's autonomy and affective response, as outlined above, holds certain additional risks that could further undermine the legitimacy of theatre practices seeking to effect political change at the present time, irrespective of the material context of the work. Jacques Rancière and those theorists drawing on his thinking focus entirely on the necessity of the spectator's essential autonomy from the ideological intention of the artist who might seek to make 'politicized art', but they too often fail to interrogate whether it is possible for the spectator to remain autonomous from the hegemonic narratives that construct the ideological norms and structures by which the spectator-subject lives. Judith Butler articulates the necessity of acknowledging our dependence on, and vulnerability to, the societal and ideological norms that condition and form our perceptions, insisting that we are not only active subjects but subjects that are also acted on: 'norms act on us from all sides, that is, in multiple and sometimes contradictory ways; they act upon a sensibility at the same time that they form it; they lead us to feel in certain ways, and those feelings can enter into our thinking even, as we might well end up thinking about them' (2015b: 5). For Butler, with Zeynep Gambetti and Leticia Sabsay, the idea that the subject's perceptions can be independent of, or impervious to, ideological norms is derived from discredited 'masculinist models of autonomy' (Butler et al. 2016: 6):

> If nothing acts on or against my will or without my advanced knowledge, then there is only sovereignty, the posture of control over the property that I have and that I am, a seemingly sturdy and self-centred form of the thinking 'I' that seeks to cloak those fault lines in the self that cannot be overcome. What form of politics is supported by this adamant mode of disavowal? Is this not the masculinist account of sovereignty that, as feminists, we are called on to dismantle? (Butler 2016: 23)

Butler's insistence that we acknowledge the subject's vulnerability as an essential element of the subject's capacity to resist is something that I will engage with more critically in Chapter 8. Here, however, it is clear that such vulnerability to ideological norms prevents both the 'real' spectator of the previous chapter and the theorized autonomous spectator of this one from interpreting a piece of theatre from some kind of neutral, or non-ideological, vantage point around which all possible responses will hover with equal attraction. If, as Slavoj Žižek argues, there is an 'inherent impossibility of isolating a reality whose consistency is not maintained by ideological mechanisms, a reality that does not disintegrate the moment we subtract from it its ideological component' (1994: 15–16), then the would-be-autonomous responses of the individual spectator are always-already imbricated in and, arguably, steered by ideological mechanisms in the moment of meeting with the artwork itself. I will also return to Žižek's theory in more detail in Chapter 8, but what is critical to note here is that both he and Judith Butler substantiate my response to Rancière's notion of autonomy: the spectator is not a free subject at risk of being ideologically interpellated by a piece of theatre (or anything else) but an already ideological subject.

While I am certainly not arguing, after Althusser ([1971] 2008), that the dominant ideological structures of contemporary neoliberalism are monolithic or inescapable, I am suggesting, after Butler and Žižek, that it is nonetheless entirely possible that even if the autonomy of the spectator from the ideological intention of the theatre artist can be secured, the spectator's autonomy from the ideological pressures of the contemporary political moment is much less straightforward to uphold. This is a critical blind spot in Rancière's thinking, as also noted by Simon Bayly, who contends that the would-be political act of dissensus envisaged by Rancière 'appears magically inoculated against the effects of the police order, preserving its militant challenge to the distribution of the sensible in a way that seems entirely implausible under contemporary cultural conditions' (2009: 25).

Notwithstanding Rancière's insistence, explored in depth in Chapter 6, that the subject is far from sovereign in her autonomy, but is ultimately relational and vulnerable on much the same terms as those offered by Butler, Rancière nonetheless fails to acknowledge that this understanding of subjectivity inevitably limits the autonomy of the spectator-subject in their perceptions and response. Thus, there is no acknowledgement that artistic practices that discredit all notions of ideological intention are, in effect, enabling the spectator to respond affectively from a position that is already-ideologically interpellated, to some degree or other, within the dominant ideological hegemony. Furthermore, in the absence of any kind of ideological steer or challenge to such a hegemony, they may well prefer to leave the ideological lens through which they have learned to perceive the world undisturbed. This is, of course, no new critique of theatre that prioritizes affective response, as extensively argued by Bertolt Brecht, among many others, but it is no less critical to bear in mind in the return to a discourse of affect at this particular historical moment. I will do so throughout this study, proposing that Althusser's concerns regarding the ideological interpellation of the subject may not be quite as comprehensively overcome as Rancière's own divergence from Althusser might suggest.

Conclusion

By briefly examining Rancière's notion of emancipation in the context of applied theatre, I have proposed that, for those at the sharp edge of neoliberal capitalism, the attempt of the artist to uphold the spectator's autonomy can indeed be understood as progressively political in the way Rancière intends, given that it constitutes a redistribution of pleasurable affective and emotional capital to those for whom it is most often limited in range and supply. However, I have questioned to what degree an unfettered logic of autonomous response can be understood as progressively political when removed from contexts of cultural and economic deprivation and relocated in the professional circuit that is this book's field of study. In such a context, I argue, and without any additional mechanisms to disrupt the wider inegalitarian distribution of the sensible beyond the theatre, the impact on the spectator might more accurately be described as therapeutic or libertarian, a thread I return to in more depth in Chapter 6. I concluded my introduction to Rancière with a further caution that reverberates throughout this study: a spectator's response may be autonomous from the artist's intention, but no response can be wholly autonomous from the influence of the ideological structures of neoliberalism by which the contemporary spectator, to a greater or lesser degree, might be said to be shaped.

3

Precarious Spectators

In the previous chapter, I detailed the rise of the autonomous spectator and examined the significant influence of Jacques Rancière's discourse of the emancipated spectator in the field of contemporary political theatre. I concluded with the caution that given each spectator meets any dramaturgical practice from positions that are always-already imbricated in ideological structures, it cannot be assumed that the spectator's response is 'autonomous' and free from ideological influence, even if it can be asserted to be autonomous, as Rancière would argue, from the artist's intention or the ideological steer of the work itself.

In this chapter, while I will certainly not argue that the dominant ideological structures of contemporary neoliberalism are monolithic or inescapable, I will suggest that they should, at the very least, be taken into account in any theoretical prefiguration of the contemporary spectator-subject, notwithstanding the individuality of constituent audience members or the importance of divergent factors of socio-economic background, ideological affiliation, cultural or national identity, race, gender, age or sexual orientation. This prefiguration is designed to counter the implied ideological neutrality of the autonomous spectator, and to locate the need for dramaturgical strategies and political steer that might rather provoke the contemporary spectator-subject to resist the seductive ideological interpellation of their time.

Subject of/to neoliberalism

The contemporary subject of the developed world has been variously considered as individualized (Bauman 2001; Beck 1992), precarious (Bourdieu 1997; Standing 2011) and ironic (Chouliaraki 2012) and is commonly located as emerging during the most recent wave of global capitalism characterized by the acceleration and intensification of neoliberalism around the beginning of the 1990s and continuing through the time of writing. Paul Mason's succinct description of neoliberalism will serve us well here:

Neoliberalism is the doctrine of uncontrolled markets: it says that the best route to prosperity is individuals pursuing their own self-interest, and the market is the only way to express that self-interest. It says the state should be small (except for its riot squad and secret police); that financial speculation is good; that inequality is good; that the natural state of humankind is to be a bunch of ruthless individuals, competing with each other. (Mason 2015: xi)

Mason's emphasis on the individualism of neoliberalism and the subsequent validation of competition and inequality are particularly relevant to this study, as is his contestation that neoliberalism is a form of capitalism quite distinct from those that went before it. Neoliberalism is, he argues, the latest manifestation of the '*learning* organism' that is capitalism, an organism that 'morphs and mutates in response to danger, creating patterns and structures barely recognizable to the generation that came before' (2015: xiii).

For Luc Boltanski and Eve Chiapello, each regeneration of capitalism requires a 'spirit' that 'legitimates and constrains the accumulation process' that is the sole aim of capitalism (2005: 24). Because such a process is ultimately amoral, in order to have the necessary buy-in from its human subjects it 'mobilizes "already-existing" things whose legitimacy is guaranteed, to which it is going to give a new twist by combining them with the exigency of capital accumulation' (2005: 20). In the case of the neoliberal phase of global capitalism, Boltanski and Chiapello identify the spirit called upon to justify renewed and emboldened efforts of accumulation as that of autonomy. As I will return to in the following chapter, the notion of autonomy is ascendant in the post-Marxist era and is perceived by a particular school of left-wing political theorists as a liberation from the steer, or inegalitarian imposition, of authoritarian modes of Marxism. However, as I will pursue here, the ascendency of autonomy also marked a confrontation with the second phase of capitalism, in reaction against its regulated working conditions, hierarchical management structures and regulatory frameworks. One particular strand of the anti-capitalist protests of 1968, a strand defined by Boltanski and Chiapello as the 'artistic critique' (2005: 38), called above everything else for greater freedom and autonomy for the individual worker. Yet, as an unintended consequence, Boltanski and Chiapello argue, 'autonomy was exchanged for security, opening the way for a new spirit of capitalism extolling the virtues of mobility and adaptability, whereas the previous spirit was unquestionably more concerned with security than with liberty' (2005: 199). The price to be paid for the ascendency of autonomy is clearly articulated by sociologist Zygmunt Bauman, 'the kind of freedom ...

envisaged would come with a price-tag attached ... The price in question is insecurity' (2001: 44).

While the price to be paid is not paid by all subjects equally, neither is it the case that anyone is immune from the ideological impact of a historical moment that is increasingly characterized by its precariousness. It is, without doubt, those at the hard edge of late neoliberalism who suffer the most from its effects, and Boltanski and Chiapello explore in detail the particular implications for those who are the greatest losers within the latest manifestation of capitalism as I will also outline below. For Judith Butler, precaritization is a political process that indeed 'acclimatizes ... [whole] populations over time to insecurity and hopelessness' (2015a: 15), but which also needs to be understood as engendering 'a heightened sense of expendability or disposability that is differentially distributed throughout society' (2015a: 15).

Despite the importance of maintaining an awareness that different socio-economic groups and individuals will inevitably feel the impacts of socio-economic changes to (sometimes vastly) differing degrees and so might require different dramaturgies of political intervention as I will discuss in later chapters, I am not limiting the implications of a broader definition of precarity, or its consequences, to those subjects most exploited by the economic relations of late neoliberalism, as Guy Standing and some others are inclined to do. My argument in this chapter rather works on the understanding that the contemporary state of 'precarity', as defined initially by Pierre Bourdieu (1997), and 'individualization', as defined initially by Ulrich Beck (1992), are consequences of late neoliberalism that penetrate all previously defined social classes with the possible exception of the tiny minority (the so-called 1 per cent) who hold significant global economic control.

As Bauman contends, drawing on Ulrich Beck, individualization has long been an increasingly significant aspect of modernization: 'a "progress" plotted along the axes of emancipation, growing autonomy and freedom of self-assertion' (Bauman 2001: 46). But the insecurity and precarity engendered by the third phase of capitalism's celebration of disconnectedness, mobility and flexibility constitute a world in which the values of commitment, collectivity and solidarity are increasingly difficult to resurrect:

> In a network world, everyone thus lives in a state of permanent anxiety about being disconnected, rejected, abandoned on the spot by those who move around. This is why today local roots, loyalty and stability paradoxically constitute factors of *job insecurity* and are, moreover, increasingly experienced as such. (Boltanski and Chiapello 2005: 364, original emphasis)

Perhaps the most invidious implication of precarious individualization, as Pierre Bourdieu most notably anticipated, is that the capacity to envision better futures becomes critically impaired because the subject's hold on the present is too tenuous. Bourdieu argues persuasively that the state of precariousness 'renders the whole future uncertain, it prevents all rational anticipation and, in particular, the basic belief and hope in the future that one needs in order to rebel, especially collectively, against present conditions, even the most intolerable' (Bourdieu 1998: 82). To have thoughts of changing the future, Bourdieu argues, people must firstly feel in control of their present situation, which is increasingly nebulous and uncertain. Even if the agency and will to change could be summoned, the knowledge of what precisely might constitute the most beneficial course of action is increasingly difficult to calculate. As Bauman explains, 'the apparent lack of any link between what you do and what happens to you, between "doing" and "suffering", is what makes chaos odious, repugnant and frightening' (2001: 32):

> Choices must be made without the conviction that the moves will bring anticipated results, that today's investments will bring gains tomorrow and that steering clear of options which seem bad today will not turn tomorrow into a painful loss. It is not clear whom and in what to trust, since no one seems to be in control of how things are going – no one can issue a reliable guarantee that they will indeed go in the anticipated direction. (2001: 44–5)

If, as Bauman drawing on Pierre Bourdieu (1998) concludes, 'the ability to make future projections ... is the *conditio sine qua non* of all "transformative" thought', then 'the collapse of confidence and the fading will for political engagement and collective action' are crucial hurdles that must be confronted (Bauman 2001: 29). Boltanski and Chiapello likewise confirm that the growth of 'anomie', or anxiety, began to accelerate after the 1970s 'not only as a mechanical result of the growth in job insecurity and poverty, but also as the mark of an elimination of the purchase that people can have on their social environment, with a consequent fading of their belief in the future as a vanishing point which can orientate action and thus retrospectively confer meaning on the present' (2005: 421).

The dominant affective impact of the economic and social changes described above in the early years of neoliberalism, as highlighted by Boltanksi and Chiapello, Beck, Bauman and Bourdieu, among many others, is anxiety. Sara Ahmed graphically describes anxiety as 'sticky: rather like Velcro, it tends to pick up whatever comes near. Or we could say that anxiety gives us a certain kind of angle on what comes near' (2010: 36). Throughout her work on emotions and affects Ahmed is clear that these neither reside solely in the individual, impacting outwards onto the individual's social environment, nor do they reside solely in the environment to then infect the individual, but rather arise from the relationship between the two, the impression the object leaves on the subject and the subject's impressions towards the object (Ahmed 2014: 6). Thus, the anxiety that is induced by the social conditions of disconnectedness, abandonment and insecurity will both impress itself on the subject's internal well-being and 'stick' in turn to their perception and experience of the world around them. If we accept Nigel Thrift's account of the rapid consolidation of practical knowledges of affective response, moreover, we might conclude that such affects of anxiety are not unforeseen consequences of the changes to the individual's social environment but 'a form of landscape engineering that is gradually pulling itself into existence, producing new forms of power as it goes' (Thrift 2004: 68). In a later study Thrift suggests that the proliferation of mass media has furthered such forms of power, providing a 'kind of affective platform in the public mind in a way which promotes anxiety and can sometimes even be likened to obsession or compulsion' (2008: 242). Ben Anderson agrees that where public emotion was once a source of threat to the dominant order, 'what is argued by theorists of the present conjuncture is that the excess of affect is now not so much regulated as induced, not so much prohibited as solicited' (2010: 168). Anxiety is solicited precisely because it acts as a form of control. It reduces the individual's capacity to care for the other and motivates competitiveness and antagonism between insecure individuals where there was once a sense of shared oppression or collective resistance. Bauman argues that historically because the working class was made up of 'people endowed with fewer resources, and thus with less choice, [they] had to compensate for their individual weaknesses by the 'power of numbers' – by closing ranks and engaging in collective action' (2001: 46). But notions of collectivity and care for the other – the rational response of the historical working class to its conditions of oppression – can no longer be assumed to be so in the more precarious landscape of the twenty-first century. Bauman rather proposes that 'the distinctive feature of the stories told in our times is that they articulate individual lives in a way that excludes or suppresses ... the possibility of tracking down the links connecting individual fate to the ways and means by which society as a whole operates' (2001: 9). For this reason, the 'added value' (9) of collective action is hard to accept and the endpoint of looking beyond one's own precariousness to engage with any wider communal predicament becomes increasingly nebulous.

This is the predicament of what Boltanski and Chiapello identify as the 'reticular', or networked, world that was to characterize twenty-first-century neoliberalism in which 'social life is composed of a proliferation of encounters and temporary, but reactivatable connections with various groups, operated at potentially considerable social, professional, geographical and cultural distance' (2005: 104). This is because the globalization of capital has rendered the capacity of any business to be geographically unrooted, flexible and mobile, one of the greatest strengths in the game of accumulation. While this mobility can financially profit those at the top, it has proved calamitous for those at the bottom, as Boltanski and Chiapello caution:

> That is why it is a significant error to include in the same category the flexibility and job insecurity of the temp with the mobility of the consumer or multinational. In one instance, flexibility is chosen, is a source of strength, is assertive; in the other, it is imposed, and turns out to be the reverse of freedom. The mobility of the exploiter has as its counterpart the flexibility of the exploited. (2005: 369)

This is because the mobility of the multinational organizations, their capacity to move operations over great distances very quickly, removes their reliance on a local, loyal workforce that might, as a consequence of such reliance, be empowered to insist on certain levels of job security and fair renumeration. In the days of union bargaining power, as Bauman argues, 'the owners and the shareholders depended for their income on the good will of the workers as much as the workers depended for their livelihood on the jobs they offered' (2001: 36). Today, however, capital is not tied geographically to any one location or labour pool, resulting in a situation whereby

> the mobile partners may simply take their belongings elsewhere and there will be no one left to negotiate with. For those in the handicapped and weaker position, the sole method of keeping the mobile managers and volatile shareholders in place ... is to entice them to come and stay by *a convincing display of their own weakness and lack of resistance.* (Bauman 2001: 36, emphasis mine)

Thus, in the global neoliberal labour market, the rational response to conditions that threaten individual security is no longer to be stronger in collectivity but rather to offer, as Bauman concludes, 'a convincing display of weakness'. Critically, then, 'the new hierarchy of power is marked at the top by the ability to move fast and at short notice, and at the bottom by the inability to slow down those moves, let alone arrest them, coupled with its own immobility' (Bauman 2001: 35).

Regardless of the distinctions rightly made between the impact on those at the 'top' and those at the 'bottom', Boltanski and Chiapello nevertheless propose that the competitive individualism induced by the demands of mobility, flexibility and disconnectedness 'in turn triggers other phenomena of exploitation, with everyone except those situated at the two ends of the chain being simultaneously exploiter and exploited' (2005: 365). Thus, there is no easy binary equivalent to the Marxist division between the proletariat and the bourgeoisie to define the current state of precarity. Rather there is a wholesale shift from structural arrangements characterized by collective communities of interest engaged in collective power disputes to structural arrangements characterized by disparate individual manoeuvrings for advantage permeating every level of social and industrial relations.

Political scientist Gary Olson warns that, under neoliberalism, the human subject may be forced to adapt their instinctive behavioural patterns and moral codes in order to survive under the new terms of their social arrangements. He defines this as 'a *culturally acquired empathy-deficit disorder*' which has '*its roots in the dominant socioeconomic system*' (2013: 57, original emphasis). Empathy, he argues, 'is less likely to manifest itself under conditions of attachment *insecurity* because the individual is more likely to be self-absorbed, personally distressed, and empathically unavailable' (55, original emphasis). Bruce McConachie, moreover, recognizes that all cognitive activity is shaped by the particular social and individual contexts in which the human brain develops, noting that 'all cultural practices and beliefs – from shopping to religion – get embedded in the synapses of the mind/brain; there is no culture without cognition and no cognition without nature' (2008: 4). This has particular ramifications for those growing up under neoliberalism, now around three decades strong, given that, as sociologist John Bone warns, the social maps that the human brain is shaping throughout the subject's early years and adolescence form 'a default way of thinking that is very difficult to overturn, leaving even those who are motivated to initiate resistance limited in their capacity to imagine alternatives' (Bone 2010: 725).

The ironic spectator-subject

In the field of sociology, Lilie Chouliaraki joins the chorus of interdisciplinary voices brought into dialogue above to identify the failure of traditional frameworks of solidarity to inspire, in the contemporary spectator-subject, the necessity of compassionate action towards the other. Chouliaraki's concern in *The Ironic Spectator* (2012) is with the spectator of humanitarian appeals rather than political theatres, and her analysis examines how the dramaturgies of such appeals have been reconceived over the past thirty years to accommodate the changes in the spectator-subject that have been discussed thus far in this chapter. Such changes are equally pertinent to the desired aims of humanitarianism and the desired aims of political theatres, despite the important distinctions in the aims themselves and the dramaturgies through which they are pursued. Critically for this study, I will now outline how Chouliaraki's analysis not only substantiates the individualization of the neoliberal spectator-subject identified thus far in this chapter but also importantly foregrounds a 'new emotionality' (1) as the key motivation for the undertaking of altruistic activity, introducing us to the importance of the production of individualized affective impact for the would-be altruistic spectator-subject of contemporary political dramaturgies, as will be further explored in the course of this and subsequent chapters.

In accordance with the theorists discussed throughout this chapter, it is Chouliaraki's conviction that 'there is something distinct about the ways in which the self figures in contemporary humanitarianism' (1) that is shaped by specific 'changes in the ethics of solidarity' (3). The historical humanitarian paradigm of pity for the other that could engender the narratives of either salvation (in the Christian-humanist tradition) or revolution (in the Marxist tradition), Chouliaraki argues, has fallen into disrepute. Historical humanitarian appeals, such as Oxfam's photo-realist representations of starving African children in the 1970s, were based on representations of suffering that were designed to engage the spectator in pity for the other and subsequent action to alleviate their suffering. But two paradoxes were to arise, according to Chouliaraki, from the dramaturgies of such a paradigm that threatened the efficacy of the appeals. The first is one of authenticity whereby the spectator-subject becomes suspicious of any representation of suffering that might present as 'authentic' and so lay claim to the right to the spectator-subject's emotional attachment or active response (36–8). Consequently, the appeal for response is rejected, and the spectator-subject can justify their emotional detachment from the call by recourse to their scepticism of its authenticity. The second paradox is one of agency (39–42). This arises from additional critiques of mimetic representations of suffering designed to inspire the act of pity, which asserted such dramaturgies were colluding in the objectification of the 'other' through portraying them in a state of naked life. By so doing, the other becomes distinguished as the 'they' (to whom these things happen) from the 'us' (to whom they don't) through a process of dehumanization that consolidates the postcolonial power imbalance and global inequity that makes the humanitarian imaginary necessary in the first place. Consequently, the act of pity is revealed as an imperialist act that perpetuates the state of inequality, and so inactivity can again be justified on ethical and political grounds.

As a result of these paradoxes, Chouliaraki concludes, such historical dramaturgies are no longer effective, yet, in her view, 'critical theory responds with a pessimistic narrative that leaves little or no ground for the promise of cosmopolitan solidarity' (29). Chouliaraki characterizes this pessimistic narrative as a 'post-humanitarian' disposition (174) steered by notions of an ironic solidary which rather situates the pleasures of the self at the heart of moral action, as I will further detail below. In this sense, Chouliaraki's ironic spectator-subject is the now-ubiquitous manifestation of the 'ironist' of earlier epochs, sceptical of appearances and cynical that anything can mean what it claims to.

If irony, at its broadest, consists of the gap between what is ostensibly indicated and what is meant, or what is intended and what actually occurs, then irony can, as has often been remarked, be understood as characteristic of our age of sceptical doubt. Poststructuralism has decisively demonstrated that meaning is contingent, that context is all and, consequently, that anything might well mean other than it appears to. Likewise, poststructuralist relativism more broadly has undermined historical reliance on religion, science and law as foundational concepts that can provide stable interpretations of meaning or that can be relied upon to deliver what they promise. If the ironist, as Glenn S. Holland claims, 'sees that meaning is not invariably determined by language and semantics, that expectations can be frustrated, and that events are not always determined by human aspirations' (2000: 38), then, surely, we are all ironists now, all too aware that 'the world is messy and not subject to human control or desire' (2000: 38).

The ironist was historically associated with high social standing and privilege, as Linda Hutcheon's extensive taxonomy evidences: 'irony has been called an intellectual attitude, an aristocratic and even anti-social one on the part of the ironist … a kind of omniscient, omnipotent god-figure, smiling down – with irony – upon the rest of us' (1994: 54). In our historical moment, however, there is no detached location on which the ironist can perch with any certainty, as the perch itself is recognized as yet another delusion that might, at any point, collapse. No longer the mark of privileged or divine perspective, irony has become the self-defensive mechanism of all those living in an age of precarity. If the spectator-subject can no longer afford to make themselves vulnerable by caring for the plight of the other, as outlined throughout this chapter, then their best ethical validation of this position is recourse to avowed scepticism of the authenticity of the other's right to make such a request of them. Thus, the move from 'an ethics of *pity* to an ethics of *irony*', despite the validity of the critiques of the former, nonetheless marks, as Chouliaraki concludes, 'the retreat of an other-oriented morality, where doing good to others is about our common humanity and asks nothing back, and the emergence of a self-oriented morality, where doing good to others is about "how I feel" and must, therefore, be rewarded by minor gratifications to the self' (2012: 3).

The ironic paradigm, Chouliaraki argues, marks 'a profound shift in the epistemic basis of humanitarianism away from the moral gravity of distant suffering-qua-suffering and towards a reliance to "our own" truths as a guarantee of the authenticity of suffering' (174). Thus, ethical responses to universal truth claims give way to personal projects of feel-good self-fulfilment, as exemplified by the 'armband activism' of the 'Make Poverty History' campaign (195) and the 'find your feeling quiz', an online quiz in which the user is asked to choose from a range of emotional responses towards the subjects of an appeal before being offered a particular self-identification such as 'warm and fluffy' or 'inspired and excited' and invited to 'click on the link' and 'find out more about ActionAid' (1).

The turn to self-expression and the 'new emotionality of appeals' (17), in the humanitarian context, is a strategic move, Chouliaraki argues, in response to the compassion fatigue arising from the paradoxes of authenticity and agency and is driven by extensive public consultation and the preferences identified through market research. Such a turn 'takes the emotionality of the donor, rather than the vulnerability of the distant other, as a key motivation for solidarity' (17). This shift from seeking to have an 'effect' on the plight of others by our actions to seeking to 'affect' how we feel about ourselves is central both to the ironic paradigm that Chouliaraki identifies in her study and to the shifts in political dramaturgies and spectatorship that this book seeks in turn to examine.

Crucially for both, Chouliaraki is clear that invitations designed with the ironic spectator in mind are ultimately constitutive, that is, they play a key role in shaping the spectator that they seek to address:

> Rhetorical irony ... does not simply appeal to a pre-existing public already aware of the precarious truths of solidarity but, as the performativity of the imaginary suggests ... creates this sceptical disposition through its very representations of suffering. (177)

It is also important to register that how we feel about ourselves is no longer a private matter, nor can it be understood, in the age of irony, in terms of authentic emotional response. In his study of how social media impacts the contemporary subject's propensity to publicly display personal emotions and affiliations, Graham Meikle argues that the so-called culture of sharing is not motivated by the desire to give to others so much as by the need to perform the self: 'public media become personalized, as each of these messages is embedded within a new context, as part of an individual user's performance of online identity. And those same users make their personal comments and opinions and emotions, their prejudices and beliefs, their secrets and their virtues, visible to others' (Meikle 2016: 191). Thus, the technologies of social media contribute to the ideological shaping of the ironic spectator-subject in many ways, one of which being that of the need – and the capability – to perform endless desired 'versions of oneself, as we display our tastes and opinions for others' (Meikle 2016: 787).

This has important implications for the theorized spectator-subject of this study, whose need to display their identifications and affiliations to an audience of others is not only restricted to online communications but also within face-to-face public contexts such as that of the theatre audience. In Chapter 7, I return in more detail to the dangers of the encouragement of offline 'virtue signalling' by egalitarian-leaning political dramaturgies that seek affirmation of a particular ideological affiliation from their spectators. Here, however, it is worth further noting that the contemporary compulsion to publicly perform and display identity and affiliation in the age of social media may also determine, to an even greater degree than previously, the dangers of the political being entirely commodified within the theatrical landscape. The return to Marxist and post-Marxist theory over recent years, as noted in the Introduction, has rendered such affiliations fashionable once more and, given that the digital visibility of the events we choose to go to and our responses to them enable us to display our chosen affiliations in the public sphere, the growth in politically engaged theatres may have as much to do with the increased market value of the thematics of migration, war and inequality as the political currency of the work itself.

Of course, the attraction of politically themed theatre for artists and audiences who wish to be identified as affiliated with such concerns doesn't necessarily negate its political potential, nor does the wish to be identified as affiliated with particular political concerns necessarily preclude commitment or genuine engagement – it may even be an important motivating factor for both. This, indeed, is the basis of Chouliaraki's analysis of the ironic structures of humanitarian campaigns: they are designed precisely to nudge the ironic spectator, through the offer of the opportunity to express and display affiliation, into giving money to the cause and contributing to actual political effect. Nonetheless, the risk remains that the performance of solidarity, pity or political affiliation might also serve as a non-performative in Sara Ahmed's terms (2012: 117). That is to say that the performance itself, be that the attendance at the political theatre show or the applause or tears for the suffering 'other' on the stage, may be a surrogate for political action, rather than the motivation for pursuing it.

Conclusion

In this chapter, the notion of the autonomous spectator has been challenged by the theorized spectator-subject of neoliberalism. Such a subject has been configured across numerous disciplines and without significant contestation, as ideologically interpellated as precarious, anxious, lacking in empathy, ironic, narcissistic and unable to envisage political or personal change in the future. The impetus for political action is consequently less often the desire to have a material 'effect' on the plight of suffering others and more often a desire to enhance pleasurable 'affects' of how we feel about ourselves. Consequently, the potential efficacy of the mechanisms and strategies of historical political theatres performed for human subjects under earlier phases of capitalism can no longer be taken for granted. Yet this damning indictment of the contemporary human subject is not without hope, and it is precisely by better understanding how the prevailing ideology seeks to constrain or redirect political agency in these ways that the contemporary political dramaturgies under investigation in Part Two of this study will be best able to design their invitations to spectator-subjects to resist the hegemonic ideological interpellation of their time or to subvert it to radical effect.

Part Two

Contemporary Political Dramaturgies

4

Political Logics and Contemporary Dramaturgies

In Part One of this book my analysis of contemporary theatre spectatorship has been structured by three key configurations: the theorized spectator who I propose is an essential aesthetic element of any dramaturgical invitation; the autonomous spectator who, I have argued, dominates contemporary theorizations of the political and assumes the right of autonomous response and freedom from the ideological steer or political intentions of the artist; and the precarious, or ironic, spectator-subject who is, to some degree, shaped by the contours of the contemporary ideological moment of neoliberalism – a figuration that thus contests the possibility of any pure autonomy of response that is altogether free from ideological steer. This theorized figuration of the precarious spectator-subject will inhabit the dramaturgical analyses that will feature in the subsequent chapters of this study, but before proceeding to undertake this examination it is first necessary in this introductory chapter to think through how we might more precisely define the political tensions, or logics, at play in the dramaturgies in question.

Despite the proliferation, within theatre studies, of different conceptions of the political since the poststructuralist fracturing of the singular ideological steer of the historical Marxist-leaning model, there persists a lack of specificity when defining the ideological logics of the various 'politicals' that are in play across dramatic and postdramatic forms of theatre, as well as within dramaturgies that transcend or problematize the limitations of this binary. Rather than a detailed analysis of the 'what' of the political, which has commonly been assumed across all models to be broadly radical or oppositional to the neoliberal status quo, the debate has rather focused on *where* any given 'political' might be located: are the politics to be found in the form or the content; the reception or the intention; the performance or the process? There is thus an absence, in our discipline to date, of an analytical framework that might allow a more detailed interrogation of what mode of political is operating in any given instance. In this chapter, I will thus propose that a new framework of analysis focusing on the interplay of the twin logics of autonomy and egalitarianism can bring much-needed critical detail to any analysis of theatres engaged in multiple notions of the political. This, in turn, will enable further insights into the ideological implications of the dramaturgical invitations and provocations to the contemporary spectator-subject that will be undertaken throughout this study.

To that end, this chapter will align the poststructuralist challenges to the Marxist-leaning model of political theatre with Ernesto Laclau and Chantal Mouffe's proposal for a project of radical democracy ([1985] 2014), one of the earliest and most influential investigations into how the poststructuralist demands for pluralism and autonomy might be upheld in post-Marxist left-wing political theory without necessitating the abandonment of the collective egalitarian imaginary.

Laclau and Mouffe's thesis argues that, with the advent of poststructuralism, a tendency away from equality towards liberty, defined as a logic of autonomy, was introduced into the discourse of left-wing radicalism. From this point on, the logic of autonomy was to exist in continual tension with the project's hitherto singular aim of collectively sought equality, defined by Laclau and Mouffe as the logic of equivalence and reconfigured in this study as a logic of egalitarianism. This chapter examines how political philosophy has responded to the advent of the logic of autonomy and proposes that an understanding of the necessary tension between the logics of autonomy and egalitarianism can provide a useful axis around which the intended spectatorship of contemporary political dramaturgies can be understood to revolve.

The project of radical democracy

In *Hegemony and Socialist Strategy: Towards a Radical Democratic Politics*, Laclau and Mouffe locate Marxism as a vital stage in what they term, after Tocqueville, the 'democratic revolution' ([1985] 2014: 136). This revolution first began to emerge in the historical period defined by the French Revolution as a consequence of 'the end of a society of a hierarchic and inegalitarian type, ruled by a theological-political logic in which the social order had its foundation in divine will' (138). Laclau and Mouffe argue that this democratic revolution is thenceforward driven by an 'egalitarian imaginary' which traversed through the seminal moment of Marxism and is sustained in the present day, enabling us 'to establish a continuity between the struggles of the nineteenth century ... and the social movements of the present' (143). The egalitarian imaginary can be best understood as the discursive context through which existing relationships of subordination, previously unacknowledged or accepted as legitimate differentiations within a fixed, 'natural' order (e.g. women are inferior to men, the peasant is inferior to the aristocrat), can be reconstituted as illegitimate and potentially antagonistic relationships of oppression. Laclau and Mouffe identify the rapid expansion of this discursive context in the mid-twentieth century leading to a 'new extension of egalitarian equivalences' (142) that underpinned a 'series of highly diverse struggles: urban, ecological, anti-authoritarian, anti-institutional, feminist, anti-racist, ethnic, regional or that of sexual minorities' (143). At this point in history, they argue, such a 'proliferation of particularisms' (148) caused a shift in the balance between equality and liberty, the 'two great themes of the democratic imaginary' (148), from the historical tendency for equality to dominate to the rapid ascendency of liberty as the term of priority.

There are a number of converging narratives that chart this ascendency and, arguably, two key historical moments. As noted in the previous chapter, one particular strand of the anti-capitalist protests of 1968 was the critique of the regulated working conditions, hierarchical management structures and regulatory frameworks of that particular wave of capitalism, a critique which called, above all else, in Luc Boltanski and Eve Chiapello's account, for greater freedom and autonomy (2005). While Jacques Rancière refutes the tension identified by Boltanski and Chiapello between the workers who advocated primarily for greater equality and the students who advocated primarily for greater liberty (Rancière 2009: 34–5), it was without doubt one key moment in European history when increased liberty was established as being as prominent an aim of the Left as the goal of greater equality. The second watershed moment, I am suggesting, was the fall of the Berlin Wall in 1989. Given the increasingly oppressive expansion of the Soviet Union and the evident fact that this particular interpretation of Marxism had not only failed to achieve an egalitarian society but had all but abandoned the 'theme' of liberty in so doing, the Western European Left, post-1989, had to locate themselves not only in opposition to capitalism but also in opposition to the discredited State-Communism of the Soviet Union's colonization of Eastern Europe. Thus, an increasing emphasis on liberty and autonomy was central to any recuperation of communist ideals for thinkers such as Michael Hardt and Antonio Negri, as I will discuss further below, and Jacques Rancière, who I discussed in Chapter 2 and will return to in Chapter 6.

The post-Marxist landscape described by Laclau and Mouffe can be seen to be reflected in the broadening scope of politically engaged theatres in the 1980s which likewise set out to acknowledge a broader, and more complex, social terrain than that identified by traditional Marxism, on which multiple, overlapping and sometimes contradictory antagonistic relationships could be identified and challenged, including those of gender, sexuality and race as well as relationships of economic or class oppression.[1] Yet the pluralism of antagonisms does not, in and of itself, necessitate the momentum of the pendulum to swing from equality towards liberty. The dynamic ultimately responsible for this was the consequent displacement of the Marxist imperative from its foundational authority within the metanarrative of class struggle. In a poststructuralist landscape, the once-unified egalitarian imaginary was fractured into a multiplicity of struggles that demanded their own autonomy from any collective metanarrative or singular ideological vision and, potentially, from each other. Left-wing politics no longer had either foundational authority or a scientific and realizable objective to be pursued. The ground had been pulled from under it and poststructuralist rethinking, such as that of Laclau and Mouffe, began to reconstitute the project of radical democracy as an ongoing contestation that had to relinquish the very idea of an ultimate destination.

The risks posed by the ascendency of 'liberty' over 'equality' thus lay in the challenge to the certainties at the heart of the Marxist ideological project. Laclau and Mouffe's new political imaginary was required 'to identify the discursive conditions for the emergence of a collective action, directed towards struggling against inequalities and challenging relations of subordination' ([1985] 2014: 137), in the absence of the authority of the Marxist vision that had been based on the privileged point of rupture given to the antagonism between the working class and the bourgeoisie. In this absence, the now diverse, and sometimes contradictory, antagonisms could not be fixed in relation to each other, nor given authority over each other, begging questions as to how the egalitarian imaginary might be sustained to enable a democratic *movement* for equality to be formed from these various constituent parts.

The danger was that the right of each antagonism to exist on its own terms and *not* be held equivalent to, subservient to or authoritative over another would permit the collective egalitarian project of Marxism to splinter into ideologically free-floating antagonistic battles fought on their own terms, with no care for a wider equality that might extend beyond the one in direct question.

As Laclau and Mouffe elaborate, 'ecology [and other similar movements] ... may be anti-capitalist, anti-industrialist, authoritarian, libertarian, socialist, reactionary, and so on' ([1985] 2014: 152). For precisely that reason,

---

[1]   See Milling 2012: 76–90 and Saunders 2015: 50–2 for a discussion of this shift in the British context.

'it is ... an error to think, as many do, that they spontaneously take their place in the context of left-wing politics [...] the forms of resistance to new forms of subordination are polysemic and can perfectly well be articulated into an anti-democratic discourse' (152–3).

This possibility underpinned the scepticism held by staunch advocates of the Marxist theatre tradition towards the emergence of the postmodern (later postdramatic) aesthetics of new models of political performance. If the new modes of resistance could not be tied to the certainties of Marxism, then how to guarantee that they would work in support of the egalitarian imaginary as proposed by Laclau and Mouffe? As discussed in Chapter 2, the poststructuralist moment, through its insistence on plurality and contingency, logically led to a discrediting of ideological steer in its demand for the autonomy of individual interpretation. This was seen by many to be a real threat to any possibility of collective struggle and was charged, as we saw in Baz Kershaw's indictment of Martin Esslin noted in Chapter 2, with giving way to an individualism and subjectivity that *might* be harnessed to the project of radical democracy but might equally well be ideologically harnessed (even if not explicitly) elsewhere. Laclau and Mouffe also caution that

> the democratic revolution is simply the terrain upon which there operates a logic of displacement supported by an egalitarian imaginary, but that ... does not predetermine the *direction* in which this imaginary will operate .... the discursive compass of the democratic revolution opens the way for political logics as diverse as right-wing populism and totalitarianism on the one hand, and a radical democracy on the other. ([1985] 2014: 152)

With the advent of poststructuralism, a tendency away from equality towards liberty, defined by Laclau and Mouffe as a logic of autonomy, was introduced into the discourse of left-wing radicalism. From this point on, the logic of autonomy was to exist in continual tension with the project's hitherto singular aim of collectively sought equality, defined by Laclau and Mouffe as the logic of equivalence.

The twin logics

The twin logics of autonomy and equivalence sustain, for Laclau and Mouffe, the necessary tension in the contemporary project for radical democracy that is essential to prevent the totalitarian victory of either logic over the other

([1985] 2014: 165–6). In both cases, Laclau and Mouffe argue, 'we are dealing with discourses which seek, through their categories, to dominate the social as a *totality*' (166, original emphasis). For the logic of equivalence, taken in isolation, would seek to forge 'a unique and indivisible struggle' in which 'all unevenness had been eliminated' (166). To avoid replicating the ideological determinism of Marxism, as they understand it, Laclau and Mouffe argue that 'the precariousness of every equivalence demands that it be complemented/ limited by the logic of autonomy. It is for this reason that the demand for *equality* is not sufficient but needs to be balanced by the demand for *liberty*, which leads us to speak of a radical and *plural* democracy' (167, original emphasis). However, in order to secure the project's collective ideological direction, they argue, each democratic struggle, however autonomous, needs to produce '*effects* of equivalence with other struggles in a different political space' (164, my emphasis):

> For the defence of the interests of the workers not to be made at the expense of the rights of women, immigrants or consumers, it is necessary to establish an equivalence between these different struggles. It is only on this condition that struggles against power become truly democratic, and that the demanding of rights is not carried out on the basis of an individualistic problematic, but in the context of respect for the rights to equality of other subordinated groups. (167)

Thus, to work together, in necessary tension, for the furtherance of radical democracy, both logics are required to acknowledge their moment of totality as a 'horizon', a tactic which will ensure, by definition, that 'this ultimate moment never arrives' thus enabling 'the incompatibility between equivalence and autonomy' to disappear (166). If closure, in both instances, were not to be with-held, then the two logics would remain inherently incompatible and contradictory, the first holding to a transparency of the social as 'the uniqueness and intelligibility of a system of equivalences' and the second holding to a transparency of the social as 'the uniqueness and intelligibility of a system of differences' (166):

> Between the logic of complete identity and that of pure difference, the experience of democracy should consist of the recognition of the multiplicity of social logics along with the necessity of their articulation. But this articulation should be constantly re-created and renegotiated, and there is no final point at which a balance will be definitely achieved. (172)

The twin logics of Laclau and Mouffe, corresponding somewhat to the twin themes of equality and liberty as noted above,[2] offer this study the precise characteristics of the axis around which the various, and contesting, 'politicals' of contemporary dramaturgies continually revolve. I have reconfigured, for its new context, the logic of equivalence as a logic of egalitarianism. This logic is named after the egalitarian imaginary defined by Laclau and Mouffe that stretches from the pre-Marxist French Revolution to the diverse antagonistic struggles of the present day and marks the conviction, within such a logic, that the theme of equality takes precedence within the equality/liberty dyad of radical democracy. It is this logic that dominated the historical Marxist-driven political theatres, before the ascendency, in European political theory and theatre practice and analysis, of the logic of autonomy introduced by the poststructuralist moment. The spectator of practice in which the egalitarian logic dominates is offered an egalitarian (and so ideological) view of the world to which they are invited to subscribe and an egalitarian (and so ideological) collective project in which they are invited to participate.

The logic of autonomy conversely grants priority to liberty over equality, in the conviction that the latter can only be asserted through the advancement of the former. The spectator of practice in which the autonomous logic dominates is granted the autonomy of individual interpretation and invited to take precisely what they want from the experience. The logic of autonomy intervenes in the previously singular, ideological narrative of Marxism to insist on a plurality of antagonisms within the political sphere and the contingency and autonomy of their individual articulations. This can be seen to correlate, as discussed in Chapter 2, with the desired emancipation of the spectator from singular, ideological (commonly Marxist) interpretations of historical political theatres and the insistence on the plurality of meanings and the autonomy of each individual spectator's response. But critically, in the same way that Laclau and Mouffe insist on the necessity for both logics to persist in tension with each other, contemporary politically engaged theatres straddle more or less precisely the uneasy tension between the two.

While some Marxist theorists remained deeply suspicious of the poststructuralist challenge to the egalitarian imaginary of Marxism, many others, including Jacques Rancière to be further discussed in Chapter 6, diverted from the resolutely determinist Marxism of thinkers such as Louis Althusser to embrace the logic of autonomy as the springboard for a

---

[2] In her later text, *The Democratic Paradox*, Mouffe (2005) focuses on equality/liberty as the twin themes of a liberal, rather than social or radical, democracy, which extends the ideological terrain much further to the right than the radical democracy that is under discussion in this study.

refashioning of a new conception of a post-Marxist egalitarian discourse. Much of Mouffe's own research subsequent to *Hegemony* is dedicated to the development of her agonistic theory that I'll examine in Chapters 7 and 8. This later theory is underpinned by her rejection of determinist Marxism and her reconceptualization of 'the political' as the inevitable and interminable eruption of conflicting desires within a society in which consensus would (indeed must) never be achieved (Mouffe 2013). Such conflict, Mouffe argues, is inevitable due to the philosophical premise that 'every identity is relational and that the affirmation of a difference is a precondition for the existence of any identity' (2013: 5).[3] Once this is understood, Mouffe continues, 'we can understand why politics, which always deals with collective identities, is about the constitution of a "we" which requires as its very condition of possibility the demarcation of a "they"' (2013: 5). It is simply not possible, Mouffe argues, for such a demarcation to be eradicated and consensus to be reached as such an aspiration ignores the political basis of the social in which political identities are formed. For Mouffe, the critical thing is to prevent the we/ they relationships from becoming the locus of antagonism, a friend/enemy relation, which occurs when 'the others, who up to now were considered as simply different, start to be perceived as putting into question *our* identity and threatening *our* existence' (2013: 5, original emphasis). This can be achieved by seeking to accept the conflict, but to manage it as a relation of agonism, an acknowledgement and validation of opposing positions that are held and fought for within democratic structures. An agonistic opposition, for Mouffe, is one held by an adversary, rather than an enemy. For Mouffe, the task within a liberal democracy is to convert potential antagonisms to agonisms: forms of dissent or conflict that can operate within a broadly democratic framework without hope of resolution, but as a way of preventing anti-democratic eruptions or social collapse. Because if the democratic structure does not permit the confrontation of democratic political positions, and moves instead towards establishing consensus, 'there is always the danger that this democratic confrontation will be replaced by a confrontation between non-negotiable moral values or essentialist forms of identifications' (2013: 7).

Mouffe's theories of agonism are increasingly invoked in the analysis of contemporary political dramaturgies, often in tandem with the necessity

---

[3] Mouffe uses the concept of 'constitutive outside' to underpin this argument, a concept that she traces back to Henry Staten (1985) who draws on Derrida's notions of supplement, trace and difference to 'highlight the fact that the creation of an identity always implies the establishment of difference' (Mouffe 2013: 4–5). The concept is central to poststructuralist theory and is also used by Judith Butler whose theories feature later in this study. Butler draws on the notion of the constitutive outside in relation to gender and identity: 'the constitutive outside means that identity always requires precisely that which it cannot abide' (1993: 188).

to uphold the autonomy and contingency of the spectator's response. This book follows the publication of *Performing Antagonism,* a substantial and wide-ranging edited collection, also inspired by Mouffe's scholarship, that 'seeks to delineate a radical democratic politics that we might yet forge' (Fisher 2017: 3). Tony Fisher's model of a 'tragic conception of the political' (12) explicitly repeats the operation that Laclau and Mouffe perform on Marxism, envisioning 'a properly democratic politics [that] understands the constitutive *lack* upon which it is founded' (12, original emphasis). In this way Fisher seeks to reconfigure radical political dramaturgies as tragic in light of the acknowledgement that in place of the future Marxist utopia there is now only agonistic conflict without end.

If Mouffe's agonistic theory seeks to manage the necessary tensions between autonomy (the demands of different identitarian communities and individuals) and equivalence (the attempt to establish equivalence between them in common cause for an egalitarian and democratic social), other schools of anti-determinist post-Marxist thought have rather embraced the ascendency of autonomy as the essential singular logic through which equality is asserted. As the flip side of the precarious subject outlined in the previous chapter, Michael Hardt and Antonio Negri configure the networked, individualized subject of neoliberalism as best placed to use the liberty, autonomy and disconnectedness that neoliberalism has bestowed on them, as the very potential for disruption and revolt. Critically, they argue that 'these struggles do not link horizontally, but each one leaps vertically, directly to the virtual center of Empire' (2000: 58). In a significant diversion from Mouffe, Hardt and Negri thus constitute the non-equivalence of such autonomous struggles as a strength rather than a potential danger that needs to be managed. Revolt, for the autonomists, becomes 'a new type of communication that functions not on the basis of resemblances but on the basis of differences: a communication of singularities' (Hardt and Negri 2000: 57).

By granting autonomy to the individual subject of neoliberalism, Hardt and Negri seek to oppose in one movement both the hegemonic power of neoliberal structures and the counter-hegemonic ideological authority of the socialist political party or leadership that historically harnessed and directed the working class reconfigured, in Hardt and Negri's terminology, as the multitude. Drawing on Gilles Deleuze and Félix Guattari's understanding of 'a new context, a new milieu of maximum plurality and uncontainable singularization' (Hardt and Negri 2000: 25), Hardt and Negri reject Mouffe's democratic framework of managed agonistic debate, and its reliance on representational political structures of parties, directives and leaders, to advocate instead for the leaderless movements of autonomous individuals, with different demands but common resistance to capitalism, exemplified by movements such as Occupy. The autonomists' opposition to institutional structures and hierarchies of production places their thinking at some distance from the institutional models of theatre practice under examination in this study, but Hardt and Negri's faith in the revolutionary potential of the autonomy of singularities is clearly echoed in Rancière's political philosophy, outlined in Chapter 2 and to be further explored in some detail in Chapter 6.

Looking ahead

In the remainder of this study, I will argue that held in tension with the egalitarian logic, the logic of autonomy has the potential, as Laclau and Mouffe propose, to disrupt the determinism of historical Marxism *and in so doing* drive forwards the egalitarian imaginary. But despite the evident political and philosophical gains in the ascendency of such a logic, the remainder of this study nonetheless proposes that when severed from the wider project of egalitarianism, the logic of autonomy may be more accurately characterized as libertarian in its freedom from any responsibility beyond the protection of individual sovereignty, as discussed in Chapter 2. To undertake a dramaturgical operation that can be conceived within Mouffe's framework as progressively political in its challenge to neoliberalism, the uneasy tension between the twin logics of autonomy and egalitarianism, I argue, must be upheld.

In the following two chapters, I will thus seek to interrogate and correct the sometimes overly enthusiastic embrace of the logic of autonomy that has threatened, in recent discourses of political theatre, to suppress, or discredit, its twin logic of egalitarianism. This interrogation will be undertaken here by an examination of the radical potential of the ideological steer that underpins the egalitarian logic. Across the two chapters, I will examine how ideological steer can counterbalance dramaturgies driven by the logic of autonomy to productively political effect. In Chapters 7 and 8, I turn my attention to dramaturgies in which the egalitarian logic dominates. Here, I examine the influential trends of theatres of real people and verbatim practice that seek to engage the spectator in the empathy operation with the 'other' and outline how the historical conception of the empathy operation has been reconfigured under the influence of the poststructuralist logic of autonomy. In Chapter 7, I identify the political risks involved with an overly egalitarian dramaturgical logic that refuses to acknowledge the pluralism of antagonisms in the contemporary moment, and the consequent dangers of a cosmopolitan, utopian consensus. In Chapter 8, I conclude by arguing for the political potential of explicitly egalitarian ideological steer in the particular context of the dispossessed, precarious spectator.

5

Questions of Irony and Interpellation

In the previous chapter, I set up a framework of analysis that proposed that the political dramaturgies under examination in the second part of this study might be productively understood as operating across the field of tension between the two political logics of egalitarianism and autonomy. The spectator of practice in which the egalitarian logic dominates is offered an egalitarian (and so ideological) view of the world to which they are invited to subscribe and an egalitarian (and so ideological) collective project in which they are invited to participate. The spectator of practice in which the autonomous logic dominates is granted the autonomy of individual interpretation and invited to take precisely what they want from the experience. Throughout this study I argue that, since the poststructuralist moment, the logic of autonomy has been in the ascendency, and the challenge for contemporary political theatres has been how to best uphold the poststructuralist demands for pluralism and autonomy without necessitating the abandonment of the collective egalitarian imaginary of Marxism.

In this chapter, I will focus on the dramaturgical strategy of ironic interpellation of the spectator, examining how such interpellation operates in both stable and unstable manifestations that can be seen to map onto, respectively, the logics of egalitarianism and autonomy outlined in the previous chapter. Irony as a political strategy has a long history, but this chapter is particularly concerned to examine what political purchase contemporary ironic invitations can retain when addressed to the spectator-subject of neoliberalism I configured in Chapter 3. There I defined this spectator-subject as precarious, individualized and, most pertinently for this chapter, always-already ironic.

In the first part of the chapter, I will focus on the most common use of irony within political dramaturgies of recent years, drawing on the ironic interpellation of the spectator in Made in China's *Gym Party* (2013), to exemplify how spectators are ironically configured as faithful neoliberal subjects in order to instil reflection on, and ultimately rejection of, their complicity in neoliberal structures, thus gesturing to the possibilities of resistance and revolt. Having assessed the efficacy of, what might be termed, broadly stable irony with a strong egalitarian steer, the chapter will then turn to an analysis of Martin Crimp's *In the Republic of Happiness* (2012). The juxtaposition of stable and unstable irony that winds through every aspect of this production, I will argue, maps onto the tension identified in the previous chapter between the egalitarian and autonomous logics of contemporary political dramaturgies. My analysis of this particular production demonstrates that there remains political potential in contemporary employment of unstable irony, and its subsequent demolition of collective interpretation, only when it is tempered by egalitarian steer that is enacted through a more stable form of ironic interpellation. However, I conclude by highlighting certain limitations of ironic dramaturgies to achieve political efficacy in the neoliberal moment by examining the potential affects and effects on the always-already ironic spectator-subject to whom their invitation is made.

Ironic interpellation

The concept of interpellation is commonly utilized within theatre studies as a means of describing how a performance addresses or positions its spectators. The term is adopted from Louis Althusser's seminal essay, 'Ideology and Ideological State Apparatuses' (in Althusser [1971] 2008), which describes how the ideological apparatuses of the state constituted and confirmed the state's subjects within the prevailing hegemonic structures of capitalism. Following a brief introduction to the concept of interpellation, I will explore how contemporary theatre makers provocatively mimic the ideological interpellation described by Althusser to ironically constitute their spectators as individualized subjects of neoliberalism in order that each spectator can recognize, reflect on and ultimately resist, beyond the theatre, the interpellation and identification of the prevailing ideology of our time.

In his essay, Althusser proposes that in order to maintain power the dominant class is required to control not only the repressive state apparatuses (RSAs) which function by violence but also the ideological state apparatuses (ISAs) which would include churches, schools, families, legal and cultural institutions, among others. The ISAs are primarily essential, Althusser argues, to ensure that the existing social formation (capitalism) can 'reproduce the conditions of production' at the same time as it produces ([1971] 2008: 1). It does this, he explains, by ensuring that all subjects are appropriately equipped for, and willing to inhabit, the role which they are required to play in the ongoing capitalist project:

> The reproduction of labour power requires not only a reproduction of
> its skills, but also, at the same time, a reproduction of its submission to

the rules of the established order, i.e. a reproduction of submission to the ruling ideology for the workers, and a reproduction of the ability to manipulate the ruling ideology correctly for the agents of exploitation and repression, so that they, too, will provide for the domination of the ruling class 'in words'. In other words, the school (but also other State institutions like the Church, or other apparatuses like the Army) teaches 'know-how', but in forms which ensure *subjection to the ruling ideology* or the mastery of its 'practice'. All the agents of production, exploitation and repression, not to speak of the 'professionals of ideology' (Marx), must in one way or another be 'steeped' in this ideology in order to perform their tasks 'conscientiously' – the tasks of the exploited (the proletarians), of the exploiters (the capitalists), of the exploiters' auxiliaries (the managers), or of the high priests of the ruling ideology (its 'functionaries'), etc. (6–7, original emphasis)

Althusser describes the act of making a subject (i.e. one who is a recognized subject both acting ostensibly under their own free will within the capitalist structures of the State and, at the same time one, *subjected to* its ideological hegemony) as occurring through a process of interpellation, whereby the individual is hailed (*interpellé*) as a subject and recognizes himself or herself as such, thus complying with his or her accepted place in the hegemonic order. However, as Althusser explains, his allegory of the policeman's call of 'hey you', to which the individual turns in recognition to accept his or her interpellation into the law of ideology, must not be understood sequentially: in the material reality of the transaction, 'these things happen without any succession. The existence of ideology and the hailing or interpellation of individuals as subjects are one and the same thing' (49). In this sense, as he emphasizes, '*individuals are always-already subjects*' (50).

As discussed in Chapter 3, the contemporary spectator-subject could not be so neatly interpellated into the specific and distinct roles Althusser draws from Marxist theory (the exploited, the exploiter, etc.). Given the permeation of precarity and individualization throughout every level of social and industrial relations, neoliberal subjects, beyond those at each extreme, most often occupy the roles of exploiter and exploited at one and the same time. Furthermore, as I will detail below, Althusser's pessimistic determinism is mostly rejected by subsequent theorists. Nonetheless, the premise of Althusser's analysis, I believe, remains helpful for an initial understanding of how subjects and subjectivities continue to be constituted to a greater or lesser degree through today's hegemonic norms and, more critically, how the act of interpellation can be subject to ironic *détournement* and used against itself for oppositional ends in contemporary political dramaturgies.

Judith Butler's notion of performativity, initially conceived in relation to gender identities, extends the notion of ideological interpellation as wielding its power not through a single 'hail' but through constant repetition and iteration of ideological norms. It is, as Butler confirms, the force of historical normalization that enables each repetition of the hegemonic norm to carry such weight and to be both a consequence of and a further sedimentation of the ideological interpellation of the subject which requires constant cultural, social and political reiteration to maintain its power (1993: 187–8). Like Rancière's insistence on the assertion of an equality that would break the power of ideological interpellation, Butler's earlier work challenges the pessimistic determinism of Althusser that locates ideological interpellation as almost irrevocable, stressing both 'the impossibility of a full recognition' in any instance (Butler 1993: 226), and the subject's potential and agency to consciously reject the call. Although in her later work Butler (2016) gives more lengthy consideration to the importance and political potential of the subject's vulnerability to ideological norms, as I will further explore in Chapters 6 and 8, she continues to insist that the subject remains active and able to resist, despite her inevitable vulnerability to ideological interpellation. Throughout her body of work Butler has sought to advance Althusser's thinking by stressing that interpellation extends well beyond a literal understanding of the verbal 'hail' and can be effected through all and any means and methods of cultural and social positioning: 'the discourse that inaugurates the subject need not take the form of a voice at all' (Butler 1997a: 31). Defined in her work as 'the normative force of performativity', Butler is clear, furthermore, that ideological interpellation can take effect 'not only through reiteration, but through exclusion as well' (1993: 188).

Butler's influence on contemporary performance practice often manifests itself in the strategy to be examined in this chapter, the ironic and provocative reiteration of the interpellation of the hegemonic ideological call. The hail of gender, in Butler's groundbreaking thinking on interpellation and performativity, is reiterated in the form of drag to enable a recognition of its performative, as opposed to essential, quality. In the same way, I will argue in this chapter, each spectator is hailed precisely *as if they were* a faithful subject of (subject to) neoliberalism, but the hail is undertaken as a citation within an ironic framework so as to reveal the naturalized as ideological and to induce self-reflection and self-critique on the part of the spectator. In Made in China's *Gym Party*, as I will now explore, the audience is characterized through the form of the production as game show spectators who have attended to see games that have winners and losers. These games hold the potential to humiliate performers and spectators alike and operate to validate or punish individuals on a whim or personal preference. As the games move from silliness to cruelty, spectators are invited to reflect on their own complicity with the ideological norms of their society into which they have, here, been ironically and provocatively re-interpellated.

Stable irony and misrecognition

Gym Party[1] consists of three performers who are competing to win on that particular evening by seeking to accrue the most points from a series of activities performed for the audience. These include game show–type challenges, such as who can cram the most marshmallows in their mouth, who can get across the stage fastest after spinning around for a minute, who can solicit the most audience votes for being the most attractive, the richest or the one we would save from certain death (18). The social and political critique that underpins the show is at times both explicit and sophisticated. In conversation with one of the company's co-creators, Tim Cowbury, he outlined the genesis of the piece as moving from an initial interest in competition to an explicit critique of the emphasis within neoliberalism on the individual. To this end, the actors adopt self-parodic performance personae who initially talk a lot about their commitment to each other as a collective:

Jess	We're a pack up here. We have love for each other
Chris	we're a group
Ira	a whole
Jess	We're up here and ok you're over there, but we are all in this together (6)

However, as it turns out, each of them is prepared to viciously abuse each other, in order to win. At the end of round two, for example, the losers are treated to, what are described in the script as, 'round two penalizations: body and personality shaming' in which

---

[1] *Gym Party* was produced by the UK theatre company Made in China and co-created by Tim Cowbury and Jessica Latowicki, with Christopher Brett Bailey and Ira Brand. I attended productions at Summerhall, at the Edinburgh Fringe Festival in August 2013, and at Manchester Royal Exchange, April 2014. Citations are taken from the unpublished script that was kindly made available to me by the company.

a) the first loser (whoever came second in round two) places the podium centre stage and has their personality verbally assassinated, via the microphone, by the second loser (whoever came last in round two).
b) the second loser strips to underwear and has their body verbally assassinated by the first loser. (19)

The audience, in line with the ideological game of the piece itself, is likewise identified as a group or a collective but, as the piece progresses, spectators from 'the pack' who have been picked out, named and commented on as individuals are later pitted against each other:

Chris *(choosing two audience members)*
  You two came here together tonight, didn't you? I'll bet one of you earns more than the other.
  Do you earn more, or does (s)he? Who's got more friends? Who gets more attention for their looks? (24–5)

The audience is, through the dramaturgies of the familiar game show format, lulled into playing the role of spectator in popular rituals of light entertainment, cheering the winner of each round, participating in the voting and enjoying the competition. However, the ever-present underbelly of the format is exposed in the later stages of the show: the losing performers are forced to undergo psychological bullying and physical harm (such as making their noses bleed), ultimately relying on the initiative and compassion of a self-selecting member of the audience to step up and dance with one of them during the final round to put an end to the cruelty. Through its explicit division of the collective 'group' into individuals who are then placed publicly in implicit or explicit competition against each other, the piece aims to highlight not only the dark side of reality game shows but the individualist direction of contemporary society more widely and the cruelty that is the inevitable result of such a turn. As Cowbury and I discussed, the piece also aims to evoke comparisons between the passive and acquiescent silence of a theatre audience, and the passive and acquiescent silence of today's citizen. In both cases, passive acceptance of individual instances of exploitation or abuse is taken as a consensus for the status quo, however cruel, to continue. As critic Joyce McMillan noted, 'the point seems to be that if we accept without question a culture of rampant individualism and competition, we end up robbed of both empathy and morality' (2013).

The invitation to each spectator to recognize how they were being interpellated by the piece and to reflect on their complicity with the culture under critique was, I would argue, ultimately intended to provoke in its audience the critique of neoliberalism that McMillan identifies. This locates the ironic structures in question as relatively stable and the egalitarian logic as dominating within this performance, given that the satirical dramaturgical address is intended to ultimately convey condemnation of the individualism it is seemingly celebrating. Drawing on Wayne C. Booth (1974), who coined the distinction between stable and unstable irony, Glenn S. Holland concludes that

> the person posing the riddle provides a series of clues to its intended solution within the riddle itself, and the person attempting to solve the riddle must recognize the clues and interpret them properly to find the answer. Understood as such, stable irony is a neatly controlled and exact form of communication; I lead you to understand my intended meaning, and you, an alert and intelligent reader following my lead, do in fact understand it. (Holland 2000: 24)

Yet when operating on the contemporary ironic spectator-subject, I will now suggest that stable irony is not so easily able to rely on 'controlled and exact' communication with its audience as may have been assumed to be the case in the past, although it has to be said that the possibility of 'controlled and exact' communication of any art form, and theatre in particular, is a difficult premise to uphold in any historical context.

The discernible reactions from the audience on the nights I attended, and the critical reviews published on the performance, reflected three broad patterns of response. First was the response of those spectator-subjects who perfectly embodied the prefigured spectator of the production. The horizons of these spectator-subjects had been well imagined, their ideological starting points consistent with the playful interpellation enacted by the show. Furthermore, they were able to recognize the ways in which they had been ironically interpellated by the show and reflect on their own complicity with neoliberal individualism. Such spectator-subjects were responsive in the way the piece intended – from the initial easy laughter at the game show antics to the ultimate response shared by Jake Orr, reviewer of 'A Younger Theatre', who wrote that 'it's not often I leave a show with a sickness in my stomach, but Made in China caused a devastating blow to me, a punch with force that I'm unlikely to forget any time soon' (Orr 2013).

There was also, however, the second response from those whose laughter didn't fade but who continued to enjoy the scenes of humiliation and cruelty that ensued, perhaps unaware of the reality of the performers' suffering or perhaps entertained by it. On the video documentation of one performance, there is a telling moment when the performers throw only a few chocolates into the audience as reward for participation which causes a stampede of competitive grabbing for the spoils, and at the performance I attended at the Edinburgh festival the evident enjoyment of many audience members didn't seem to correlate with any possible appreciation of the actual physical pain, or at least discomfort, the performers were undergoing in the ritual undertaken on losing.

Drawing on Ulrich Beck, Zygmunt Bauman proposes that historical models of revolt or revolution are now unsustainable, that the individualized society under global capitalism requires a certain 'collective courage in political experiments' but that the capacity or propensity of individuals to undertake such experiments is in short supply (Bauman 2001: 51). My own fear was that the 'chocolate-grabbers' in the *Gym Party* footage might have been too deeply entrenched in the game to be capable of anything more than getting out of it the entertainment on offer. The 'bang for your buck', in the words of one performer (24), might well have been the chocolate, or the good time of the commodity event, and some spectators may have been having too much of a good time enjoying the spectacles of competition and humiliation to empathize and reflect on the cruelty they were presented with and their own complicity in the proceedings. As critic Lyn Gardner concluded, 'as audience members, we are all drawn into the game and compromised – because when it comes down to it, we all want to be on the winning team' (Gardner 2013).

A third response was my own – the spectator who resisted their interpellation as a good neoliberal subject because the dramaturgical structures of the competitive, participatory game show were not ones that this spectator took any pleasure in or felt any complicity with. The winner of one round declares to the audience 'I'd like to thank all of you, who've just endorsed it' (19), but my overriding feeling was, despite the integrity of the political aims of the work, that I had not asked for, or endorsed, the show that I had been both given and blamed for. In fact, I had elected to opt out of the game to the degree that I refused to vote, or participate, during the show, but my resistant act of abstention from the assumed collective body of the audience was not one that could be acknowledged within the show's critical framework, and so I was held as guilty by proxy due to my presence in the audience collective. While the 'culture of rampant individualism and competition', in critic Joyce McMillan's words (2013), that *Gym Party* was both adopting and critiquing was one that seemed familiar and initially non-threatening to many in the audience, for this spectator it was rather experienced instantly as a reflection of the hegemonic culture it was only later to critique.

None of the above responses are more pertinent than any other, and the complexity of the piece, which is not fully captured in the above analysis, enabled a diversity of response that was underpinned by a broad critique of competitive capitalism which could have been read and experienced in many different ways. However, my particular analysis of *Gym Party* seeks to demonstrate that in the context of ironic spectator-subjects even relatively stable ironic interpellation may not be the most 'controlled and exact form' of political communication. Key to its potential political efficacy is its capacity to imagine its spectators well. If the horizon of expectation of the audience is misjudged, or if it varies too widely among individual spectators, then attempts at provocative repetition of ideological interpellation will rather land on some spectators as misrecognition. Thus, the call that each spectator is intended to recognize and turn to, in reality, might be heard by some spectators as addressed to another subject who is not them. This will result, as Judith Butler proposes, in a rejection of the hail from which the spectator will turn in non-recognition. My own response to *Gym Party* was precisely this rejection; the spectator-subject hailed by that particular performance was not one I recognized in myself, and so the political effect of recognition and then revulsion, the 'devastating blow' noted by Jake Orr (2013), missed its mark on this particular spectator.

This is perhaps the danger of broadly stable ironic interpellation that is specifically designed to reiterate ideological norms: that it relies too much on a collective horizon of expectation from its audience. The hail might be guaranteed to land provocatively on some spectators but risks potentially alienating others. In their application of provocative interpellation of the audience, politically engaged artists thus seek to carry out a delicate balancing act. Their interpellation to audience members *as if they were* subjects of (and subjected to) the ideological norm must be pitched with precision. It must hit, in the first place, the 'matching' ideological norm of the spectator and then be accelerated to such a degree that the critique of such a position becomes evident to the spectator who then catches themselves in complicity with the implications and consequences of ideological behaviour of which they are, themselves, culpable. In any one performance the audience might be made up of spectators who will be accurately pitched to and productively brought to realization; spectators who will be accurately pitched to but fail to pick up on the potential for self-critique; spectators who will be accurately pitched to, pick up on the potential for self-critique, but reject it; and spectators who will not feel accurately pitched to and so will reject the need for self-critique and any alleged complicity from the outset.

Regardless of the complexities of achieving intended efficacy through ironic interpellation, such dramaturgical structures themselves would be condemned by Jacques Rancière as undemocratic, given the assumption of mastery, as outlined in the Introduction, that is manifest in the ironic procedure, whereby the artist intends a broadly common interpretation on the part of the spectator who will be invited to interpret the irony correctly. Moreover, the use of stable irony seeks to construct and constitute like-minded and temporarily privileged communities that are aligned with the author/artist/speaker, and so necessarily excludes those who are not able to read the clues they are given. As Holland observes,

> Irony develops a temporary ad hoc intellectual community, a community not only of similar beliefs but of similar mental capacity and processes. We, who understand irony, recognize the ironist as 'one of us,' and we recognize ourselves as the alert and intelligent people the ironist covertly addresses while leaving those less fortunate in the dark. The pleasure derived from the recognition of irony is compounded by our awareness of our own competence as its audience. (2000: 57)

Thus, the limitations of the stable irony of political satire, as understood through a Rancièrean framework of the political, would be identified as its intellectual operation of mastery and its division of potential audiences into those 'parts' who have the capacity to 'get it' and those who are excluded from the count. The dramaturgical structures of *Gym Party* would fall under, what Rancière terms, the Marxist critical tradition in which the critical procedure intends a 'dual effect: an awareness of the hidden reality and a feeling of guilt about the denied reality' (2009: 27). In *Gym Party* the hidden reality is the violent cruelty of the competitive, individualist society that neoliberalism has engendered, and the guilt is invoked through the way the piece highlights the spectator's complicity in, and enjoyment of, the neoliberal game. Given Rancière's insistence on autonomy for the spectator from the ideological steer of artistic intention, as discussed in Chapter 2, it is not surprising that a dramaturgical strategy that prioritizes the egalitarian logic through stable and satirical ironic strategies would cause Rancière concern.

The employment of unstable irony, on the other hand, defined by Wayne C. Booth as occurring when 'the truth asserted or implied is that no stable reconstruction can be made out of the ruins revealed through the irony' (1974: 240), might operate precisely in tandem with the ascendency of the logic of autonomous interpretation. Unstable irony, as Holland proposes, 'leaves us to wallow through the quicksand of absolute relativism where there is no such thing as a correct interpretation, but where there are only interesting ones' (2000: 25). To explore the potential of unstable irony, within the discourse of political dramaturgies, I will now turn to Martin Crimp's *In the Republic of*

Happiness[2] before engaging further with Rancière's scepticism of the ironic operation. In putting Crimp and Rancière into dialogue I will identify the political potential of both stable and unstable irony before highlighting the stubborn limitations of contemporary ironic dramaturgies of all shades that seek to further the project of radical democracy.

Unstable irony in the 'Republic of Happiness'

In the Republic of Happiness (*Republic*) is a performance in three parts which, taken together, offer an elucidating exposition, and deepening, of the sociological terrain this study has mapped out thus far. The precision of Crimp's sociological analysis is unsurprising given his known engagement with the work of Richard Sennett and Frank Furedi, among others, as noted by Vicky Angelaki in her chapter-length study of *Republic*, 'Utopia to Dystopia: Martin Crimp and the Illusion of Insularity' (2017: 149). Angelaki proposes that this particular play 'delivers the optimal amalgamation of these sociologists' approaches and their application to theatre' (149) and demonstrates Crimp's conviction that 'to tie happiness to individualist neoliberalism is a utopia, from which not only isolation, but also dystopias spring' (138). Dominic Cooke, then artistic director of the Royal Court and director of *In the Republic of Happiness*, reports that Crimp saw his own critique of individualism in *Republic* as a mirror image of Ionesco's *Rhinoceros*, which Crimp had previously translated: 'The biggest threat [in *Republic*] was not the denial of our individuality but the belief in it. By believing in our right to create our own story and bring about our own happiness we deny the significance of the many other stories, individual and collective, that exist in the world and how they shape us' (Cooke 2014: 410).

Part One of *Republic* is entitled 'Destruction of the Family' and features an ostensibly naturalistic, if dysfunctional, family Christmas dinner that is abruptly interrupted by Uncle Bob, who appears through a wall to ruin the dinner, before the naturalistic set itself is dismantled by stagehands. Part Two is entitled 'The Five Essential Freedoms of the Individual' and consists of five choric sections of text, some spoken and some sung, delivered directly to the audience in the first person by the ensemble that appeared in the first part, but now divested of any characterization. In Part Three, entitled 'In the Republic of Happiness', we are reacquainted with the

---

[2] First performance, 6 December 2012 at the Royal Court Theatre, London. All performance observations are taken from the production on 15 December 2012 and all citations from the published playtext.

characters of Uncle Bob and his wife or girlfriend, Madeleine, from Part
One, now inhabiting a strange, brutal and context-less existence in which
Uncle Bob is rendered dislocated and disoriented, clinging to Madeleine's
version of reality and attempting to repeat and perform her assertions of
a happiness that is clearly beyond his grasp to experience or understand.
Despite Madeleine's stories of the citizens of the Republic and her tales
of the renown of Uncle Bob's public lectures, the two appear to be eerily
alone, with Uncle Bob now reduced to a pitiful figure, physically and
emotionally abused by Madeleine. He can neither remember nor make
any sense of the stories she tells him. This disorientation, Cooke suggests,
arises from scenarios the actors had explored in rehearsal, 'the idea of
Bob awakening to the horrifying possibility that the reality he lives in is
an illusion, a stage set. There is nothing beyond it. Madeleine's story is all
that exists' (Cooke 2014: 411). Desperately, Bob attempts to repeat after
her the words of their '100% Happy Song', as if speaking, or singing, the
state of happiness as a self-evident and transparent truth will summon it
into existence:

Uncle Bob   The earth – plus Mum and Dad – the bedside lamp –
                  the state – have … have
Madeleine (*sotto voce*) have burned to ash.
Uncle Bob   have burned to ash –
                  yes everything's just great.
                  Hum hum hum
                  hum the happy song. (Crimp 2012: 89)

Even, it seems, the only happiness on offer, the happiness learned from
Madeleine that he can barely summon, is a catastrophic, apocalyptic one.

In her monograph *The Plays of Martin Crimp: Making Theatre Strange*,
Vicky Angelaki notes 'the consistent presence of subtext in Crimp's theatre'
(2012: 1), which is often employed to ironic affect: 'an undercurrent of hidden
communication and activity, which Crimp cultivates and invites spectators to
uncover … encouraging them to peer through the information immediately
available' (1). Opening with a family sat around the table for Christmas
dinner, *Republic* initially locates itself as the latest manifestation of a long
tradition in Crimp's work where, as both Angelaki (2012: 92) and Aloysia
Rousseau observe, 'the home is everything but welcoming' (Rousseau 2014:
344). Yet, this is where straightforward parallels with Crimp's earlier, highly
ironic, evocations of home and family come to an end. Because in the earlier
work both Angelaki (2012: 87–120) and Rousseau (2014) address – including
Definitely the Bahamas, *Getting Attention* and *The Country* – the irony

persists and deepens through the characters' insistent depiction of 'these domestic dystopias as fictitious havens' (Rousseau 2014: 344). Here, irony is working its classic and stable function: the spectator-subject is made aware, through Crimp's dramaturgical design, that all is not what it seems and is invited to see through the characters' avowals of contentment, or innocence, or ignorance that anything is wrong, to pierce through to the darkness of suburban dysfunction and complicity that characterizes much of Crimp's oeuvre.

Conversely, *Republic* discards ironic subterfuge to a degree that increasingly abandons subtext in favour of satirical farce. The failed attempts by Mum, in the first few lines of dialogue, to shroud what is really meant by saying something different is blown apart in Hazel's reaction to her sister Debbie's pregnancy:

Hazel	So why doesn't she just get rid of it?
Mum	Hazel doesn't mean that.
Hazel	Yes I do – if the world isn't 'good enough'.
Granny	That's not a nice thing to say, Hazel.
Mum	She doesn't actually mean it.
Hazel	Yes I do. (Crimp 2012: 9)

This opening exchange is swiftly followed by Granny's tales of buying Grandad pornography and her confession of malicious joy in taking taxis that in two minutes will cost her more than a binman would earn in an hour (14). The explicit detail and unashamed delivery of the text – 'on nights like that the taxi is glorious … and the fact that other people are having to suffer and work just to pay for such basic things as electricity makes it even sweeter still' (Crimp 2012: 14) – make it difficult to locate irony in Crimp's characterizations within this first part of the play, as it has featured in much of his previous work. If irony is fundamentally about meaning something other than that which is said or portraying a character who is proclaiming a certain set of values in order to indicate that their behaviour is quite the opposite, then here we are given grotesquely honest characterizations that say precisely what they mean and so appear to be monstrous in their egoism and are intended to be perceived as such. The scene culminates in a speech that is designed to trump everything that has gone before it. The unexpected and sudden appearance of Uncle Bob is at the request of his wife, or girlfriend, Madeleine, who wishes him to tell the family 'before we both leave – before we both irreversibly vanish … how much she hates you – yes hates you and abhors this family' (22). Uncle Bob's declaration of Madeleine's abhorrence of the family dominates the text for six pages and goes into grotesque detail regarding each individual member of the family. Granny and Grandad 'smell like flood-damaged carpet' (23); Mum, Uncle Bob's sister, inspires Madeleine to want to 'take your head ... between her two hands and bang it against a wall ... repeatedly against a wall until what she calls your your your your *teeth* – yes – break in your mouth' (25); and of Heather and Debbie she asks 'Wasn't there a test ... Why couldn't your sister screen them out?' (27).

Crimp's 'Republic of Happiness', then, on its surface, announces the death of all irony: a republic of transparency and equivalence, where what is meant is said and where what is said is the only truth there is. This is confirmed in the refrain sung by Madeleine at the end of Part One:

> It's a new kind of world
> and it doesn't come cheap
> and you'll only survive
> if you don't go deep
> (so I never
> no I never
> no I never go deep) (Crimp 2012: 37)

What is celebrated in the Republic that constitutes the end of irony is the rise of the sole and transparent truth of the solipsistic and libertarian individual, a rise that is quite clearly intended by Crimp to be read critically and ironically by the spectator in deeply complex and multifarious ways. Firstly, we are offered a Republic that celebrates the end of irony, the end of any depth beneath or beyond the transparent and self-evident truths of the individual. Secondly, Crimp's irony operates in his naming of such a Republic as Happiness when its consequences and reality are clearly intended to be read as catastrophically tragic. But thirdly, confronted by Crimp's ironic portrayal of a Republic that declares the end of irony, the spectator, arguably, experiences the collapse of stable and unstable irony into endlessly unstable irony, as Holland describes:

> Unstable irony is ... not only different from stable irony, it is actively destructive of stable irony as well. Unstable irony, as its label indicates, is the shifting sand under the building the interpreter of stable irony thought he had built upon a rock ... The shifting sands of unstable irony allow no building to be constructed after the demolition of the surface meaning of the ironic work, and the interpreter must either despair or build what shelter he or she can from the debris left. (Holland 2000: 24–5)

The difficulty with unstable irony is that its lack of directed meaning prevents it from settling once it has demolished the surface, or appearance, that was its original target. Rather it freefalls into the demolition of all certain meaning, thus demolishing along with the object of critique the foundations on which the critique was built in the first place. Thus, the unstable layers of irony employed by Crimp not only destabilize the Republic of Happiness but also destabilize the authority of his ironic attack of it, arguably leaving the spectator-subject without any moral or political indicator as to how to read the Republic, or the play itself.

This demolition of any clear narrative interpretation (Where are Madeleine and Uncle Bob in Part Three? Is it real or imagined? Are they alone? What has happened to the rest of the world?) invokes the legacy of absurdism that often underpins the work of Crimp; and the insistence on the spectator's need to create their own answers clearly exposes the logic of autonomy that underpins the multiple and unstable ironic operations of the play. But this autonomy, I will now argue, is tempered by the egalitarian steer of Part Two that is explicitly and unashamedly polemic in its satire, albeit remaining resolutely untethered from any fixed narrative meaning.

'It's deeper than that'

The form of theatrical presentation shifts from the naturalism of the family Christmas dinner in Part One to the choric direct address of Part Two, but the declarations of the chorus are as lacking in subtlety as the dialogue spoken by the characters in Part One, with each contribution stressing more and more emphatically that there is nothing here deeper than the truths that are spoken:

> when I say I'm happy to separate my legs, I mean it. I mean what I say.
> I mean what I mean.
> I mean what I say I mean: I mean I am happy to separate my legs – look.
> […]
> It's not one of those horrible things where people all mean the opposite
> of what they say.
> No way am I speaking in code – (2012: 47)

The subject, here spoken by multiple performers, ostensibly refutes any possibility of irony, as Crimp's characterizations had done throughout Part One. But this subject, like the Republic itself, is the very object of Crimp's ironic treatment. It isn't necessarily clear from the performance that different performers are, in fact, speaking different lines at random each night, improvising in order with a text they all know in its entirety (Cooke 2014: 411). But it is apparent in performance that there is no fit between the lines spoken and the performer speaking them or between the lines spoken and the performer's previous character. It is also apparent in performance, as the lines are grabbed at by the performers, as Angelaki describes, in 'a race for time' (2017: 156) that here is competitive individualism at work in the very dramaturgy of the production. Yet this hyper-individualist subject, even as she/he speaks, is spoken by interchangeable and multiple voices, thus contradicting the theme of the unique individual even as it is celebrated. In the opening section, the subject claims to 'write the script of my own life', and the irony is explicit: 'Nobody looks like me. Nobody speaks the way I do now. Nobody can imitate this way of speaking ... I am the one who makes me what I am – okay? I've got my own voice: I don't repeat what other people say' (41). Thus, Crimp's dramaturgical structure gives the lie to the statement of each 'I' who claims they are unique and self-determining yet are spoken by anyone in accordance with a given script.

'Passive dialogism' has long been a dramaturgical device of Crimp's, as Elisabeth Angel-Perez discusses, occurring when a character's language is inhabited by someone else, a device that is employed by Crimp to stage a 'literally dis-located postmodern subject' (2014: 355). Yet, whereas 'Anne' in *The Treatment* and *Attempts on Her Life*, the focus of Angel-Perez's analysis, is presented as dislocated and commodified by the hollowing out of her individual subjectivity by others, in *Republic* Crimp shifts focus from the tragic dislocation of the sovereign individual to the subject's illusory insistence on its unity and power, locating the latter as the very threat to the Utopia the neoliberal subject seeks to inhabit. As Angelaki observes, 'the anonymous speakers believe they represent themselves and their own beliefs, but, in reality, stories, experiences and treatment mechanisms are interchangeable' (2017: 153–4).

Thus, the irony of Part Two is both stable and explicit. The extremity of the statements alone could leave few audience members in doubt that this is a savage satirical exposé of the monstrous nature of the neoliberal individualized subject, rather than – as the subtitles suggest – a celebration of the freedom of the individual:

> Can't write my own script? – can't turn a sex crime to my advantage? – can't turn a chicken sandwich or the scream of an abducted child to my own personal advantage?
> *Wrong!* (Crimp 2012: 45)

As throughout the play, the songs in Part Two are delivered with naivety and put to music that composer Roald van Oosten describes as 'innocent and playful ... a sweet kind of synthetic, with toy instruments and the like' (2014: 412) providing the ironic disjunction between their delivery and the darkness of the narrative they are espousing. When the chorus gaily sings 'There's nothing political about my holiday hat' (Crimp 2012: 53), the implicit suggestion is not only that there is something political about the holiday hat (though what precisely is left open) but, more importantly, that there is something political about every individual choice, however banal it might appear.

The stable irony of Part Two thus sets the context for the spectator's interpretation of Part Three and in so doing, I propose, offers the egalitarian, specifically ideological, steer that tempers the risk of nihilism that cannot easily constitute progressively political practice. In conclusion to Part Two, the designer, Miriam Buether, 'designed a room that appeared through the floor, pushing the previous set out of view', reflecting the fact, as Cooke observes, that 'individualism denies history, wipes it out. New realities are created like skyscrapers in a financial district wiping out everything that had gone before' (Cooke 2014: 411). Sequentially, the audience is able to read Uncle Bob's collapse as a logical consequence of the Republic of the Individual that has been played out in Part Two. Like the precarious spectator-subject discussed in Chapter 3 of this study, Uncle Bob is condemned to an endless individualized present that is seemingly devoid of past, future or wider context. His anxiety is chronic, incapacitating his ability to know fact from fiction. He attempts to construct a replica of happiness from someone else's words and knows nothing beyond the transparent surface of his own present existence. He has little sense of agency and no critical apparatus for understanding how to challenge the world he appears to exist in, beyond two fleeting moments – that constitute the only shadow of resistance within the play itself – when he mutters inwardly to himself: 'but it's deeper than that, it's deeper than that, the whole thing goes much / deeper than that' (Crimp 2012: 84, 88). The audience, I would argue, is thus charged to pick up this barely audible cue from Uncle Bob to demand that this world of surface Crimp presents cannot be accepted for what it seems to be or be tolerated to continue. It has to, we have to, surely, go deeper than that.

Crimp himself distinguishes his own process of making strange from Brechtian alienation, as Angelaki notes, 'implicating the audience', rather than 'establishing objective distance from the events we see on stage' (2017: 146). Yet, I would argue that there is something of the *Lehrstück* about *Republic*, albeit in a post-Brechtian,[3] rather than Brechtian, framework.

---

[3]   See Barnett 2013 for an extended discussion of post-Brechtian theatre.

Crimp offers his audience a mirror to their reality; a 'Republic of Happiness' constructed on the neoliberal conviction in the unassailable freedoms of the individual, magnified, here, until the over-familiar becomes strange. Such satirical magnification exposes the horror of the logical consequences of the ironic disposition that prevails in the real world of the audience and shows the ironic spectator the fate that might be waiting for each and every one of them through the contemporary 'Everyman' of Uncle Bob. The ambiguity of the aesthetic form of Crimp's post-Brechtian *Lehrstück* is a necessary dramaturgical choice given its addressee: a Royal Court audience who are, generally speaking, highly educated in contemporary cultural norms and consequently demanding of the intellectual open-endedness of the logic of autonomy, and the depth required by both stable and unstable irony, in order to enjoy the opportunity to employ their own interpretative capacity. This is in no sense meant pejoratively of such an audience, of which I am clearly a part, but merely stating what is too often, in the analysis of politically engaged theatre in such contexts, left unsaid: that audiences need to enjoy the theatre on which they spend – often not inconsiderable – amounts of time and money, or they would simply not attend. In foregrounding the logic of autonomy, the political dramaturgies of the contemporary moment are constructed to appeal, in the main, to audiences who will appreciate their complexity and open-endedness. A dramatic moral fable about the fate of the individualistic everyman would not, I would argue, have functioned so effectively in the context of the Royal Court as Crimp's post-Brechtian manipulation of the dramatic form had the capacity to do. Nonetheless, it is notable that *Republic* additionally demonstrates, as I noted in my Introduction to this study, that it would be a fallacy to align dramatic form with ideological steer and the postdramatic with the logic of autonomy, given that the egalitarian logic is emphasized in Part Two, the section that departs from the recognizable dramatic features of Parts One and Three and draws instead on well-established postdramatic dramaturgical form.

Ironic interpellation of the ironic spectator

Despite the political potential of the ironic dramaturgies under analysis in this chapter, there are still certain limitations to the ironic interpellation of the ironic and precarious spectator-subject who is both the subject and addressee of the satire employed by Made in China and Martin Crimp. Irony has a tendency, as noted above, to offer the vantage point of superiority, enabling the spectator-subject to see what the characters caught up in the event are seemingly unable to and establishing a community of privileged insight. Consequently, the intention of inducing an awareness of the spectator's own uneasy complicity with neoliberal individualization might be evaded through the ironic spectator-subject's sense of individual superiority and subsequent condemnation of the behaviour of 'people unlike them' from within an audience of people they felt to be more or less like themselves arriving at a more or less consensual interpretation. Thus, the ironic dramaturgies of both *Republic* and *Gym Party* might risk bolstering a sense of the exclusive and certain community that Rancière so distrusts: the one described by Holland as 'not only of similar beliefs but of similar mental capacity and processes ... the alert and intelligent people the ironist covertly addresses while leaving those less fortunate in the dark' (2000: 57). *Republic* was, after all, produced as the Royal Court's Christmas play, appealing to an audience who, by implication, had chosen this for their festive entertainment, rather than the pantomime down the road in Shaftesbury Avenue.

Furthermore, *Republic* only presents characters who are the distorted mirror image of the mostly middle-class audience that Crimp's work is designed to address. While Part Three gestures to the tragic downfall of the individual whose fate is the warning to the equally individualized spectator-subject, the oppression and inequality of the wider world that is excluded from Crimp's Republic is also absent in the play, save for a few very minor appearances, such as Granny's enjoyment of the poverty of those emptying the bins. This would leave the play open to the ironic spectator-subject continuing to exclude such concerns and the existence of such others from her own reflection which is focused entirely inwards in narcissistic self-critique, or rueful, but not unenjoyable, acknowledgement of guilty culpability of behaviour that, given the absence of wider social concerns, has no real consequence.

Lilie Chouliaraki notes that the most significant limitation to the political efficacy of ironic dramaturgies is when the spectator-subject's political activity is invoked only through stories about people like them and the potentially narcissistic feel-good appeal of participating in such a community (2012: 185). Consequently, the 'suffering other', the one whose life experience sits furthest from our own, is systematically dehumanized, as she is progressively eliminated from the story altogether. If this is troubling on an ethical level, the political dangers are also great, as the narcissistic move simultaneously eliminates any need for the spectator-subject to ask or respond to the question 'why'. If the 'suffering other' is removed from the equation, then the cause of such suffering and the demand to address larger questions of systemic injustice and inequality falls away with them. As Chouliaraki concludes, once the 'truth of the self' becomes the only grounds for public action, the burning question arising from the ironic paradigm of solidarity persists: 'How does such truth provide a place through which we can recognize the vulnerable other as an other with her or his own humanity?' (182). The necessity to challenge potentially narcissistic ironic structures of exclusion and to facilitate the return of the 'other' to confront the individualized spectator-subject is addressed in detail in subsequent chapters. Here, however, I will now highlight the second significant limitation of irony's political efficacy that can also be seen, from a very different perspective, as central to Rancière's sceptical assessment of the ironic operation that underpins the artistic tradition of political critique.

There is, fittingly enough, an underlying irony in the use of unstable ironic dramaturgical structures that ultimately rely for their political efficacy on the commitment and agency of an ironic and individualized spectator-subject who is characterized by her propensity to remain precariously uncommitted and her incapacity to undertake decisive action towards better futures. The reach of individualization under neoliberalism renders its subjects, for the most part, not only oppressed by but simultaneously complicit in, and benefitting from, capital's ideological stranglehold. Thus, a knowledge of the oppressive consequences of an individualized society might not, in many cases, be enough to persuade the spectator-subject to let go of the compensatory benefits such a society can deliver, especially if we find ourselves on the winning side, as many in the Royal Court auditorium might calculate themselves to be.

In addition to the risk that the ironic spectator-subject might turn away from the political call for action in a state of detached amusement, there is the risk that the precarious spectator-subject might be frozen by the dystopia they are confronted with and their own incapacity to know what they can possibly do to prevent it. Here, ironic dramaturgies risk mirroring the structures of neoliberalism which are insistent in their call to the individual to take responsibility for their own fate while at the same time rendering the precarious spectator-subject incapable of so doing. Perhaps the most dangerous implication – for politically engaged theatres – of an individualized subject-spectator that Zygmunt Bauman, drawing on Beck and Beck-Gernsheim, identifies is that 'you are, on the one hand, made responsible for yourself, but on the other hand are "dependent on conditions which completely elude your grasp" (and in most cases also your knowledge); under such conditions, "how one lives becomes the *biographical solution of systemic contradictions*"' (Beck and Beck-Gernsheim 1995: 7 and Beck 1992: 137 in Bauman 2001: 5). In other words, as Bauman continues, 'risks and contradictions go on being socially produced; it is just the duty and the necessity of coping with them which is being individualized' (2001: 47). There is thus a danger that any provocation to the individual spectator to effect change, which does not also offer any kind of indication as to what can be done, might simply replicate the ideological workings of global capitalism by charging the individual with responsibility for the state of the world while leaving them unequipped to understand how best to change it and without any power to do so.

Crimp's theatre is lucid in its ideological challenge to the spectator – this is hell, this is the logical consequence of neoliberal individualism, this must be resisted – but leaves the interpretation of what must, or can, be done to an individual spectator-subject who, according to the theorists examined in Chapter 3, is least equipped to respond. In a sense, *Republic* holds up the individualized subject for scrutiny, but takes the risk that those who are invited to look are equally individualized spectator-subjects, who might be more inclined, in the first instance, to laugh ironically or, in the second, to turn away in hopeless terror, given that a scepticism of agency and the reduced capacity to imagine alternative futures are part of their own, as well as Uncle Bob's, contemporary predicament.

The third and final restraint on the potential of ironic dramaturgies to operate politically in the contemporary moment is proposed by Jacques Rancière. Above and beyond his scepticism of stable irony, as discussed above, Rancière identifies the operation of mastery at the heart of any dramaturgical structure, including that of unstable irony, 'where one searches for the hidden beneath the apparent' (2004: 46). In his essay 'The Misadventures of Critical Thought', Rancière argues that in both the Marxist critical tradition and the postmodern critique of Marxist demystification (despite the latter's disavowal of dialectic) 'it is always a question of showing the spectator what she does not know how to see, and making her feel ashamed of what she does not want to see' (2009: 29–30). Thus, the tradition of political critique in both its Marxist and postmodernist manifestations – modes which I would argue Crimp's work productively straddles – continues 'to denounce an ability to know and a desire to ignore. And ... point[s] to a culpability at the heart of that denial' (31).

Rancière rejects the political efficacy of both critique and counter-critique due to the central figure in both of, what he terms, 'the poor cretin of an individual consumer, drowned by the flood of commodities and images and seduced by their false promises' (2009: 45–6). He locates the origin of this figure as far back as the second half of the nineteenth century, a phantom that manifested in the bourgeois subject's fear of a society in which too many individuals were becoming capable of participation in the articulation and interpretation of 'words, images and forms of lived experience' (2009: 46). For Rancière, as will be examined at length in the following chapter, the critique of individualism that he posits at the door of both left and right in contemporary political thought (and of which this study would likely be charged) is a continuation of the 'diagnosis of incapacity' that the privileged parts of society have historically invoked to prevent those who are not counted from insisting on their right and capacity to disrupt the existing distribution of the sensible (2009: 47). Rancière argues that the procedures of critical thought invoked under both Marxist and postmodern auspices 'have as their goal treating the incapable: those who do not know how to see, who do not understand the meaning of what they see, who do not know how to transform acquired knowledge into activist energy' (2009: 47).

Rancière thus proposes that the critical tradition in its entirety, along with its assumption of incapacity, is discarded and a new approach forged: 'an egalitarian or anarchist theoretical position that does not presuppose this vertical relationship of top to bottom' (2004: 46). Rancière's topography of the political, as explored in depth in Chapter 2, can, in its embrace of both egalitarianism and anarchy, be seen to operate at the node of maximum tension that is the pivot around which I have argued the twin logics of contemporary political theatre revolve. A critical distinction between Rancière's argument and the one advanced throughout this study is that, for Rancière, these two seemingly incompatible logics are not conceived as forever in productive tension, as my own theoretical framework proposes; rather the parameters of what constitutes 'political art' must be conceptually reworked in order that the 'anarchic' logic of autonomy becomes the only guarantee of the egalitarian, or democratic political, as will be further discussed in the following chapter.

Conclusion

In this chapter, I have examined the dramaturgical practice of provocative and ironic interpellation of the spectator, whereby spectators are ironically configured as faithful neoliberal subjects in order to instil reflection on, and ultimately rejection of, their complicity in neoliberal structures, thus gesturing to the possibilities of resistance and revolt. I cautioned that such a strategy was, nonetheless, vulnerable to the anticipation of a collective horizon of ideological expectation from its audience. Conversely, the hail might be guaranteed to land provocatively on some spectators while risking alienating others.

In my analysis of Crimp's *In the Republic of Happiness* I argued that a sustained tension between the logics of autonomy and egalitarianism could counter a potentially absurdist and nihilistic ironic instability with ideological steer that invites its audience to consider a more egalitarian politics.

Nonetheless, I highlighted three challenges for all ironic dramaturgies operating in the contemporary moment, given that their invitations are addressed to a spectator-subject of neoliberalism who is, herself, always-already precarious and ironic. For an ironic spectator-subject, the call to arms can induce self-reflexive narcissism and occlude the other, be deflected as inconsequential or evaded as a charge from which the spectator considers themselves superior and immune. For a precarious spectator-subject, the call to arms can immobilize, replicating the operation of neoliberalism in its accusation to the individual to take responsibility for systemic injustice without any clear direction as to how this might be done.

Compounding both of these challenges, Rancière would argue that the incapacitated, ironic or precarious spectator-subject is not a given around which political dramaturgies need to be shaped but has been precisely created and sustained by those who require such a figure to justify the efficacy and political intention of such dramaturgical structures. This is the basis of his rejection of the critical machine that 'unveils the impotence of the imbeciles' (2009: 48) and his proposal for a new approach to 'uncouple the link between the emancipatory logic of capacity and the critical logic of collective inveiglement' (2009: 48). This approach has been hugely influential in the formation of a new sense of the 'political' in contemporary performance dramaturgies, and it is to this that the next chapter will turn.

6

Questions of Autonomy and Affect

In Chapter 4, I set up a framework of analysis that proposed that the political dramaturgies under examination in the second part of this study might be productively understood as operating across the field of tension between the two political logics of egalitarianism and autonomy. The spectator of practice in which the egalitarian logic dominates is offered an egalitarian (and so ideological) view of the world to which they are invited to subscribe and an egalitarian (and so ideological) collective project in which they are invited to participate. The spectator of practice in which the autonomous logic dominates is granted the autonomy of individual interpretation and invited to take precisely what they want from the experience. Throughout this study I argue that, since the poststructuralist moment, the logic of autonomy has been in the ascendency, and the challenge for contemporary political theatres has been how to best uphold the poststructuralist demands for pluralism and autonomy without necessitating the abandonment of the collective egalitarian imaginary of Marxism.

In Chapter 2, I highlighted the influence of Jacques Rancière's theories of emancipated spectatorship on the growing dominance of the logic of autonomy within the discourse of contemporary political theatres and the subsequent scepticism towards the political efficacy of the egalitarian logic and notions of collectivism that operate under its auspices. Given that this study seeks to interrogate and correct a sometimes overly enthusiastic embrace of the logic of autonomy and to re-examine the radical potential of the somewhat discredited ideological steer of egalitarianism, it is necessary to return here to Rancière's particular understanding of the political and how this has been extensively applied within contemporary theatre analysis and practice.

In this chapter, I thus seek to examine how Rancière's assertion of the spectator's emancipation is explicitly aligned to a radical politics of unintended aesthetic affect that has significantly influenced contemporary artistic analysis. This chapter will explore how Rancière and those drawing on him seek to extricate the individual subject from its sovereign, bourgeois history where it stands as the enemy of the collective and to relocate it as autonomous, vulnerable, contingent and partial, only achieving meaning through difference from, and in relation to, others. This reclaiming of the individual from historical capitalism and the neoliberal moment, to serve as an autonomous agent within the contemporary communist imaginary, is vital both to Rancière's own political project and to the radical narrative of the autonomous spectator I have been interrogating throughout this study. It underpins the politics of the turn to unintended and individualized affective response that has been influenced by Rancière's thinking and presents the autonomous spectator as a radically oppositional figure to that of the collective audience or certain community, which are rather located as ideologically regressive throwbacks to the authoritarian consequences of the State-Communism that evolved in the USSR.

While there has been fascinating work to come out of the auspices of such thinking, in theatre studies and beyond, I highlight some existing concerns with the limitations of Rancière's framework, and I offer my own thoughts on how the application of his thinking within certain material contexts of theatre practice raises still further questions about the alleged radicalism of the logic of autonomy when severed from the logic of egalitarianism altogether. Ultimately, this chapter argues for the importance of a material analysis of the context in which dissensus takes place, a re-harnessing of affect within the theatre to effect beyond it, and the necessity for the logic of autonomy to remain counterbalanced by a logic of egalitarianism that connects the individual response with a wider collective.

Following my engagement with the political project that Rancière proposes, I have chosen to offer Kieran Hurley's *Heads Up* (2016) as a lucid example of theatre that explores the current thinking on autonomous affect in both form and content, but in which the political charge, while enhanced by the affective experience of the form, is driven by the egalitarian logic of the narrative content. I then enter into a more sustained conversation with the theory and practice of Andy Smith, drawing on *Commonwealth* (2012) and *Summit* ([2017] 2018) in particular. I will argue that Smith's work clearly seeks affective impact and operates consciously within the logic of autonomy examined in this chapter, but nevertheless seeks political effect through attempts to bridge the divide between the material and microcosmic event of the performance and the inegalitarian injustices in the world beyond it. Thus, while the autonomy of individual response is upheld, the individual spectator is explicitly located within, and invited to take responsibility for, a wider collective. I will suggest that through employing a gentle and sincere counter-hegemonic interpellation of the spectator-subject as an already-radical agent of change, Smith's work is also able, through the imaginative employment of egalitarian ideological steer, to actively counter the potential limitations of a precarious and ironic spectator-subject always-already imbricated in neoliberalism and primed to respond from that ideological position.

Affect and theatrical communism

In *Passionate Amateurs: Theatre, Communism and Love* (2013), Nicholas Ridout aligns his project with Rancière's aesthetic efficacy in an explicit rejection of the historical emphasis, within the political theatre discourse, on political intention and outcome. Ridout argues that the politics of theatre should not be understood in terms of theatre's sociopolitical agency, that is as something that takes place within the theatre that *then* has a political effect on the world beyond it, but as affective labour taking place in the very real world of the theatre: 'a real place, where real people go to work, and where their work takes the form of "conversation"' (2013: 124). For Ridout, 'the act of dedicating oneself to acting and speaking together … is, in and of itself, a political act' (2013: 16). Thus, rather than looking to theatre to contribute to a broader movement of communism beyond it, Ridout's 'gamble', as he terms it, is to seek 'communism in a certain potentiality within theatrical practice' (2013: 5), a potentiality which might find a way to prefigure egalitarian politics within the work itself: 'to actualize in collective or socially oriented artistic practices something that is elsewhere only an idea or a vision of the future' (2013: 15).

Ridout's understanding of the political role that affective response plays in this 'gamble' is different from the redistributive potential of the pleasurable affects to be gained from emotions such as joy and excitation, as primarily explored in Chapter 2. He rather seeks to discern an 'affective affiliation with communism' not understood as a 'utopian imaginary outside capitalist relations' but rather 'nurtured deep within the cultural form – theatre – that most often reproduces them' (2013: 143). Beyond affective response as understood in James Thompson's terms as politically charged due to its severance from intended meaning and capacity to induce unanticipated, subjective associations, Ridout also understands affect as something less quantifiable than the emotions that capture its tangible aspects under terms such as joy, surprise or excitation. Rather it constitutes, most profoundly for him, something he describes as 'social or affective heat or … warmth' (2013: 146) that exposes the felt, or sensed, relations between individuals in such a way that highlights the interdependency, or sociality, of the human subject. He suggests that theatre may be 'a way of making known to ourselves the conditions of our being-social, understood not as a full community of individuals but as a network of relations of exposure, a "theatrical communism", perhaps' (148).

The community, for Ridout, as for Rancière, is not the placeholder for the power from which the individual can be nourished and sustained nor is its formation the goal of egalitarian politics. The 'uncertain' community, as Rancière terms it (2004: 36), conversely configures a non-determined collective of individuals responding to the aesthetic event who are empowered to be equal in their democratic right to autonomous interpretation. In this way, the emphasis on autonomous response in Rancière's thinking evades the charge of individualism and rather aligns the notion of the autonomous individual with democratic equality and necessary difference:

> What our performances – be they teaching or playing, speaking, writing, making art or looking at it – verify is ... the capacity of anonymous people, the capacity that makes everyone equal to everyone else. This capacity is exercised through irreducible distances; it is exercised by an unpredictable interplay of associations and dissociations. (2009: 17)

Rancière terms this 'being together apart' (2009: 53) which, in one sense, can be understood as 'together' in a shared capacity to respond to the work but 'apart' given the separate and distinct nature of each individual's subjective response. In a deeper sense, Rancière's philosophy posits the relational nature of subjectivity, so that each individual's 'apartness' can only be formed and constituted in relation to the shifting networks of the multiple subjectivities of any given, temporary and contingent community. Following Rancière's notion of 'together apart', Ridout speaks of 'solitude in relation' (2013: 28): a theatre that establishes 'some kind of distance; in which participants are always separated from one another rather than merged with one another in an achieved community of the event' (2013: 11). This distance from the other, Ridout argues, is what constitutes the political potential, or 'theatrical communism', of the act of performance:

> Instead of seeking communion with others, one opens oneself to the experience of encounters with others as marking simultaneously the limit of one's self, and the place where one's self, such as it is, begins. That is to say, in a recognition that one's self, as such, is constituted, not by its integrity and individuality, but precisely by its appearance in relation to others. (2013: 10)

Thus, Ridout argues, it is in a more radical opening of the self to the encounter with the other that a more egalitarian and less individualist mode of 'being together' might be nurtured. And it is in such an opening that the 'social or affective heat' that constitutes the affective resonance more fully articulated by Nigel Thrift and other affect theorists is located.

Thrift introduces affect as a new 'structure of attention' (2004: 67) that enables an expansion of sensory connections and capacities to be engaged, to the point at which, following Spinoza, 'there is no longer a subject, but only individuating affective states of an anonymous force' (Spinoza cited in Thrift 2008: 13). For Thrift, the political potential of attending to 'the kind of affect associated with embodied practices' (2004: 69–70) is to develop what he terms '*skilful comportment* which allows us to be open to receiving new affectively charged disclosive spaces' (2004: 70, original emphasis), a skill set which the theatre might be well placed to advance. Also relevant for this study is his additional identification of 'the model of tending':

> Here the simple political imperative is to widen the potential number of interactions a living thing can enter into, to widen the margin of 'play', and, like all living things, but to a greater degree, increasing the number of transformations of the effects of one sensory mode into another. (2004: 70)

By attending to the affective resonances that occur in the relations between individuals (including non-human animals and objects) beyond the familiar conceptualizations of already-known emotions, Thrift argues that we will open up new forms of relation and new sensory modes of awareness that have the capacity to model 'new political forms' or 'new counterpublics' (Thrift 2008: 22). Thrift recognizes the peculiar capacity of arts practice to best model 'affectively charged disclosive spaces' (2008: 189–90), and Ridout further proposes that this may indeed be the communist potential of theatre:

> The experience of listening among others acquires a peculiar condition, in which the intensities of both solitude and relation are amplified, so that inside a theatre auditorium one feels oneself both more alone and more related than one does on the outside in so-called real life. (2013: 162)

Drawing on Jean-Luc Nancy, Ridout claims 'listening' as 'the mode of attentiveness in which we simultaneously sense ourselves and ourselves sensing our relation with others' (2013: 153). Through such attentiveness the affective resonances that are engaged by an increased openness to sensory impression are expanded and deepened, and the awareness of self is perceptible only as an affect of the whole and in relation to the other. The political potential of such attentiveness is particularly acute, Ridout suggests, in dramaturgies that feature direct and personal address to the audience, where

> we are simply invited to give our attention, to assist, by means of our presence, at the making public of what might otherwise have been thought and imagined in solitude, in the hope, perhaps, that the simple but difficult act of making it public in this way, the act of offering it for the attention of others, might place that solitude in new relations. (2013: 154–5)

Strategies to enhance attentiveness and affective resonance were clearly perceptible in my own experience of Kieran Hurley's *Heads Up*,[1] which I'm going to draw on briefly here to illustrate how both sensory affects and less categorizable affective charge 'in which we simultaneously sense ourselves and ourselves sensing our relation with others' (Ridout 2013: 153) can be brought into play.

In common with many other contemporary storytelling artists, Hurley opens by greeting the audience in his own person, before embedding our presence in the real time and place of the performance at the centre of the fictional narrative: 'This is a story about the end of the world. It is a story about a city. Like this one. Here and now. It is a story about me. And it is a story about you. It begins, as it ends. With a breath' (2016: 92). And Hurley breathes in deeply, amplified by the microphone in front of him.

The 'you', in English, is ambiguous, covering both singular and plural address. In this first section Hurley delivered it to the collective audience. The 'you', however, that followed was addressed variously to individual spectators as the narrative progressed: 'You hold on tight to the air in your lungs … [y]ou step into the marble corridor … You are Mercy. That is your name' (2016: 99). As we are introduced to the other characters – Ash, Leon, Abdullah – we are likewise addressed by Hurley in the second-person individual. As Hurley switches seamlessly from one distinct narrative to the next, the 'you' remains constant. 'I', as I attend to each narrative, am all of these people. All the other 'I's in the audience are all of these people. And more than the people. As Mercy, the character whose narrative starts it all, the investment banker who

---

[1] *Heads Up* was first presented at Summerhall at the Edinburgh Fringe Festival, August 2016. I attended a later production at the Sheffield Crucible on 16 March 2017. Citations are taken from the Kindle Edition of the playtext and indicate the location numeric given.

deals in futures, the prophet of the end of the world, you, we, I grow, at the climax of the performance, to a mythical figure 1,000 feet high:

> You are what is here! You are the stuff that is here, that lives here. Towering high above the city, you are the city! You are re-development and planning process and new investment and corporate interest. You are gentrification and demolition and forgotten past. You are residential zones, commercial zones, casino, police station, mayor's house, school …. You are gum on the bus seats … you are the weather, the sun, the moon and the air. You are all the lives that live and that lived …. You are breath.
>
> And you are Ash, alone in the toilet cubicle …
>
> And you are Leon, lost, gasping into the wheel of a freshly crashed Porsche …
>
> And you are Abdullah, trapped behind the counter, monitored, surveyed …
>
> And you are Mercy, one thousand feet tall …
>
> And you are a man, sat at a desk, telling a story about the end of the world.
>
> And you are sat in a room in this city, listening to a man tell a story which he has told you is about the end of the world. (2016: 357–79)

The dramaturgy of the writing feels underpinned by Spinoza's philosophy: 'there is no longer a subject, but only individuating affective states of an anonymous force' (Spinoza cited in Thrift 2008: 13). The affective force of the writing is underpinned by the sensory attention of the performance itself: Hurley is dressed in a suit, but with bare feet. He sits behind a small table which is crammed with a microphone and a semicircle of small lights that uplight his face with shadows, with only a single rigged light from behind. At points in the narrative he operates two lights facing out to the audience to flash blindingly then go dark. His intensive and almost relentless delivery has the force of a high-speed train, and is punctuated with tension-inducing drumbeats and underscored throughout by self-operated music that shifts register as one narrative gives way to another with unexpected and affective irregularity.

Through the attentive social listening, imaginative projection of a pluralist and shifting subjectivity and expanded sensory experience that resulted, Ridout's affective charge was at work, opening narrator and spectators out towards new configurations of what might be 'understood as a society rather than a community; a changeable association made of multiple conversations, across the intimate distances of the public space'

(Ridout 2013: 137). Such theatres thus act, under the terms of Ridout's gamble, 'as a kind of "communist" enclave' (12) or what Fredric Jameson has termed 'utopian enclaves' – spaces which 'remain as it were momentarily beyond the reach of the social … at the same time that they offer a space in which new wish images of the social can be elaborated and experimented on' (Jameson 2005: 16 cited in Roberts 2009: 355). I will shortly argue, however, that, for me, it was not so much the sensory, affective charge of Hurley's production that constituted the radical, or egalitarian politics of the work, but rather the specifics of the narrative content that was able to offer an ideological steer to counterbalance the autonomous and individualized experience provided by the sensory affects. But first I would like to look more closely at the politics of the enclave itself, which might be said to characterize the vast majority of contemporary theatre featured on the European touring and festival circuits.

Utopian enclaves

Ridout's exploration of the affective – and for him thus political – potential of contemporary theatre sits within the auspices of, and draws explicitly on, 'the widespread revival and flourishing of revolutionary "enclave" and microtopian thinking' identified by John Roberts (2009: 359). Roberts highlights the convergence in contemporary relational art practice of 'a utopian communalism and cultural communism' (363) that recalls the early work of Marx. Here, communist relations precisely offered 'the production and collective exchange *of* singularities' (357, original emphasis), an emancipatory potential of Marxism that was betrayed by the authoritarian State-Communism that subsequently evolved in the USSR. Marx's vision of the *'re-aestheticisation* of experience' (356, original emphasis) can be usefully aligned both with Thrift's notion of the deepening and broadening of affective receptivity and with Rancière's insistence on the egalitarian right of all subjects to engage creatively, disruptively and on their own terms with the given aesthetics of their environment.

It is significant, as John Roberts suggests, that recent philosophical and artistic attempts to recuperate such a vision can be understood not so much as a challenge to neoliberalism but more a reaction against 'the retardation of cultural form and conservative foreclosure of the senses' under State-Communism as existed in Europe until the end of the 1980s (2009: 356). If the phantom of the communist state, or 'the Party', ghosted Marxist political theatre, evoking a theological author and arbiter of a political art designed to forge ideologically coherent communities from its audience, then the move of contemporary left-leaning political philosophers such as Rancière, in common with Badiou, Nancy, Guattari and Negri as discussed by Roberts, is to precisely reverse this understanding of political effect. This is undertaken, as we have seen, by a scepticism towards political intention, certain communities and ideological steer and a turn towards the political currency of unintended affects and the autonomy of the individual.

The philosophical counter-move against a discredited politics of State-Communism and its authoritarian misappropriations of the emancipatory communism originally envisioned by Marx is clearly reflected in the ways in which a new communist imaginary begins to take shape in the practice and theory of those seeking to 'move on' from old notions of political theatre. The new communist imaginary, as Ridout argues, encapsulates the political promise of affect that is located in the relationality of the theatre act itself and not in any political efficacy beyond it. In both the wider philosophical discourse explored by Roberts, and the theatre practice and theory undertaken within its parameters, the notion of an agent acting on others to produce effective political outcomes is rejected in favour of spaces which seek to be, above all, democratic in their relationships in order to secure an unpredictable diversity of affects and effects that are in no way predetermined by the artist.

When set against the totalitarianism of the State-Communism they seek to depart from, such practices offer a welcome space for performative prefigurations of new, relational and ultimately progressive modes of subjectivity that might bring to mind, in a very different ideological and dramaturgical context, Augusto Boal's recommendation that theatre should act as a 'rehearsal for revolution' (Boal [1979] 2008: 98). Yet, the capacity of capitalism, as explored in Chapter 3, to subsume all experimentation arising in opposition to it would seem to be particularly well placed, in our neoliberal age, to seize on utopian enclaves that celebrate the liberation of the individual from membership of, or loyalty to, ideological communities. Ridout himself expresses a concern that '"autonomist" thought' may be susceptible to co-option by capitalist structures (2013: 14) but my own scepticism of the assumed radicalism of Rancière's logic of autonomy goes much deeper. My real concern, seeded in Chapter 2, is that despite the rhetoric of progressive, or even communist, politics that pervades such discourses, Rancière's notion of political dissensus does not appear to extend beyond the enclave to disrupt the wider material context of production on which the equality that is afforded the participants of such communities implicitly or explicitly relies.

Grant Kester (2004), as Roberts notes, is just one critic who cautions against 'an enclave mentality that prefers the idealised production of aestheticised singularity, over and above work that enriches already existing lines of communal dialogue (specifically through class and race)' (Roberts 2009: 365). Peter Hallward likewise expresses unease at Rancière's reluctance to say very much at all 'about the concrete (if not "objective") forms of empowerment required to lend this affirmation [of universal equality] consequential force' (Hallward 2005: 40). For Hallward, there remains a suspicion that, in certain contexts, Rancière's 'trenchant egalitarianism', which is irrevocably upheld as binding in the face of real, material inequalities, can too easily be read as 'an almost passive acceptance of de facto inequalities' (Hallward 2005: 42), and this is exacerbated, I would argue, when the 'trenchant egalitarianism' is applied in artistic spaces that are cut off from the wider inegalitarian distribution of the sensible. Following Hallward, Janelle Reinelt further emphasizes that 'without a follow-up move to consolidate gains', what we are left with may be 'just a gesture – a momentary redistribution of the sensible' (2015: 246) with no consequence beyond the time and space of the theatre event. The danger with prefigurative politics of egalitarianism, when confined within the utopian enclaves of performance, is that the 'communist imaginary' remains precisely that, as Dmitry Vilensky argues: not a 'hypothesis of communism', which 'is practical' and 'you set out to prove', but 'speculation that has no consequences' (Riff and Vilensky 2009: 465). As Simon Bayly cautions, 'Rancière's theory may encourage us to do little more than "play at" politics or equality, and his egalitarianism, no less than Schiller's notion of play, risks confinement to the "unsubstantial kingdom of the imagination"' (2009: 128–9).

David Riff gives a very clear account of the options open to the artist or scholar working in resistance to, yet supported by the inequalities of, global capitalism:

> To do something, you have the option of either inventing your own collective practice, or to work in the existing institutions, whose own practices contradict your own. But once you are either here or there, you find that you have been installed as a readymade on a certain cultural field, and that you have been given a set of privileges, which even include free collaboration and political radicalism, for example. Society is outsourcing its politics to art, and that has become extremely profitable. The challenge is to *work through* that reification for a common cause. (Riff and Vilensky 2009: 469, original emphasis)

I would reiterate here my concern that unless Rancière's logic of autonomy is counterbalanced with egalitarian steer, and contemporary political theatre is permitted to *intend* an effect that reaches *beyond* the enclave, the wider distribution of the sensible is arguably consolidated, regardless of how it might be momentarily interrupted in the microcosm of that particular, temporary cultural community. Within the aesthetic-politico enclaves of the European touring or festival circuit, for example, the spectator might dis-identify from their allocated role in which they constitute a 'no-part' under the conventional terms of the authorship of artistic creation, and the subsequent assertion of their equality to create through interpretation might well constitute a certain kind of formalist democratic politics. But when this enclave is contextualized within the macrocosmic social distribution of the sensible, there are rarely any 'no parts' to be found within such an enclave; the spectators are for the most part counted and authorized within various designated cultural roles from student, to artist, to producer, to curator, to critic, to cosmopolitan purveyor of culture. In a vital sense, the exclusion of the no-parts within the social distribution of the sensible is replicated by their regular absence from such enclaves in which only those who are already counted are benefitting from the affective resonance of the theatre – be that the 'joy, pleasure, awe' proposed by Thompson or the political charge of a new sense of the social proposed by Ridout.

Thus, without taking up the challenge to '*work through*' and break out of what Riff terms our own 'respective golden cages' (2009: 470), the resistance, or politics, or aesthetic redistribution of the sensible, that takes place *within* those golden cages is always going to run the risk, in Gail Day's provocative and Rancièrean terms, of containing artists and scholars within 'their accepted place of fiddling with sensoria while the world burns' (Day 2009: 403). This, for me, is the difficulty with the way in which 'the political' has been reconfigured, following Rancière, as radically progressive and yet contained within the theatre event itself, barred from seeking intended efficacy beyond it. It enables artists and audience to feel, and indeed to reflect, that they are contributing to the project of radical democracy; yet this affective and cognitive activity can too easily become, in Sara Ahmed's terms, a non-performative (Ahmed 2012: 117), thus echoing the risk run by ironic dramaturgies as noted in the previous chapter. When such activity is severed from the inegalitarian context in which the enclave sits, the politics that are operational within the space may more accurately be described as libertarian, as I argued in Chapter 2, than communist. Such practice does not then so much constitute a rehearsal as it does a surrogate, in Ahmed's terms, for the active contestation of inequality beyond the enclave. More generously, it might be worth removing such practice from the discursive framework of political theatres altogether to better understand and appreciate the important philosophical, aesthetic or therapeutic work that is taking place. This would certainly be one benefit of this study's aim to narrow the field of what constitutes 'the political' and to more clearly distinguish work driven entirely by the logic of autonomy from political dramaturgies that are characterized by the tension between both logics and intent on challenging the inegalitarian injustices of the neoliberal context in which they exist.

Beyond the contexts of deprivation and inequality addressed in Chapter 2, it seems to me that affect within the theatre act that seeks to operate under the auspices of a post-Marxist project of radical democracy must be re-harnessed to the egalitarian logic that permits the artist to intend an ideological interpretation or effect of the work – notwithstanding the impossibility of such an end to be secured. Without such a move, theatre practice which is driven solely by the logic of autonomy might be dangerously blind to the degree in which its own models of practice might be complicit in propagating the inequalities of contemporary hegemonic structures, in which individual autonomy is also prized. To return to Kieran Hurley's *Heads Up*, the dominant political charge here, I would argue, despite the turn to affect being explicit in the form of the piece, is driven by the egalitarian logic of the content. The narrative drive of the piece offers little in the sense of political hope or message, the 'heads up' of the title being a warning that the world is coming to an end, which it then ostensibly does. The affective charge, for this spectator, was a combination of thrill, tension and the increasing pace at which the end of the world was approaching us as we listened and reflected together in the audience. Yet it is the micro-narratives of the piece that all deal – either explicitly or obliquely – with the pressures of living at this point in history and operate as searing critiques of neoliberal capitalism.

Leon, the coke-snorting pop star, remains obsessed with getting media coverage for a random cause he has championed to save the bees, while ignoring the fact that his girlfriend is giving birth to their child. Ash, a schoolgirl who has been the victim of sexting, and mostly dwells in the online world of computer games, offers a grim perspective on growing up in a networked world. Abdullah, a worker in a fast-food outlet, has been named and shamed to his colleagues by a mystery shopper for not being 'people perfect' and ends up in a violent battle with a protester against consumerism who he mistakes for a second mystery shopper. Mercy is an investment banker, making vast sums of money by predicting which way the markets will go in the future and capitalizing on disasters around the world. During the course of the story she has an epiphany and becomes a prophet of a different future, abandoning her old life and walking the streets to warn people that the end of the world is approaching. Given the direct address noted above – that each character is introduced as 'you' to the audience – we are personally, and as explored in the previous chapter, provocatively interpellated into each one of these narratives that emerge from a capitalist world order gone badly wrong that is now facing the poetically logical conclusion.

To return to Nicholas Ridout's gamble on the communist potential of theatre, the affective charge of the logic of autonomy is pulsing through *Heads Up*, as we are invited to give our individual attention to Hurley's direct address, audioscape and scenographic design that are designed to connect each individual spectator to the uncertain community of the audience who are sharing uniquely phenomenological experiences of the piece. But I would argue that without the specific narrative content of *Heads Up*, it would be difficult to claim the performance as aligned to a radical political project of the kind that Laclau and Mouffe describe. Rather, it is the materialist analysis of the narrative content as a searing critique of the neoliberal world inhabited by both performer and audience, and the implicit threat of the inevitable endgame were we to permit this to continue, that constitutes the egalitarian logic that invites the audience to look beyond reflection on their present, individual experience in the moment and extend it to the collective conditions and inequalities of neoliberalism that are in operation beyond the utopian enclave of the theatre event. The 'recognition that one's self, as such, is constituted not by its integrity and individuality but precisely by its appearance in relation to others' (Ridout 2013: 10) is provoked, I would argue, more by Hurley's alignment of each individual in the audience to the characters of the text and the proposed interrelation of every material aspect of an unequal world and doomed planet that is the subject of the narrative than it is to the affective charge of 'the experience of listening among others', pleasurable and exhilarating though that may be (Ridout 2013: 162).

Prologues to change

I will now turn to the work of Andy Smith that I will argue also explicitly seeks affective and effective impact, but which resists the narrative drive to the particular political perspectives that are the backbone of *Heads Up*. Smith rather develops his own dramaturgical strategies to somewhat differently bridge the divide between the utopian enclave of the performance and the world of inequality beyond it. As well as resisting, to some degree, the meaning-making role of narrative, Smith also notably rejects the provocative and ironic interpellation discussed in the previous chapter. Instead, I will argue, his dramaturgies operate a gentle and sincere counter-hegemonic interpellation of his spectators that challenges Rancière's scepticism of ideological steer. By interpellating the collective audience *differently* and constituting them as *ideologically other* to the precarious and powerless subject of neoliberalism, Smith's work seeks to destabilize the force of hegemonic interpellation and steers an egalitarian logic beyond the enclave that invites his audience to be moved by the performance in directions that remain open, but nonetheless signposted, to potentially egalitarian and collectivist outcomes.

Smith has written, in his doctoral thesis, of his exploration of a 'counter-cultural' theatre practice that 'articulates ideas and thoughts toward social and political change today' (2014: 8). His theoretical arguments and practical experimentation are heavily influenced by the philosophical frameworks explored in this chapter, in particular his conviction, shared with Read and Ridout, that 'the action of gathering together' facilitates 'the activity of reflection and contemplation' and thus holds 'the potential to be political and social' (9). Smith, like those he draws on, is hesitant to revert to old models of political theatre, rejecting the 'political play' (103), a 'clear dramatic dialectic' (15), and 'a request at [*sic*] end of the evening for us all to leave the theatre and take to the streets in a defined political action' (15).

He is also committed to the autonomy of the spectator, writing in a footnote that *Commonwealth* is 'attempting to offer the audience some capacity for their interpretation' (2014: 75), enabling 'each member to bring their own preoccupations to the piece, and think about what "things" they might apply to their own context' (75). He describes his own attempts to level the perceived hierarchy between artist and audience, stating that 'I do not look to separate myself from the audience, casting them as a "they" to whom "I" the performer speak and offer information ... Neither am I interested in imparting what I believe to be the "right answers"' (16). His early use of the moniker 'a smith' was precisely to this end, 'a reduction of myself in order to create more space for the audience who are there to see the work' (98).

Although the influence of Rancière and others who advocate a new communist imaginary is evident in both Smith's practice and theory (Smith 2014: 102–7), I will suggest below that Smith's work might not be quite so far removed from previous theatres of political intention as he intimates. He writes,

> In each work, I *appeal* to those gathered in the theatre *to reflect on and ask questions of the world in which we live*, and in doing so *consider our individual and collective capacity to shape it.* Through this activity I also *ask an audience to recognise* ... it is not the entity of the play or performance that we should rely upon to undertake such a change, but us, the people who are involved in its making through our acts of presentation and reception. (2014: 14, my emphasis)

As highlighted, Smith's use of these particular terms is significant in the context of this study. As an artist he may be leaving space for each spectator's autonomous reading of the work, but he nevertheless *appeals* and *asks* an audience to undertake specifically political actions: to reflect and ask questions of the world beyond, and to recognize their responsibility and agency to make changes in that world. Smith's intentions for his work echo the rhetoric of much that is claimed for the notion of 'the political' explored in this chapter but, in Smith's case, as I will discuss below, his work literally puts into play the operation he outlines above. That is to say that the audience is directly invited to contemplate specifically political questions concerning the state of the world beyond the theatre and their own relationship to them, thus emphasizing a strong egalitarian logic at the heart of the work to counterbalance the influence of Rancière's logic of autonomy. In this way, I would argue, Smith's work acts, if not as a rehearsal for revolution, perhaps at least as the prologue to a more modest possibility of change. This is made explicit in the dramaturgy and narrative of *Summit*, a piece that was produced subsequent to his doctoral work and to which I will shortly return.

Counter-hegemonic interpellation

Where artists such as Kieran Hurley and Chris Goode acknowledge the performance event as the context in which a narrative will be told, *Commonwealth* (2012) and *Summit* (2017), in common with much of Smith's work, draw explicit attention to the gathering itself as the context for a narrative that proceeds to be about that very gathering or, rather, as Smith always makes clear, a gathering just like that one. This invites self-reflection from each spectator on the part they are playing within the utopian enclave that is the subject of the narrative, as well as on its potential for political prefiguration. *Commonwealth*[2] is introduced as

> a story about people getting together, about a group of people getting together, getting together to do something, getting together to listen to a story.
> Getting together somewhere like this, in a room like this in a building like this. That sits on a street a bit like that one. That's part of a city a bit like this one. A city in a country not unlike here. Just one of many countries in a made-up world.
> And at the beginning of this story these people get together. They gather together in this room like this. (2015: 41)

---

[2] *Commonwealth* was first performed in Gateshead Town Hall on 6 May 2012. I attended a performance at the CDE Conference in Barcelona in June 2015. Citations are taken from the playtext published with Smith's *The Preston Bill* (2015).

This strategy sets the scene for the audience's focus of attention to land precisely on the material context of the particular theatre event they are attending and the implications this might have on the thinking that is to take place. This ensures that such a context is never concealed but remains highlighted as an integral part of the utopian enclave in which the imagining, or listening, or reflecting, will take place. I attended a performance of *Commonwealth* as part of an academic conference organized by CDE (Contemporary Drama in English) in June 2015. It would be difficult to describe a performance situation that more closely reflected the risks of the utopian enclave expressed by Riff, Vilensky and Day. We were seated in the room of a beautiful religious retreat on the outskirts of Barcelona, a small audience of academics many well known to each other through successive and reasonably intimate conferences organized by CDE in recent years. Each spectator was almost certainly well to the left of mainstream European political thinking, well-versed and prepared for experimental models of theatre and mostly familiar with, and well disposed towards, Smith's methods of working, as well as a number of us being well acquainted with Smith on a personal level. Yet despite the strong potential for any political charge to have been contained in one of those 'golden cages' Riff cautioned against, I will now suggest that Smith's dramaturgy may have enabled us, in Riff's terms, to '*work through* that reification for a common cause' (Riff and Vilensky 2009: 469).

The story that is told is the imagined story of another event, just like the one we are at, in which another layer of story is told: a story of people who have decided to get together to 'Do something. Listen to a story […] Just like we did. Something not unlike what we all just did' (2015: 42). These people are offered as placeholders to be occupied by each spectator. They are people who, we are told, do the sorts of things that the 'we' of Smith and his audience do, people who, every now and then, get concerned about things and feel like they want to do something: 'not a solution or cure that works things out, or a spell that would help them to just forget, but just to let them think or feel, or maybe think and feel that they aren't alone' (44). The existing community that formed the audience of which I was part is thus explicitly recreated in the shape of its fictional counterpart, enabling the spectator to reflect on the gathering they are part of and the specific community this holds without losing sight of the things that might concern them in the world beyond the enclave.

In Smith's performances, his hallmark simple phrasing, calm, even and gentle delivery, and extensive use of repetition all bring to mind the stories for young children that he acknowledges as a strong source for his work (2014: 105). In addition to the – for some spectators at least – calming quality of the children's bedtime story, remembered from their own childhood or enjoyed more recently with their own children, the affective, meditative rhythms of Smith's work, delivered in his particular cadences, also bring to mind a prayer service, a kind of secular ceremony which, like its religious counterpart, is infused with a sense of purpose and belief that in that very action agency is being realized. If Martin Crimp's work, examined in the previous chapter, might be said to have its counterpart in Catholicism, a theatrical world full of accusation and warnings of the hell to come, then Smith's work falls at the Methodist, or even Quaker, end of that analogous spectrum. Because it is devoid of ironic inflection and Smith takes care to align himself with his audience – the people 'like us' – there are no overtones of paternalism in the text that refuses to castigate those who populate it, for feeling annoyed, or under pressure, or wanting to give up because there's nothing that can be done. The small speculative stories that are offered concern people who are bothered about little things, such as the anxiety over which cheese to buy in the supermarket. These things are not parodied, as they might be in the ironic structures of Crimp, but rather validated, as part and parcel of what needs to change, of what 'we', by being there and thinking through these questions, might already be changing.

What this offers the spectator is significant in light of the limitations of ironic dramaturgies highlighted in the previous chapter. Smith brings to the audience's attention the dangers identified in Chapter 3: that neoliberalism might decrease the capacity of the precarious subject to believe that they hold agency or even to imagine what kind of action might be possible:

> There's a thought that the world, the world that they are in, is full of too many complications.
> [...]
> however much the people in this room, the people in this story want something to happen, however much they might want to make something happen, there's a thought that it's unlikely that it actually will. There's a thought that really they just can't. A thought that however hard they try, what they do or say won't have the desired effect. That if any change did really happen, then the result would be a situation pretty much the same. (2015: 53)

From this proposed horizon of expectation, the sense of impossibility, for the precarious spectator-subject, of even imagining better futures, Smith proceeds to offer the tentative possibility of agency and hope:

> They could begin to think that there are chances to resist, and think about how they might resist, resist all the things that confuse or annoy them, the big things and small things and all things between.

However big or small they might be, they are thinking there could be
chances to resist. There are chances to just stand up and say no.
Chances to stand up and say something like this:
No.
No.
No.
We don't want things to be like this.
We don't want things to be like this.
So we've made a start, we've made a start by doing this here. (2015: 56)

In his own analysis of the aims of his work, Smith cites Rebecca Solnit's
conviction that 'to hope is to give yourself to the future, and that commitment
to the future makes the present inhabitable' (Solnit 2005: 5 in Smith 2014:
33), and this is the political operation his work undertakes: to combat the
despair that nothing can anymore be done, a despair that paralyses the
precarious spectator-subject's capacity for agency in the present. In this way,
each performance is located, as Smith proposes, not as a political act in and
of itself but, I would argue, as a prologue to action, an invitation that each
individual spectator can be strengthened by and can choose, or not, to follow
up beyond the theatre event itself.

Unlike the ironic dramaturgies under discussion in the previous chapter,
Smith does not provocatively interpellate his spectators as complicit subjects
of neoliberalism leaving them feeling guilty and unsure of what they
are supposed to do, but rather recognizes them, through their imagined
counterparts in his fiction, as people who not only want to make things
better but, critically, have already made a step towards this goal by simply
being there to listen to a story. In this way, Smith's work seeks to directly
confront and counter-attack neoliberalism's interpellation of the precarious
spectator-subject described in Chapter 3: the subject who feels devoid of
agency, responsible for all the problems of the world but powerless to resolve
them and, consequently, unable to envisage better futures or the possibility
of change. In Smith's audience, the spectator-subject is rather assured that
the very little they have already done constitutes action and, furthermore,
that they are not alone: 'We are thinking that just by being here and thinking
something like this something is changing. Something could be changing. Or
at least moving, and continuing to move' (2015: 58–9).

The interpellation of each spectator as an already-active and counter-
hegemonic political agent is a bold move in a contemporary political
discourse dominated by the poststructuralist imperatives of contingency
and provisionality. As can be seen in the poststructuralists' rejection of
Althusser, as discussed in Chapter 5, it is the determinism of the idea

of ideological interpellation of the subject that is rejected as much as its particular ideological direction. Consequently, the ironic, provocative interpellation inspired by Judith Butler and examined in the previous chapter sits comfortably with poststructuralist imperatives precisely because it invites the spectator-subject to deconstruct their 'given' identity as a neoliberal subject, but resists from offering a determined, alternative subjectivity in its place. Thus, the spectator-subject is left intentionally displaced and disorientated. This also accords with Rancière's insistence that 'the place of a political subject is an interval or a gap ... between names identities, cultures, and so on' (1992: 62). Even Judith Butler's accounts of the human subject, noted in Chapter 2, that challenge the notion of autonomy Rancière would ascribe to the political subject, still advocate caution towards the practice of any subject's identity being in some way invited or determined by another. However, in a study that advocates expanded notions of subjectivity, Cristina Delgado-García suggests that through a certain reading of Judith Butler's work, a corresponding counter-hegemonic constitution of the addressee might be considered through a counter-hegemonic interpellative 'hail':

> The subject's own share in the subjectivation of the other opens up the possibility of agency, the possibility of 'speaking [to the other] in ways that have never yet been legitimated, and hence producing legitimation in new and future forms' (Butler 1997a:41). Butler's reformulation of the ways in which the subjectivising address takes place therefore considers how subjects hold the possibility of interpellating others, perhaps invoking subject positions that might be foreclosed under normative modes of subjection. (Delgado-García 2015: 58)

Delgado-García sets the scene for a further investigation of this possibility in her analysis of the characterization of the audience in Tim Crouch's *England*, although Crouch, a long-term collaborator of Andy Smith's, stops short of the counter-hegemonic interpellation explored here in *Commonwealth*. In *England*, Delgado-García argues that the spectator is configured as a 'collective subject' (2015: 145), suspended between a provocatively reiterated ideological interpellation as a cosmopolitan neoliberal consumer and an impossible identification as the Muslim widow of the man whose heart has been sold to the English protagonist. In the first instance the mode of interpellation, I would argue, is broadly ironic and likely to be resisted by the spectator who opposes neoliberal structures; in the second it is set up to be rejected as inconceivable, leaving the spectator with the invitation, or responsibility, 'to find their own position, their own praxis, within economies of power' (Delgado-García 2015: 180). In this way, Crouch's work remains in line with Butler's poststructuralist emphasis and Rancière's logic of autonomy, both of which would resist determined ideological interpellation, even when designed to be counter-hegemonic.

Smith, I believe, rather steers the spectator towards a particular position and praxis and exploits an underexplored potential in current theatre practice and scholarship with his more radical (in the sense of its contestation of poststructuralist imperatives) reconsideration of the potential for critical interpellation of spectators that directly and explicitly invokes determined 'subject positions that might be foreclosed under normative modes of subjection' (Delgado-García 2015: 58). The openness of Smith's call, the characters that are left as placeholders for each spectator to fill and the narrative gaps that are left for spectators to respond to however they choose, ensures that how each spectator interprets the political role they are offered remains a matter of personal reflection and, importantly, personal responsibility. But Smith's generous recognition of each spectator – not as a precarious subject who requires Smith's 'mastery' or guidance to gift them their agency but as someone who has already picked up that challenge for themselves and who is already taking responsibility merely by being there, would seem to me to be a potentially invigorating dramaturgical strategy that might empower spectator-subjects to reject any perceived lack of agency to envisage a different future from the one that neoliberalism would seek to bind them to.

A new sincerity

Smith's rejection of ironic interpellation enables him to embrace the 'new sincerity' that Siân Adiseshiah has identified as an increasingly common element in contemporary performance practice. Adiseshiah borrows the term from its literary counterpart in contemporary American novels, drawing on analysis from Adam Kelly and Martin Eve to note that the 'new sincerity attempts to move beyond postmodern irony, cynicism and fatigue, but is simultaneously careful not to rehabilitate an essentialist self, an expressive subjectivity' (Adiseshiah 2016: 7). Adiseshiah proposes, citing Adam Kelly, that 'the possibility of sincerity depends upon its becoming dialogic in character, always requiring a response from the other to bring it into play' (Kelly 2010: 141 in Adiseshiah 2016: 8). This highlights, in the context of live performance, 'the performative invitation to spectators to respond and attest to the potential of a sincere dialogical encounter over our personal and collective futures' (Adiseshiah 2016: 8), as we saw precisely exemplified in Smith's *Commonwealth*. Examining Forced Entertainment's *Tomorrow's Parties*, Adiseshiah argues that, in relation to this company's work, it might be more accurate to adopt the term 'critical sincerity' given that 'residues of an ironic affect continue to trouble the encounter, ironic moments exist within the space of sincerity, and the authentic is always in question' (2016: 10). Indeed, she concludes that 'the possibility of a sincere encounter over our collective futures is perhaps the (utopian) not yet' (14). Yet, while the sense of a more critical 'dialectic of sincerity' (13) is an entirely appropriate lens through which to analyse the work of Forced Entertainment, haunted as it is by the 'shadows of irony, narcissism or solipsism' (12), I will now propose that 'a sincere encounter over our collective futures' is precisely the outcome that Smith seeks in his production of *Summit*, the first of his productions in which he doesn't perform.

*Summit*³ echoes the structure of *Commonwealth* in a number of important ways, but it also represents a gear shift both for Smith and his audience, as the stakes of the political operation his theatre undertakes are thematically and dramaturgically raised. As *Commonwealth* was a story about a group of people, like the audience, gathering to hear a story, *Summit* tells the story of a group of people, like the audience, meeting at a summit: 'a big, and often international, meeting. A meeting where the stakes are high. A meeting held to discuss something – an emergency or a crisis or a disaster' (2018: 3). *Summit* is recounted by three performers through a complex and multilayered temporal structure and across multiple languages, but primarily, in the 2018 touring production, through English, Malay and British Sign Language (BSL), this last represented in the given citations, as in the published playtext, in bold. These dramaturgies of time and language underpin the particular political potency of this production and need a little further explication before locating the piece within the theoretical framework of this chapter.

At the beginning of the piece the audience is addressed, as in *Commonwealth*, as being in the time and space of the performance. The three performers then invite the audience to take part in the story that they are going to tell, the story of the Summit. All we are told at this stage, and in fact there is little more information forthcoming in the remainder of the show, is that during this Summit, unexpectedly and suddenly, the lights go out and that 'soon after this happens … things begin to change. Soon after it happens things very slowly begin to change' (2018: 6). We are then told that we are

---

³ First presented at the Spire, at the Brighton Festival in May 2017. My original argument here was developed from viewing unpublished documentation of that performance, but the details and citations given here were updated after attending a revised touring production of the piece at the University of Manchester on Friday 28 September 2018.

going to hear this story in three ways, from three perspectives and in three acts. We are told that the first act will take place 1,000 years in the future, and we are asked to imagine, after the lights come up, that we are those people in 1,000 years' time, who have gathered to hear the story of the Summit.

When the lights come up on Act One we are thanked and welcomed in a multiplicity of different languages and joyously, if ambiguously, greeted with 'we made it' (14). The self-referential layers of Smith's dramaturgy continue to expand: the performers (1,000 years in the future) tell us, their audience (1,000 years in the future), that at this Summit, which happened 1,000 years ago, people gathered in a place very like this one. Here Smith connects the future (fictional) audience with the past (fictional) audience of the Summit, with the (real) audience of the theatre venue, who now inhabit both the fictional future of the present and the fictional past of the present at the same time. Despite this ostensibly being the story of the Summit, the details remain provocatively sketchy. We hear only that at this Summit people were talking, thinking, listening, that they were ready for change. We hear that when the lights went out 'many thought that it was the end' (19), but the performers joyously confirm that it was nowhere near the end, but rather the 'actual start' (20).

The start of 'our story' (as we listen 1,000 years in the future) was this moment (1,000 years ago, or the actual moment of the performance event we are attending) when the lights went out, the moment when the change began, the moment when we 'moved forward / **And now we are *here*'** (28). 'Here', it becomes clear, is a utopia of the future, sketched out with Smith's hallmark child-like simplicity with lists of things that there are more of and things there are less of. Things there are more of include freedom, ideas, democracy, diplomacy, unity, identity, nationality, morality, ethics, equality, optimism, internationalism, automation, communication and understanding. Things there are less of include patriarchy, monarchy, hierarchy, technology, law and order, mess, capitalism, labour, pollution, population, confusion, privatization, devastation, destruction, need, greed, want, addiction, lies and misinformation, profit and loss ownership, production, global financial domination, division, disease, separation, exclusion, isolation, segregation, anger and trouble (29–36). There are multiple reference points for the British audience of 2018 as to the symptoms of the crisis that consisted of trouble:

With wars and demagogues
Referendums and exits
With terrorists
Presidents
Capitalists

And sexists
With over-consumption
And global warming
With leaders and losers
Emergencies
And warnings (38–9)

We hear that no one knew what to do, and that everything was in a mess. A Summit was ultimately called, but there is no record of what was said, all we know is that suddenly the lights went out, and soon after that, change began.

Act Two is introduced after the lights come back on, when we are told that in the next act we are going to go back in time to five years before the Summit of the story occurred. This makes it, as one performer helpfully explains in the 2018 performance, around 2013. Act Two consists of three versions of the same speech, first delivered by the performer who signs in silence, then by the performer speaking in English and then by the performer speaking in Malay. The narrative content, working from the English version, describes a familiar world where we know that 'a crisis or catastrophe of some description is on its way' (58) and in which 'things might be about to go a little bit out of control' (58). Knowingly, with a nod to the real place and time of the audience in 2018, we are warned that 'soon – maybe even in as little as five [years] … things could be happening that make us think that this really is the beginning of the end' (58). With a simultaneous nod to the fictional future of five years hence, of which the story of Act One has made us aware, we are told: 'sometimes it feels as if the lights are about to go out' (59).

As in *Commonwealth*, we are generously interpellated as people who are 'all here now because we want to do something about' the 'difficult and problematic times' we find ourselves in (57). Not only are we interpellated in our fictional 2013 subject positions but also, as the spectators, we actually are, in 2018, 'at some point in the future' who 'might be sitting or standing something like this – probably somewhere like this – wondering if there is really any way out of this mess' (58). Each performer's address concludes with a number of direct calls to arms:

> … We need campaigns. Activities. Meetings – a summit, even. We need small gestures. We need big gestures. We need ideas. We need action.
> … We need to use our imagination. We need to imagine that change might be possible.
> … If we don't do something now, or at least soon, then things might be about to begin to take a very distinct turn for the worst. (60–1)

After all three performers have spoken, we are asked in English and BSL, 'Are there any questions?' (66) before the lights go out. The third act is introduced as the Summit itself and we are warned that 'soon we will get to the moment where something happens. The moment where the lights suddenly go out ... And in that moment – or rather just after it – things begin to change. Things very slowly begin to change' (68). When the lights go out for the final time we now know, however bad things appear to be, that this is the start of the change. This is the moment when – very slowly – the 'history' of the utopian world we have witnessed 1,000 years from now will begin.

The dramaturgical temporal disjuncture thus operates politically on a number of levels. It has set up the future that is so difficult to imagine and recognized us sequentially as those who have already done something about it, those who wish to do something about it and those who are now left to pick up the invitation, if we wish, to leave the theatre and make this the moment that things – very slowly – start to change, in whichever way – large or small – we can best imagine. Here, Smith goes much further than in *Commonwealth*, raising the stakes of the political project from the personal to the global and inviting the spectators to take up the hope and conviction that the unspoken and unknown changes that initiate the fictional journey from present dystopia to future utopia can indeed start here, in the time and place of the performance, in their thoughts and actions from this point on.

Prefiguring utopia

The operation of the egalitarian logic in Smith's work is not merely the invitation to think or act towards a narrative of utopia, thus provoking the imagination of better futures, nor is it merely an explicit, and strategic, interpellation of the spectator as always-already subjectivized, thus contesting the lack of agency that is part and parcel of neoliberal subjectivity. What *Summit* also weaves through its jumps in chronology is a dramaturgical prefiguration of aspects of the 'utopia' its narrative gestures towards. In Act One, 1,000 years in the future, Smith's repetitions and rhythmic patterns are used to both aesthetic and political impact as the dialogue of the three performers criss-crosses effortlessly through a myriad of different languages:

And then one moment
Momenton
A **moment**
Listening talking **talking** listening
Hanajh

Louar
Everyone
Here
Then suddenly
Pludselig
Lights out (23–4)

Underpinning this fluent, melodic and playful convergence of languages are the gestural vocabularies of BSL not only expressed by the performer who communicated throughout in BSL but also employed seamlessly at moments by the other two performers. Juxtaposed with this pluralist address that can be followed effortlessly by all audience members, including those with hearing impairments, the second act, taking place in the fictionalized gathering of 2013, segregates the dialogue out into three distinct monologues as noted above, the first in sign, the second in English and the third in Malay. This enacts three operations that are underpinned, I would argue, by the egalitarian logic. The first is that the order, in itself, subverts the expectation of the English-speaking non-hearing-impaired spectator by firstly necessitating they are required to wait for the translation which more usually comes subsequent to the spoken, English text that is assumed as the dominant mode of communication. This displaces such a spectator-subject from their unacknowledged place of privilege in the common distribution of the sensible and engages them in the experience of the 'other' – the hearing-impaired, or non-English-speaking subject. Subsequently, a different challenge awaits this particular spectator-subject, as they are then asked to listen to the address in a language that few of them, going by usual audience demographics of Smith's work, will be able to understand. The fact that they have now 'heard' the narrative in English removes the potential mode of engagement offered by the signed version, of seeing how much they can work out from the performer's tone and body language and so – in a functional sense – makes this section redundant for the majority of the audience, who already know what has been said. Yet, this very redundancy requests a particular attention from the spectator that asks for nothing in return: the attention to someone who is speaking, who has something to say, who is sincerely expressing themselves in order to engage the listener in collaboration. The spectator can, of course, ignore this request: switch off, think about something else, look around the audience or check their phone. But to do so is to explicitly dismiss the call to acknowledge the 'other' as legitimate in her difference and to reject, in Adiseshiah's terms, 'the performative invitation … to respond and attest to the potential of a sincere dialogical encounter over our personal and collective futures' (Adiseshiah

2016: 8). By giving the speaker our full attention, we participate in the collective effort of Act Two to connect with the 'other' beyond considerations of what is easy or even what is useful for our own purposes of comprehension.

Secondly, the removal of meaning also enables our affective response to emerge as a new 'structure of attention' as Nigel Thrift proposed (2004: 67), enabling an expansion of sensory connections and capacities to be engaged as we connect with each of the speakers without access to familiar linguistic meaning. Thirdly, as we sit through and potentially work hard at connecting with those speakers whose language we are not able to speak, we remember that in the act before, in the utopia of 1,000 years in the future, a multiplicity of languages was playfully traversed. Here, there had been no waiting for 'your' speaker but an ongoing dialogue in a pluralist language that enabled everyone to follow the narrative in real time. In the Manchester performance I attended, this section was exuberant in its comedic ensemble interaction, and the audience responded with much laughter. Everyone was accommodated effortlessly by this choric, polyphonic language that had evolved over the millennium between now and then, and which left everyone entertained and no spectator-subject on the margins waiting for explanation. Here, as it is stressed in multiple languages and through repetition, there is no 'other' because we are all 'other':

Druga
Kala
Taira
Andre
Other (33)

It is not just in the future setting of Act One that elements of Utopia are prefigured, although the laughter induced in this section starkly and effectively contrasted with the gravity and silence induced by the individual speeches in Act Two. In between each of the 'fictionalized' acts, the performers on stage prefigure a kinder, more diverse, more sincere and more careful world. Smith uses his first production that is not a solo show to open the stage to Aleasha Chaunte, a black female performer; Jamie Rea, a white male Deaf performer; and Nadia Anim, a female performer of Malay heritage.[4] Within the overwhelmingly white and able-bodied world of European contemporary performance this, in itself, is a strongly egalitarian choice. Moreover, their relationships with each other are supportive and

---

[4]   In the original production Chaunte performed with Stephen Collins, a white male Deaf performer, and Nima Taleghani, a male performer of Asian ethnicity.

without competition or differential status – quite a rarity in ensemble choric performance where constructed tensions between the performers are a common strategy that offers increased dramatic potential. Most explicitly, each performer speaks to the audience with the same care and concern that Smith adopts in his solo practice, anxious to guide the audience safely through the show. 'Is everyone OK?' we are asked whenever the lights come back on, 'Is everyone following?' Likewise, we are explicitly told when the lights will go out and for how long, and when they will come back up again, as well as being given clear and detailed instructions as to who we are positioned as in any given act. The performers prepare the audience for Act Two with the information that here people will say things in three different languages, but not to worry, 'everyone is going to say pretty much the same thing' (49).

The return, in Act Three, to the present time, and the Summit of the title, sees the performers shift strategic gear for the only notable time in the show. Arguably, this is the only ghosting of irony in a show that is otherwise adamantly sincere, as the performers enact the following dialogue:

> We are going to take control … We are going to lead everyone through these turbulent times. We will not be broken. We are going to regroup and rebuild and transform.
> We want you to trust us.
> We are going to do this/for you
> /*A sudden blackout* (72–3)

As the lights go out, we know that this is the signal at which things are going to start to change. But they are not going to change due to any of the actions of the performers who, here, perform 'in role' as our 'leaders' whose authority is cut short. In this act, the performers are not sincere, but offering a manifestation of leadership that is undercut by everything that has gone before it and by its own short-lived aspirations. Because when the lights go out, the leaders have gone, and it is the audience (and the actors who reappear to take their bow) who are left to decide how things might change and to take individual responsibility for it. As Smith proposes in his thesis, with explicit reference to Rancière's rethinking of communism, his own work looks to 'instil a confidence in the audience that we are autonomous individuals in a wider and connected society' and to 'make a request to both performer and viewer to reflect on how we are acting, and consider what we might do (or already do, or be able to do) in order to make changes to the world in which we live' (2014: 16). Thus, the ironic portrayal of political leadership in the third act is obliterated into darkness, and the responsibility for action, and the choice of what that might be, passes to each autonomous individual. The egalitarian steer of the piece is thus productively challenged in this final moment by the failure of professional politicians, or artists who have the answers, but nonetheless such a logic has shaped the invitation made to the spectator by its reflection on the wider inequalities and the utopia to which the autonomous individual is now requested to respond.

Conclusion

In this chapter I have argued that the emancipation of the spectator under Rancière's rubric cannot be configured as an act of political dissensus if the individual's autonomy of response within the microcosm of the performance event is severed from any impact on the inegalitarian distribution of the sensible in the macrocosm of the world beyond. It is only when the affects generated within the enclave of performance are in some way re-harnessed to the intention of political effect on the wider, inegalitarian landscape that such affects can be seen to be operating under the auspices of radical democracy. If the logic of autonomy is entirely severed from the notion of political intention or ideological steer, then the theatre in question is libertarian in its politics and cannot productively be considered to be aligned with the project of radical democracy, however else it may be justly valued for its aesthetic, philosophical or therapeutic benefits.

I have suggested that Kieran Hurley's *Heads Up* holds its political currency not in its form, as has long been argued more broadly by postdramatic theorists such as Hans-Thies Lehmann, but in a narrative content that specifically requires each spectator to inhabit the identities of those human and non-human characters who are suffering under the consequences of neoliberalism. Andy Smith's work, conversely, retains only the barest framework of a narrative which invites each spectator to fill in the details from their own imagination and maintains a focus on the time and place of the event, even as it offers fictional iterations of it with which each spectator can continue to engage on a personal level. I have argued that Smith explores the potential of sincere, rather than ironic, interpellation and employs a self-reflexive framework of metanarratives that encourage consideration of, and reflection on, the material context of the utopian enclave by gesturing to questions of inequality and injustice in the world beyond the theatre. The egalitarian logic is also evident in the explicit invitation to each spectator to reflect on their own responsibility towards change and greater equality and justice in the future that begins when the theatre event has ended. In this way, the logic of autonomous interpretation and individual responsibility works in productive tension with the egalitarian logic of the narrative framework and the counter-hegemonic interpellation of the spectator as an already-subjectivized political agent who has the capacity, and has already begun, to alter the future. Thus, Smith's work holds the potential to contest the lack of agency that is endemic in neoliberalism and offers the precarious spectator-subject a perspective that explicitly challenges the hegemonic ideological structures that would conversely foster despair and apathy.

In addition, I argued that *Summit* began to address the absence of the other that I had noted as a particular political limitation of the ironic dramaturgies of Martin Crimp. The presence of *Summit*'s particular performers and languages on the stage actively expanded the voices of those speaking and thinking within the utopian enclaves of European contemporary performance, as well as prefiguring a world in which diversity, otherness and plurality are significantly progressed. One question, however, that might be asked of the dramaturgy of *Summit,* and it is one that the following chapter will take up, is whether the Utopia of the future, the world in which everyone is equally 'other', defies the political logic of agonism proposed by Mouffe that stipulates, as discussed in Chapter 4, that politics is ultimately constituted by the difference of 'us' and 'them' and that the antagonism of social reality cannot be eliminated in the way that Smith's Utopia optimistically proposes.

7

Questions of Empathy and Agonism

In Chapter 4, I set up a framework of analysis that proposed that the political dramaturgies under examination in the second part of this study, might be productively understood as operating across the field of tension between the two political logics of egalitarianism and autonomy. The spectator of practice in which the egalitarian logic dominates is offered an egalitarian (and so ideological) view of the world to which they are invited to subscribe and an egalitarian (and so ideological) collective project in which they are invited to participate. The spectator of practice in which the autonomous logic dominates is granted the autonomy of individual interpretation and invited to take precisely what they want from the experience. Throughout this study I argue that, since the poststructuralist moment, the logic of autonomy has been in the ascendency, and the challenge for contemporary political theatres has been how to best uphold the poststructuralist demands for pluralism and autonomy without necessitating the abandonment of the collective egalitarian imaginary of Marxism. In the previous two chapters I have argued that the logic of autonomy needs to be balanced by the logic of egalitarianism for theatre practice to be meaningfully aligned with the post-Marxist project of radical democracy.

In this and the subsequent chapter, I turn my attention to contemporary political dramaturgies in which the egalitarian logic might be said to dominate. Where Rancière critiqued ironic dramaturgies for their assumption of mastery, my key contention was the risk that they occluded 'the other' from both the stage and the critical consideration of the spectator. Recent trends in practice that seek to explicitly address this occlusion are verbatim performance and theatres of real people, whereby space is made on the stage for the autobiographical stories of testifiers or non-professional performers who are most often presumed to be other to the imagined spectator-subjects who are predicted to attend the production (Gaarde and Mumford 2016: 5).

In this chapter I turn to a seminal example of such practice, *Queens of Syria* (2016), a piece of theatre featuring Syrian refugees performing for audiences in mainstream theatres across the UK. This analysis enables me to introduce and interrogate contemporary employment of the empathy operation, whereby the spectator is required to engage with those who are considered 'other' to them, a strategy that might be expected to address the limitations of the ironic dramaturgies of the critical tradition. Given the identification, in Chapter 3, of the precarious neoliberal subject as individualized, ironic and lacking in the capacity for empathy, the need for dramaturgies that can support or encourage empathetic engagement with different others would appear to be vital at this historical moment and perhaps underlies the resurgent popularity, post-2008, of verbatim strategies and theatres staging non-professional performers to this end.

This chapter will explore, in particular, the ways in which the empathy operation has been notably reconfigured, for its contemporary employment, by the poststructuralist logic of autonomy that has been discussed throughout this study, despite the explicitly egalitarian steer of *Queens of Syria* and much comparable practice. The tension between the two logics thus enables an invitation for empathetic response to operate as politically vital in the neoliberal moment. Most importantly, I will examine how the political operation of empathy is now most commonly located in the other's resistance to being understood, thus insisting on a two-way dialogic operation that refuses to permit any easy colonization of the other. This resistance, I will argue, opens up a critical field for agonistic debate in which the complexity of the political context beyond the plight of the suffering individual might be addressed. In my analysis of *Queens of Syria*, I will explore the ways in which many of its dramaturgical choices draw on such reconfigured frameworks.

However, I will also examine how the dramaturgy of real people closes down the potential for two-way dialogic engagement between spectator and performer due to the absence of character that eliminates the critical field on which such engagement might be possible. By so doing, I will argue such practice can evade the agonistic debate, which I discussed in Chapter 4, that is required to accommodate the complexities of the political situation in question. Here, I will suggest that the potential of the egalitarian logic is hampered by the disavowal of the pluralist antagonisms insisted upon by the poststructuralist logic of autonomy and the subsequent drive to political consensus between egalitarian-leaning spectators and refugee performers. In conclusion, I will argue that the production risked raising a potentially dangerous antagonism between the consensus in the theatre and the spectres of the 'other others' who do not welcome refugees or subscribe to the cosmopolitan liberalism of the audience and who, furthermore, are unlikely to be in the auditorium to engage in dialogue or to defend themselves from the implied accusation made in their absence.

The empathy operation

In everyday psychological terms, empathy is generally understood as the operation by which an individual is able to cognitively understand and emotionally relate to the feelings of another. Where such capacity is lacking, the individual's cognitive and/or emotional ability is defined as impaired, as in the diagnostics of conditions characterized by socio- and psychopathy, or challenged, as proposed by research into the autistic spectrum. Such diagnostics of impairment or deficit implicitly assume the capacity to empathize as a 'normal' human characteristic, although the degree to which this capacity is socially learned or biologically innate is far from settled and well beyond the remit of this study to pursue. On the one hand, cognitive scientists point to the mirror neurons in our brain that fire in the same way when we see someone else perform an action as they do when we ourselves perform it. Mirror neurons, as Lyndsay B. Cummings observes, 'have led many to claim that we have an innate connection to the actions, intentions, and feelings of others' (2016: 4). However, as Bruce McConachie notes, 'sensori-motor coupling and imaginary transposition' are only the first two stages of the four-stage process that might ultimately lead to 'a kind of golden-rule ethics, which induces empathisers to treat other empathisers with fairness and respect' (2013: 193).

Any conviction that the 'golden rule' empathetic engagement that McConachie notes might be accessed by an 'innate', biological capacity of the human subject is challenged on many fronts. In Chapter 3, I proposed that one of the consequences of narcissistic individualization has been what Gary M. Olson defines as 'a *culturally acquired empathy-deficit disorder*' which has '*its roots in the dominant socioeconomic system*' (2013: 57, original emphasis). Empathy, he argues, 'is less likely to manifest itself under conditions of attachment *insecurity* because the individual is more likely to be self-absorbed, personally distressed, and empathically unavailable' (2013: 55, original emphasis). Furthermore, it is widely accepted that such an instinctive capacity, even if it is established as scientific fact, tends to diminish and ultimately disappear, when the suffering is located at distance from our immediate social circle. As Anthony M. Clohesy explains, any biological instinct for ethical engagement is intuitively aroused to care for family and close community, but this intuitive sense of ethics is not always adequate to stretch to those 'distant others' with whom we hold less in common (2013: 66).

Theatre has, since the *Poetics* of Aristotle, been celebrated for its potential to awaken the spectator-subject's capacity for empathy with the distant other, and it is not surprising that Lilie Chouliaraki (2012), discussed in Chapter 3, ultimately advocates a return to 'theatrical structures' within the communicative structures of humanitarianism as a vital means of challenging the dominant ironic paradigm that has emerged in recent decades. For Chouliaraki, the 'theatrical structure of solidarity' is one in which 'the encounter between western spectator and vulnerable other takes place as an ethical and political event', as opposed to the 'mirror structure' she sees as symptomatic of the ironic paradigm, 'where this encounter is reduced to an often narcissistic self-reflection that involves people like "us"' (4). Chouliaraki's use of the descriptor 'theatrical' is drawn from Aristotelian models of theatre, the critical characteristic being the distance between the spectator and the staging of representations of the other. She is inclined to resist the contemporary retreat from such structures within the humanitarian imaginary, arguing instead for revised and revitalized renewal of the historical theatrical structures of humanitarian communication. To this end she proposes a paradigm that constitutes 'solidarity as "agonism"' (188) that can return the 'suffering other' to centre stage, but this time as an agent within her own historical context as opposed to a victim, or charitable project, that can offer satisfaction to the Western subject.

For theatre scholars, it is clear that in her revision of the historical 'theatrical structures' of the humanitarian imaginary, Chouliaraki is arguing for a Brechtian dramaturgy, one in which empathetic engagement 'is combined with judgement so as not to collapse into narcissistic emotion' (2012: 23). Her insistence on 'the mobilization of empathy and the challenge of judgement' as the 'two key functions of theatrical imagination' (192) gives her adoption of the term 'theatrical' a resolutely Brechtian flavour. However, Chouliaraki prioritizes the first key function over the second, in a reversal of Brecht's understanding of emotional engagement as an affective means to a critical, rational end. Drawing on Dana R. Villa, Chouliaraki rather argues that 'it is, therefore, the way in which the sufferer's voice participates in the dramatization of suffering that can make a difference to our affective engagement with it ... solidarity does not solely depend upon "the rigorous logical unfolding of an argument ... but rather [on] imaginative mobility and the capacity to represent the perspective of others"' (Villa 1999: 96 in Chouliaraki 2012: 193). This reversal in emphasis may well reflect the reconsideration of the potential of emotional and affective strategies within contemporary political dramaturgies that has been examined at points throughout this study.

Chouliaraki's proposed 'solidarity of agonism' brings Mouffe's agonistic framework, as introduced in Chapter 4, back into the foreground as a key point of reference for politically engaged theatres at this point in time. In many ways comparable to Rancière's call for dissensus, examined in Chapters 2 and 6, Mouffe's idea of the political is driven by the necessity for the continual disruption of consensus and the insistence on the incorporation and valorization of the voices of those who have been written out of any strategically constituted consensus of the social. Furthermore, both Mouffe and Rancière, in common with Chouliaraki, afford particular attention to the importance of affect and emotion. As Mouffe argues, the prime task of agonistic politics is 'not to eliminate passions from the sphere of the public, in order to render a rational consensus possible, but to mobilize those passions towards democratic designs' (2005: 103).

In this chapter, my examination of the political dramaturgies of the staging of those who are 'other' to their audience will seek to interrogate whether such dramaturgies hold the potential to operate within an agonistic framework of solidarity, in which the other is enabled to appear on the stage as an agent within her own historical context and in which consensus is disrupted. This will involve an interrogation of the empathy operation that is requested from the spectator, and to that end I will now explore the ways in which contemporary theorists have looked to reconfigure empathy's political potential following the historical critiques of its limitations.

Empathy reconfigured

In her history of empathy, Cummings seeks to contest the long-standing claim that empathy facilitates the capacity for the subject to know or experience how the other is feeling. She argues that this emphasis on the brain's cognitive, emotional and imaginative activity has led those sceptical of such other-orientated credentials, such as Charles Edward Gauss, cited in Cummings's study, to stress that 'the vital properties which we experience in or attribute to any person or object outside of ourselves are the projections of our own feelings and thoughts' (Gauss 1973: 85 in Cummings 2016: 5). Thus, to claim to empathize or know how another might feel is always an act of imagination, rather than one of knowledge, and so cannot be relied on to correspond to the reality experienced by the other. Moreover, the claim to know another is, by definition, to position oneself as knowing all of that which can be known, given that the imagined version of the other must be constructed from what is known to the self. In Chouliaraki's model of the humanitarian imaginary, she argues that there is an assertion of power in the claim to know someone who, in the uni-directional model of the photo image, or analogously in the dramatic representation of suffering, is unable to know the spectator-subject back on equal terms or to respond to how their own subjectivity is being constructed in the mind of the spectator-subject through the operation of empathy. To assume that the other's experience can be known through the operation of empathy is a diminishment of their capacity to be other than or more than that which the spectator-subject can know. Furthermore, in cases where the lack of personal knowledge of such experience is extreme, the other is precisely reduced to the specifics of that experience. The starving African child in the photo-image exists in relation to their starvation, they can be no more than hungry and suffering. Likewise, the refugee is afforded only their loss and displacement, defined and known by their lack of full humanity, by one who is characterized by a relative completeness of humanity in their display of unreturnable generosity. The double-edged nature of compassion that might arise from an encounter with victimhood is that it secures the paternalistic power of the subject to bestow gifts on the other that cannot be returned and so consolidates the inequality of the relationship.

In her study of the cultural politics of emotions, Sara Ahmed cites Elizabeth V. Spelman to emphasize that 'compassion, like other forms of caring, may also reinforce the very patterns of economic and political subordination responsible for such suffering' (Spelman 1997: 7 in Ahmed 2014: 22). The operations of empathy within such a context lead not only to compassion for the other's suffering, Ahmed suggests, but to a feeling of generosity that reflects back onto the subject and risks being transformed into 'fetishism' (2014: 22) that 'forgets the gifts made by others ... as well as prior relations of debt accrued over time' (22), a transformation that is especially acute in a post-colonialist context. Again, this leads empathy, like a boomerang, through the vehicle of the suffering other to return back to the subject who has employed it and is now able to bask in a 'feel-good' self-reflection. Whether such affect is best understood as egoistic, altruistic or, as Anthony M. Clohesy argues after Martin Hoffman, a bridge between the two, the empathy operation under such terms seems to move no closer than the ironic structures examined in Chapter 5 to shifting the emphasis from the feelings of the subject-self to the concerns or requirements of the other (Hoffman 1990: 54 in Clohesy 2013: 18).

Cummings likewise proposes that the difference of the other must be upheld in operations of empathy. Drawing on the work of Edith Stein, Cummings emphasizes that the 'other can "lead" the empathizer to places to which he or she may not have access' (2016: 13). She views those moments whereby the spectator-subject is unable to know or feel the other's experience not as a failure of empathy but 'rather as an opportunity for the empathizer to recognize the need for an expanded worldview' that 'may give us cause to reflect on our *own* behaviour, knowledge (or lack thereof), and orientation to the world' (2016: 13). While this does, again, suggest the return of attention to the self, it is a return that is critically self-reflexive, rather than emotionally self-indulgent, as it may locate the self precisely *as another subject's other*. This was the manoeuvre I identified at work in the previous chapter's discussion of Andy Smith's *Summit*. Through three sequential versions of the same monologue – the first in British Sign Language, the second in English and the third in Malay – the English-speaking non-hearing-impaired spectator was challenged to confront the difference of the 'other' in a way that encouraged them to reflect on their own customary location of dominance within communication structures and perceive themselves, unusually, as 'other' to two of the three speaking subjects.

The political validation of empathy, through its recognition of the unconquerable difference of the other and subsequent acknowledgement of the failure of the subject's capacity to colonize such difference, becomes vital in the reconfiguration of empathy explored in this, and the following, chapter. Anthony M. Clohesy, drawing on the philosopher Martin Heidegger, argues that this is precisely where the ethical value, and ultimately the politics, of empathy can be located, proposing that the political potential of 'the empathetic experience of difference' is that it pierces 'the "armour of unity" that has grown thick on us over time' (5). That is to say that the inevitable acknowledgement of our incapacity to know the other evidences not only the difference of the other but, more importantly, the incompleteness, or otherness, of the subject-self's own identity and self-narrative to others. This acknowledgement then exposes the illusion of wholeness and sovereignty that underpins the subject's conception of selfhood, and the violence that the subject has enacted (and will continue to enact) towards others in order to sustain such an illusion. The violence, Clohesy argues, lies in the denial of the other's singularity, the denial that there exists anything beyond that which we can know and the denial that beyond the subject's own orientation they are not the centre or privileged perspective against which otherness can be measured. He concludes that 'it is this unsettling aspect of the empathic experience of difference that is of the utmost ethical significance because, ultimately, ethics must be about guiding us away from the familiarity and security of "home" to the more unfamiliar and inhospitable terrain of Difference from which we continually stray' (2013: 6).

Clohesy thus directly addresses how the ethical and political potential of empathy lies in its capacity to make us strangers to ourselves and so enables the operation of empathy to be extended beyond those and that with whom we feel ourselves to be 'at home'. The dislocation caused by the operation of empathy, he argues, 'is important because it allows us to see how our immersion within "relations of proximity" *conceals* our obligations to distant others' (2013: 27, original emphasis). Clohesy's understanding of 'proximity', aligned, as he remarks, with Bourdieu's notion of *habitus*, both encompasses and is deeper than literal geographical or social location: 'proximity should be seen to include *all* those aspects of our identities and lives that we accept in an uncritical way, all of those unexamined opinions, attitudes and prejudices, all of those moods and dispositions that are constitutive of our "being at home" in the world' (2013: 29). For Clohesy, such extended relations of proximity might conspire in the concealment of 'our obligation to recognize others [those who fall outside of such relations] in a spirit of equality and solidarity' and 'an understanding of the conditions for justice' (29). The disruption enacted by the empathic movement causes a partial loss of identity and thus forces the subject to confront the provisional, fallible and finite nature of their 'being at home' in the world: to confront, in Heideggerian terms, the 'uncanniness' of their true being which, in turn, might 'reconfigure the terms of our relations to strangers and the obligations we owe to them' (29).

This necessary confrontation with 'Difference' – the fallible, contingent and fractured nature of identity that cannot be determined or secured – is strongly underpinned by advocates of the poststructuralist logic of autonomy that has been examined throughout this study. Ernesto Laclau and Chantal Mouffe, discussed in Chapter 4, explicitly align the logic of autonomy with 'the uniqueness and intelligibility of a system of differences' (166) that risks the political anarchy of unreconcilable and entirely disparate antagonisms between multiple subjects and others. Jacques Rancière, as discussed in Chapter 6, argues precisely for such anarchy: 'the capacity of anonymous people, the capacity that makes everyone equal to everyone else ... [and] is exercised through irreducible distances ... an unpredictable interplay of associations and dissociations' (2009: 17). In the following chapter, I will return again to the discourse of 'Difference' to highlight some potential difficulties that an unquestioning adoption of the logic of autonomy might raise. But here, I will now focus on the radical potential of this reconfigured empathy operation and how it might be put to work politically in the context of theatre.

Cummings insists, to this end, on exploring the potential of what she terms 'dialogic empathy', an operation of empathy that resists the temptation to 'possess some part of another's experience without heeding warnings that our understanding is flawed or our empathy unwelcome' (2016: 17–18). She draws on Martin Buber's understanding of dialogue that 'consists in neither attempting to force one's perspective on another nor in passively accepting the other's perspective ... Dialogue occurs in an open exchange in which all parties are honest about their positions in the moment while remaining open to new perspectives' (Cummings 2016: 18). Thus, for Cummings, 'a dialogic empathy ... is one that does not "arrive" at understanding, but rather emerges in the moment-to-moment engagement with another' (19). Cummings draws heavily on theorizations of empathy within the context of psychological and psychoanalytical discourses in which the subject (therapist) and the other (client) are engaged in one-to-one and face-to-face dialogue. Such operations cannot be straightforwardly applied to the situation of theatre in which the spectator-subject is often plural and rarely given the opportunity to engage in literal dialogue with the actor-other who has a script to follow. But Cummings suggests dialogic empathy can be undertaken via dramaturgical strategies that interrupt the operations of a potentially unidirectional empathetic engagement with the actor-other and 'challenge our interpretative acumen, reminding us either overtly or subtly that we may not know as much as we think we do' (17). The reconfigured empathy operation, in short, emerges as 'a process that may ask us to see the world and ourselves differently' (28).

Yet, Cummings is also aware of the danger that empathetic engagement with the individual protagonist, however reconfigured, might divert the spectator's attention from wider systemic causes of inequality. This concern has long-held sway in political theatre history and is a significant driver of the strong documentary theatre tradition, most recently the re-emergence of verbatim theatre, that often eschews the journey of the individual protagonist in favour of a plurality of voices and perspectives. Cummings usefully distinguishes the historical moment of empathy's emergence in the early twentieth century from that of the emergence of sympathy in the eighteenth century by positing the latter as a manifestation of empire, whereby the ability to access the experience of the cultural 'other' was seen as a way to bind disparate communities together under colonial rule. Empathy, rather, 'became the means by which we understood others as psychologically unique beings in the age of bourgeois individualism' (2016: 15). In a concern that will continue to reverberate throughout this chapter, Cummings notes that 'in this age of ... neoliberalism, this also means that empathy risks shifting our focus from systemic conditions toward individual experiences [...] If sympathy operated, potentially, as a tool of empire, empathy may operate as a tool of global neoliberalism, separating individual experiences from the wider conditions that create them' (15). This, ultimately, risks fetishism, as cautioned by Sara Ahmed, whereby 'the transformation of the wound into an identity cuts the wound off from a history of "getting hurt" or injured' (2014: 32). Where a historical narrative of injustice is encapsulated in a singular identity narrative of suffering, the attention is paid to the wound and the present pain of the victim. This attention is displaced from the structures of inequality that permitted the wound to occur, leaving such structures unquestioned and in place to continue wounding.

Contemporary political dramaturgies of empathetic engagement are thus required to do two things in response to the historical scepticism of the empathy operation, as I will now examine in the context of *Queens of Syria*. Firstly, the spectator's attempts to colonize the other through the operation of empathy must be checked by the other's right to respond dialogically, leading the spectator to critically reflect on the unknowability of the other and the fallibility and contingency of their own narrative of self. Secondly, the spectator's attempts to empathize with individualized narratives of suffering must be managed in such a way that permits critical space for the spectator to reflect on the systemic causes of the suffering and any potential complicity they may have in the continuation of the injustice. In the following section, I will begin my analysis by countering this second caution with the possibility that the individualized narratives of *Queens of Syria* might, in fact, retain political currency in the contemporary context of mass-mediatized representations of otherness.

Strategies of re-facement

Queens of Syria was co-produced for its UK tour by Developing Artists, Refuge Productions and Young Vic Theatre.[1] The original project took place in Amman in late 2013, comprising a series of drama therapy workshops, attended by Syrian refugee women, that were geared towards a performance of Euripides' *The Trojan Women* for fellow refugees, interspersed with the refugees' own real-life stories. The touring production that I attended was adapted from this process and political context with mainstream UK audiences in mind.

In line with much contemporary verbatim practice, *Queens of Syria* adopts a mostly pluralist framework that rejects the centrality of any individual protagonist's journey. It rather offers multiple women's stories from different backgrounds and perspectives, interspersed with choral sections taken from *The Trojan Women*. Yet, the dramaturgy also enables each of the women to be particularized by detailed accounts of their individual lives, homes and customs. While this might appear to risk the individualization of suffering noted above, and so detract the spectators' attention from the wider systemic context of warfare and injustice, the emphasis of the personalized biographies was, here, I will argue, serving a different political purpose.

---

[1] I attended the performance at the Liverpool Everyman Theatre on Friday 16 July 2016. All citations are taken from video documentation of the performance, kindly made available by Developing Artists.

In the context of the mass media representation of refugees in the UK as 'swarms' or 'masses', particularly during the spring of the 2016 Brexit campaign with its infamous 'Breaking Point' poster of hundreds of refugees framed as a threat to the UK, the individualization of the women in *Queens of Syria* was an explicitly political strategy. Judith Butler and Athena Athanasiou argue for a politics of singularization as a resistance against images of dehumanized and nameless refugees making their way across Europe in the current humanitarian crisis, asking how 'does one belong when one remains nameless and unnameable?' (Butler and Athanasiou 2013: 134). The anonymous 'starving children' in the early Oxfam images, as discussed by Chouliaraki, were likewise given neither names nor biographies by which they could transcend their identity of 'wound' and be 'counted' as individual human beings of ethical equivalence to the individuals who were requested to give money for their aid.

Thus, the individual and subjective accounts of autobiographical experience offered by the women in *Queens* enabled the otherwise excluded or unwelcome other to show herself as a named individual fully human subject with agency: to face the audience in a physical encounter, to take part in the social count and to validate her right to take place and tell her own story. In the single ironic section of the piece, and a rare moment of humour, the audience is additionally held to account for their interest in the stories of the refugees. One of the women mimics a would-be host – who could be either an immigration officer or a theatre maker – with a fake smile and condescending tone asking, among other questions: 'What's it like to be a refugee? Can I make a play from your story? How come you have a smart phone? Sorry it's not sad enough, do you have a sadder story?' (61) This is an acknowledgement of the dangers of an overcompensation by a liberal theatre culture to redress, as Alison Jeffers argues, the parasitic images of refugees in mainstream media. To combat such images, the representation of refugees in theatre is often given a 'saintly glow' and 'oscillates between the extremes of gifted and traumatised', risking refugee characters becoming 'politically neutered to the point of victimhood' (Jeffers 2012: 44). Through the performer's mockery in this instance, our instinct to empathize is blocked, as Cummings would recommend, by the explicit accusation of our culpability both on account of our nation's actions and lack of hospitality, and by our own prurient attempts to empathize. We are made to understand that we have not been invited merely to gratify ourselves with empathetic engagement but to accept complicity and, where possible, take restorative action.

Moreover, the content of the women's life stories was designed to avoid the 'transformation of the wound into an identity' (Ahmed 2014: 32). The women refused to characterize themselves by their refugee status alone and offered narratives instead that reflected acts of bravery and resistance, designed to combat the mythologies of refugees as victims or threats in addition to undermining the characterizations of passivity and servility often imposed by mass media representations on the figure of the Muslim woman in the West. One woman, for example, narrated the story of the night she gave birth under bombardment. With the hospital cut off by a checkpoint, she eventually arrived only to find the medical staff unable to assist. She gave birth to her child with the help of her relative before fleeing the hospital and, ultimately, her home with her new born child and other dependents.

The dramaturgy of the piece thus offered a strong political framework in its empowerment of the women to perform stories of individual lives that demonstrated bravery, resilience and resourcefulness. Likewise, the women's descriptions of their lives before the war highlighted distinct identities as student, mother or, in one instance, a successful businesswoman who had built up her own pharmacy from scratch before having to abandon it. They also told of daily habitual practices that were particular to each individual woman and unrelated to the events that were to come, such as the Syrian tea drunk on the balcony every morning overlooking the river or the Syrian coffee drunk in a bedroom overlooking the garden with the smell of roses and basil. Everyday memories of watching women hanging out the washing on adjoining roofs or the man opening up the store across the street demonstrated both the normality and singularity of unremarkable lives.

Jacques Rancière's notion of the political is operating here through a strategy of re-facement, a manoeuvre whereby those who have been disenfranchised and de-individualized within the dominant Western narrative of the refugee crisis are afforded the right to a face, a voice, individual identities and biographies and the autonomy to speak as they wish. The political operation of the affective charge within the context of the original performance in Jordan, for performers and spectators, can also be understood within the redistributive aesthetic economy I explored in Chapter 2. Here, I argued that within such an economy the potential for resistance might indeed be said to lie in a rebalancing of the aesthetic or emotional capital that is globally weighted against the disenfranchised, or 'parts with no part', to the same degree that economical capital is recognized to be.

The radical potential of this operation of re-facement remained visible within the production that toured the UK, underpinning both the autobiographical monologues of Syrian refugees and the choric sections in which they spoke the words of the Trojan women. It was especially notable that a great number of the monologues, through which the women shared their individual stories, were presented in the form of letters to loved ones:

a sister, a mother, a brother, children. All monologues were, with one exception to which I'll return, spoken in Arabic with sur-titled translations. Thus, although presented in the form of direct address, the UK audience, I would suggest, were not the intended recipients. The performance, in these moments, was an opportunity primarily for the women to speak their thoughts aloud in a public space, to give presence to those from whom they had been separated by the war. In these moments, the telling of the stories was more paramount to the politics of the piece than any particular impact on the spectators was intended to be. The spectators' role was merely to give witness, to enable the performances of the women to 'take place'.

The text of *Trojan Women* also, it seems, offered the women the platform and mechanism – not for concrete political change which would be an impossible quest in this context but for the right to enjoy a public cry of rage and/or prayer and collective act of solidarity. At key moments in the piece we see filmed projections where one of the women speaks to camera about the aims and outcomes of the original project. On the first of these, the first performer speaks of the close connection between the Syrians' own experience and that suffered by the Women of Troy, their common despair, death of loved ones, disempowerment, exile and loss of country. She describes their 'message' as 'a scream or a sound which is being embodied in the script of the play the Trojan Women'. A second woman continues by stating the importance of the fact that the play features strong, brave women who tell their own stories: for her, it is Syrian women who have borne the brunt of the warfare and who, like coal turned to diamonds, have come out more beautiful under the pressure:

> This play gave us a space for freedom where we can express ourselves. We discover new people in each one of us. People became different from what society imposed on us. Maybe this play will not take me back home, it will not save the innocent people, and it will not bring displaced people back to their homes. But as the saying goes, to light a candle is better [than] damning the darkness. (15.00)

Through the text of Euripides, they are enabled to voice their resistance and their refusal to give in. It also empowers them to grow beyond themselves, reject the ways they have been positioned in the Western narrative of the crisis and explore the new people they are able to be. Like Hecuba, as noted in a later section, they are each of them a Queen. It is fitting, then, that for the most part, the *Trojan Women* extracts, although spoken directly out at the audience are, as in the Greek tradition, predominantly addressed to the Gods, or Fate, rather than the spectators in the theatre.

There was a single exception, when the choric address in Arabic shifted into English, and the address shifted accordingly to directly interpellate the spectators in the theatre. This underscored the re-facement of the refugees into performers with the agency to speak as they wished to an audience who were obliged to listen, thus reversing the usual power dynamic of the distribution of the sensible within European contexts of asylum-seeking. Yet, the mode of interpellation that encompassed this shift raised, as I will argue below, important questions about the capacity of the dramaturgy to offer the critical space for consideration of that very context and in so doing threatened to prevented dialogic engagement or agonistic debate between the performer and the spectator.

The critical field of character

In the extract below, the switch to English is marked by italics and is taken from the words spoken by the woman on the video of the production, rather than the surtitles which were slightly different, but without significant variation:

> You Achaeans, who swell with greater pride in your spears than your wits, why were you frightened of this boy that you committed a murder that has no precedent? Was it in case he might someday restore our fallen city? Your strength amounted to nothing then ... *But now the city has been taken and every Trojan man lies dead, you are frightened of a child. Oh, what cowards you are.* (29.00)

Because, I would suggest, the Syrian women so closely identified with the emotional experience of the Trojan women, the impact of positioning the audience as the enemy went beyond a straightforward misrecognition of the audience as characters within the framework of the fiction. The predominant framework of the piece remained autobiographical, so the choric text spoken by the women was difficult to read in the framework of the original. Nowhere did the production offer a sustained sense of the fictional context of *Trojan Women*; the text was rather used, as noted above, as an affective outlet for the women's voicing of their own experience and was framed meta-theatrically by the filmed commentary on their use of it. As a result, the audience's positioning as the enemy became loaded in relation to the women's real experience of war in Syria, rather than their fictional experience of the Trojan War. This sense of our location as real, rather than fictional, enemy was compounded by the rare switch into English for the final accusation: 'what cowards you are'.

This intentional and provocative juxtaposition of the two frameworks (real/fictional; Syria/Troy) was more explicitly delivered later in the piece. The chorus speak the lines of Hecuba, this time addressing a bundle held by one of the women, locating the action of burying the dead child in the tragedy of Euripides: 'Sadly, it is not you who will bury me. No, it is I who shall bury your pitiable corpse, an old woman. Who has lost her city and her children, giving burial to a mere boy' (41.00). Then the women sing together over the cloth that represents the dead child. At this point the same woman who had addressed the audience in English as above steps forward and addresses the audience in English again, this time in their own identities as spectators in a theatre in the UK:

> We're not here to entertain you or sing a song. I have an anger and a message to pass to you. We came from the Troy of this age … or perhaps worse … Millions of refugees, massive destruction of cities, hundreds of thousands of innocent victims who died all kinds of death …. And everyone wants to join in …. Everyone wants to bomb in our home, but no-one wants to accept us in his home, even temporarily, only the sea, opens its arms for us, without any preconditions …. We lost our home. We are being killed now and in every moment. And the most miserable point is that it's just become normal. How did killing people became normal? Shame on you. (44.00)

She is visibly moved, and many of the spectators are moved also. But in the politics of this moment, I will now argue, there is a difficulty here that arises from an over-identification of the women of Syria with the women of Troy and the consequent absence of a character that is independent of the women's own identities that can provide the critical space for actor and spectator to meet in reflection on the emotions that are being played out. This lack of character as a site of shared analytical reflection, I will further argue, may have compromised the capacity of the piece to engage the audience in critical reflection on the complex political situation of which the women's plight was a symptom and, furthermore, reduced the work's potential to uphold either the agonistic framework in which Mouffe's post-Marxist project must sit or the dialogic demands of the reconfigured operation of empathy.

In her psychoanalytical study *Acting, Spectating, and the Unconscious*, Maria Grazia Turri (2017) details the precise operation that she sees being played out between the actor (feminine in Grazia Turri's account) and the spectator (masculine in Grazia Turri's account) in terms of the empathy operation. Locating the actor's *character* as the 'emotional field' (2017: 100), equivalent to that of the patient's unconscious with which both therapist and patient seek to engage, she argues that the actor undertakes a role equivalent to that of the therapist in her task of interpreting the character in such a way that the spectator, like the patient's conscious self, is able to recognize and acknowledge his repressed emotions. Undertaken correctly, the spectator's projections of emotion onto the character will be transformed by the interpretative skill of the actor from 'beta-elements', or 'repressed emotions', into 'alpha-elements' in order that the spectator's raw, unprocessed emotions can be brought forth for acknowledgement and analysis (102). Central to Grazia Turri's argument is the need for the actor's emotional relationship with the character to be neither so close to the character's emotional experience that the character effectively disappears and the actor plays her own emotions, nor so detached from them that the character's emotions are feigned, rather than experienced (103). Grazia Turri's concern is that if the emotional engagement of the actor is not correctly pitched then one of two things is likely to occur, both of which 'equally deprive the spectator of transpersonal alpha-function' (108), that is the capacity for the spectator to critically acknowledge and analyse his own emotional responses to what he is being shown.

The actor who plays her own feelings, rather than those of the character, is the one that concerns us here, given the absence of character in theatres of real people and the untrained nature of the performers who are drawing directly on their own emotional experience. Grazia Turri's criticism is that such an actor does not approach the character as a good therapist would approach their patient's unconscious emotional state, with sufficient engagement to empathize but sufficient detachment to enable the patient to likewise inhabit a critical perspective on their emotions. Rather the actor who plays her own emotions is like the therapist who 'acts in', accepting without question the *unconscious* emotional narrative of their patient (the emotional field of character in Grazia Turri's analogy) and unable to move the patient (spectator) beyond an uncritical immersion in emotional terrain that remains repressed and unquestioned:

> Because playing by instinct equates to the withholding of understanding, the actor will not be in a position to transform the spectator's beta-elements through her alpha-function and will return them as unprocessed emotional experiences. Moreover, the actor takes the performance of the character as an opportunity to re-enact her own unprocessed emotions and in turn project her own beta-elements into the audience. (104)

Grazia Turri's argument, if the psychoanalytical basis of it is accepted, raises a fascinating series of questions for theatre of real people more broadly.

When the actor, who is untrained, is playing their own self, what are the implications of this disappearance of character that Grazia Turri locates as essential for a productive transformation in the spectator from unthinking emotional engagement to critical self-reflection?

Although offered within a very different framework of analysis, Grazia Turri's conclusions on this aspect of her study are not that far removed from those of Bertolt Brecht who also, as noted earlier in the chapter, suspected an empathy operation 'by which the audience is made to identify itself with the character on the stage and actually feel his emotions' (Willett in Brecht 1964: 16). Yet, despite Brecht's own frequent railings against empathy, this is not straightforwardly the case, and his own proposal for actor-training reflects the stages and demands of Grazia Turri's psychoanalytic model as well as holding more in common with Stanislavski's process than is often acknowledged. Here, Brecht states that the actor was first required to know the character: 'Before you assimilate a character in the play, or lose yourself in it ... you become familiar with the character', then required, explicitly, to empathize: 'The second phase is that of empathy, of the search for the truth of the character in the subjective sense ... becoming one with it' (Brecht 2015: 280). It is only in the third phase of the actor's engagement that the big break with Stanislavksi's training process occurs: 'And then comes a third phase in which you try to see the character ... from the outside, from society's standpoint' (280). At this point the actor arrives at the familiar Brechtian position, whereby 'a definite distance between the actor and the role had to be built into the manner of playing. The actor had to be able to criticize. In addition to the action of the character, another action had to be there so that selection and criticism were possible' (Brecht and Mueller 1964: 156 in Mitter 1992: 46–7).

Empathy, for Brecht, was thus a vital element of his dialectical process, from the actor's perspective at least. From the starting thesis of the empathetic engagement and immersion required by naturalistic characterization, Brecht added the anti-thesis of division and difference between the actor and the role she played. The tension between the two would result in characterizations that were designed for the spectator to analyse in the space that the actor's dialectical process opened up. The difficulty in *Queens of Syria*, as in other similar models of theatre, is that there is no character present to offer the critical space on which the actor and spectator can converge. Despite the differences between Brecht's Marxist and Grazia Turri's psychoanalytical frameworks, their conclusions point to the same issue for politicized spectator engagement in theatre models where untrained actors play themselves: the emotions of the actor *are* those which are played, and thus the untrained actor is unable – or at best will find it challenging – to carve out a space in which that is played (the performed self) is open to mutual critique or analysis.

The term 'mutual' here is important. It is, of course, very possible for the spectator to critique the actor's performed self and challenge their expressed emotions, just as it is possible for any one person to criticize or analyse another's emotional behaviour in the world beyond the theatre. But if the emotional behaviour of the performed self is unquestioned by the actor who performs it, then the judgement of the spectator falls not on the character or their own emotional response but on the real-life subject who performs before them. As Grazia Turri confirms, when confronted with an actor who plays their own emotions the spectator is either 'forced into empathy' (2017: 105) or violently rejects the empathy operation 'by becoming confused, disgusted, overwhelmed' by 'the extravagance of uncontrolled sensibility' (2017: 104). Grazia Turri and the eighteenth-century critics she draws on adopt this severity of language as it is the perceived lack of skill on the part of professional actors playing characters, not the deliberate dramaturgy of people playing themselves, that is the object of the spectator's disdain. I would suggest that when confronted by untrained performers showing their own unprocessed emotional states, the alternatives become more nuanced, yet nonetheless closely connected. For, as the fictional framework is abandoned, Syrian woman meets British spectator without any semblance of character to offer the potential meeting point for analytical engagement to open up the possibility of criticism of the character (in Brecht's argument), of transpersonal alpha-function for the spectator (in Grazia Turri's terms) or of dialogical empathy, to return to Cummings. Without this critical space, the spectator has a limited number of ways to meet the direct and explicit accusation of the performer, who is passionately confronting the faces of the English spectators, some of whom are sitting feet away from the stage. None of these responses, I will now argue, would seem to offer political efficacy for the spectator, notwithstanding the redistributive politics of the affective experience remaining inarguably potent for the performers involved.

The most visible response was offered by those spectators who I observed in tears at the close of the performance. While the precise cause of the tears would differ from spectator to spectator and can only be speculated on, it is reasonable to position this response more broadly as an emotive response of sadness and compassion at the plight of a human-like-us – the imaginative inhabitation of another's sorrow and pain that rejects any scepticism over the legitimacy or authenticity of such pain. The dramaturgy that elicits such a response risks ignoring the historical objections to the empathy operation that I outlined earlier in this chapter. Such objections suggest that immersion in one's own emotion at the plight of another can not only lead to self-gratification but also efface any critical consideration of the systemic context of the suffering. Chouliaraki's 'conception of agonistic solidarity' makes clear that both 'affective proximity to and contemplative distance from vulnerable others', both 'emotion and argument', are key requirements (192). In an overly emotional response of sadness in the face of another's pain, the second, in both instances, risks being diminished or obscured.

Furthermore, to return to Grazia Turri's analysis, there is no field of character on which critical response to, or rational debate on, the women's narrative can occur or be initiated. Chouliaraki's 'agonistic solidarity' allows, in the words of Samuel Moyn, 'both for the recognition of the other's point of view and preserve[s] a space for criticizing that point of view' (Moyn 2006: 404 in Chouliaraki 2012: 192), but it could be argued that in the dramaturgical model in which the women's suffering is narrated by the women themselves, there is no ethical space in which that narrative can become subject to critique or question. When the women reference as 'martyrs', the male relatives of theirs who have died, we are reminded that Syrians are perpetrators of the war, just as Syrians are victims of it. We do not know which 'side' these 'martyrs' were on nor what role they have or have not played in the ongoing war, or its atrocities. Through the lens of a purely compassionate humanitarianism, clearly these questions are irrelevant, if not offensive, but that is the dilemma that the dramaturgy evokes: a choice between unquestioning humanitarian empathy (which risks relocating the women as objects of our pity), or potentially unethical, and certainly insensitive, political enquiry.

This dilemma, I would argue, comes about at the meeting point between the logic of autonomy that underpinned the politics in the original context and the logic of egalitarianism that seeks to steer a specific political message through the touring production. Performing in the context of the refugee camp, the pleasure of disrupting the distribution of the sensible by speaking how, and of what, one wished constituted, under Rancière's notion of dissensus, a redistribution of the affective economy that drove the political logic of the production's original context. When such a dramaturgy migrates to the context of a public performance for an audience who are other to those who are performing their emotions, the egalitarian logic is enacted through the spectators' act of solidarity in their witnessing of the women's act of dissensus. However, once a political stance is called for, as the accusation 'shame on you' explicitly demands, the logic of egalitarianism and ideological steer begins to dominate, and at this point the space for critical dialogue and consideration of the charge becomes vitally required. As the foregrounding of the logic of autonomy in the women's right to speak as they wish, without any consideration for the reception of their words, begins to recede in the face of the explicit accusation to the spectators, the counterbalancing logic of autonomy is required to return elsewhere, to insist that the critical space is opened out beyond the singular binary configuration of victim and accused. This space is closed down in *Queens* not only due to the lack of character that would enable both actors and spectators a site of exchange at which they could meet for critical reflection but also due to the absolute conflation of the Trojan War with the current real situation in Syria, again leaving no neutral 'space' in which contestation might productively occur. In a piece that explicitly sets out a political position in relation to the war in which its Western spectators are held culpable, the complexities of the war itself require addressing, rather than being smoothed over in an over-easy analogy with the fate of the Trojans. While the women's *response* might well be analogous, as discussed above, the causes and detail of the two wars are clearly not, and yet the differences are elided, rather than explored. This is another consequence, I would suggest, of the production's original political logic, in which an analysis of the Syrian war was not the point; the focus was entirely on the material effect and affective impact of such a war on the Syrian women. Yet the global politics of the war and the responsibility of the world to welcome the refugees and heed the call for restorative action were made paramount in the touring production without the critical space being made available for the spectator to reflect on, and thoughtfully respond to, such a call.

To return to the most visible response I noted above, there may have been those spectators weeping not from a simple emotional response of grief or compassion but from a more complex acceptance of their own culpability (as a national subject, if not an individual) for the actions of their state. Such actions would include not only the UK's participation in military air strikes and lack of generosity to the refugees fleeing Syria but also the Government's perceived failure to hold – what I assumed to be a reference to President Assad – to account: 'while we are working on this project, maybe, maybe this world that stayed silent about the crimes in Syria. Maybe this world will have a hint of conscience. It can tell the criminal: Stop, it is enough. Enough! Enough with the killing and cold-blooded murder! We want to stop the war!' (61).

But the evocation of an emotional response of pity, compassion and/or shame may, I have argued, diminish, rather than facilitate, wider critical questioning of the systemic situation, given the lack of space within the particular model of theatre of real people that might accommodate more rigorous, and potentially contentious, debate. There is the danger, indeed, as I will now argue, that the interpellation of 'shame on you' in the absence of such a space is more likely to block the opportunity for dialogic engagement or agonistic debate between the performer and the spectator and might evoke complex responses that can fire in a number of different, and potentially dangerous, directions.

Shame on the 'other other'

In her discussion of shame in *The Cultural Politics of Emotion*, Sara Ahmed asks, in relation to Australia's expression of shame towards its treatment of the Aboriginal peoples, 'in allowing us to feel bad, does shame also allow the nation *to feel better?*' (2014: 102). In the context of *Queens*, a similar question might be posed: by weeping, is the spectator able to feel validated in her compassionate and culpable identity, as one who is responding in the 'right way' to injustices which have been carried out in her name, if not by her in person. Does the shame, in Ahmed's words, enable 'the restoration of an identity of which we can be proud' (2014: 110) and, importantly, allow us to "'show" ourselves to be this way or that, a showing which is always addressed to Others' (109). In more prosaic terms, can the show of shame be an implicit and unconscious form of virtue signalling to the women, and other audience members, that this particular spectator, by showing shame, by applauding the accusation of guilt, is precisely *not* guilty of the crimes of which they've been accused.

Conversely, I would suggest, there is also the alternative consequence of a solicitation of shame that can be experienced by the would-be-giver of empathy within a context of inequality, and one that was perhaps partly at the root of my discomfort as a spectator who was unable to weep. For those who are entirely conscious of the imbalance of power between their gift (be that charitable donation, compassionate act or emotional offering) and the recipient, the request for such a gift can induce a feeling of unease in the subject's own privilege within the inequality of the situation and their incapacity to change it, resulting precisely in a resistance to gifting the emotion that is solicited. But perhaps also underlying such a resistance is a more straightforward rejection of the accusation of culpability, potentially leading to the refusal to acknowledge any consequent imperative of empathy or restorative action. If the spectator is located as the one who is responsible, as well as the one who has the requisite agency to address the necessary restorative action (both of which subject positions may be rationally rejected by the precarious spectator who, as discussed in Chapter 3, experiences an absence of agency within neoliberal structures of systemic injustice), then this spectator may feel herself to be wholly misrecognized by the performer, who does not, in fact, know the spectator's ethics or politics, or the political context in which she is operating, but casts her in the designated role of one who should do differently nonetheless.

The vast cultural power differential between UK audiences and the Syrian refugees makes it uncomfortable to frame the empathetic dialogue in this way, but in essence there is little possibility of the dialogic engagement required by Cummings if one dialogic partner does not return the exchange but rather castigates and vilifies a version of the spectator that the spectator herself is powerless to respond to or amend. This perceived misrecognition of the spectator by the performer, to return to Clohesy's argument for an empathetic operation that 'compels us to confront the imagined nature of that which constitutes our deep sense of who we are' (2013: 6), is much more likely, it seems to me, to shore up the illusory 'armour of unity' (Clohesy 2013: 5) that the subject maintains to protect their sense of identity than to disrupt it. Nothing makes us cling harder to our own perceived sense of who we are than someone accusing us, without rational argument, of being worse than we believe ourselves (rightly or wrongly) to be. Thus, the confrontation that is inherent in the elicitation of shame is as likely to evoke a defensive and protectionist response as it is to lead to the acknowledgement of Difference within the spectator's subject-self, as advocated by Clohesy.

The elicitation of shame, in this instance, renders the establishment of an agonistic dialogue between performers and spectators challenging. There is antagonism directed from the performer towards the spectator, who is literally located, within the dramaturgy of the piece, as the 'enemy' of the women and the cause of their distress. The spectator can either succumb to this one-sided antagonism and offer the shame that is requested. Or they can resist and retreat. But there is not the space within the dramaturgy of the piece to meet the accusation of the women dialogically, or critically, in ways that might facilitate an agonistic debate in which the spectator might rationally contest or consider where her culpability might lie and in which the women could stand as equal dialogue partners rather than being located, in this moment, as only those to whom a great wrong had been done.

This is a final twist in the direction that the elicited emotion of shame can take, and that is the acceptance of a shame that belongs to others, but to which you are irrevocably tied. This acceptance of shame by proxy holds similar risks to the acceptance of shame on the spectator's own account, in that it can also, perhaps even more often, result in a signalling of virtue, of the one who is on the 'right side' of the debate. In this context, the acceptance of shame by proxy gives a superior sense of ethical identity to the spectator who accepts it on behalf of the other who would refuse it, as Ahmed proposed. Shame by proxy holds more dangerous consequences when it is undertaken on behalf not of a national statesperson or government but of another subject or community against which the spectator-subject locates themselves in opposition. The accusation that the West has treated refugees inhumanely, for example, as cited above, is unlikely to personally land with an audience member who has paid for a ticket to attend a production performed by Syrian refugees. But it then becomes easy for the spectator to feel shame by proxy on behalf of her fellow citizens who are being positioned by the production as less enlightened or compassionate than she feels herself to be. Not only does this increase the probability that self-gratification will be the ultimate emotional affect but, more dangerously, it ignores the spectre of the 'other other' to both spectator and performer who is raised, implicitly accused and found guilty without even being present to engage in their own implicit, and unacknowledged, representation.

The spectator experiencing shame by proxy can applaud the accusation in order to register her understanding of the pain and anger of these women and to register that she is on their side. She also implicitly cries 'shame on you' to that 'other other' who does not welcome the refugees and on whose behalf she magnanimously accepts the charge. Such a response further decreases the potential of the piece to support agonistic solidarity. Where in one sense the Syrian women are the unknowable 'other' to the magnanimous spectator, they are not 'others' in an agonistic sense, as this spectator can be understood, in Clohesy's terms, to share close proximity with the refugee through occupying the same side of the political debate. To return to the absence of agonism, from the performers' perspective the situation remains *antagonistic*; it is literally shaped by war and the framing and accusation of the enemy-other. Yet, from the magnanimous spectator's perspective, the situation is not even *agonistic*, as such a spectator would feel, in Clohesy's expanded terms, 'at home' with the women's anger at the horror of war and the imperative to show hospitality and compassion to its victims (2013: 29). Thus, performers and magnanimous spectators are in danger of becoming aligned against the 'other other': those British citizens who are, or who are perceived to be, hostile to immigrants and refugees. Not only is there no productive *agonistic* contestation between the parties present but there is a potentially lethal *antagonism* created between them towards a new 'enemy', or antagonist who is unlikely to be in the auditorium to respond self-reflexively or otherwise.

This highlights a danger that underlies the politics of the empathy operation at this particular historical juncture and in certain modes of performance. What we see happening in *Queens* constitutes a risk for all egalitarian-leaning theatres that do not acknowledge the pluralist terrain of antagonisms that the logic of autonomy insists must be recognized in the post-Marxist context. In such instances, the egalitarian-leaning dramaturgies risk the occlusion of the 'other other' from an empathetic discourse that has, like the humanitarian imaginary in its Marxist iteration, been historically structured around a binary relationship between spectator-subject and suffering other who are required to meet each other in empathetic dialogue. Yet, within contemporary political theatre addressing predominantly left-wing or socially liberal spectators, there is rarely agonism between the suffering other and the spectator-subject who is happy to empathize and/or accept the cry of shame. Both are 'at home' with the political situation and their take on who is to blame: the 'other other' who is disrupting the liberal consensus in the theatre and whose voice and presence is most often absent from the auditorium.

This is a critical and dangerous development that highlights a wider political challenge to the contemporary empathy operation in the theatre, way beyond the specifics of the invitation to shame that occurred within this production. The figure of the 'other other', I will now argue, has come about, in part, as a by-product of the cultural influence of the post-Marxist logic of autonomy and the subsequent emergence of an increasingly liberal and cosmopolitan world view, prevalent in particular among those who might be expected to form a significant majority of those attending politically engaged theatre in the West. This emergence, in itself, of course, is in many ways a force for good and a mark of real progress in the pluralist post-Marxist project of radical democracy. But there are limitations to the cosmopolitan vision of multiplicity and acceptance of difference that are vital to acknowledge, as I will now detail below.

Cosmopolitan love of difference

Clohesy, while noting that critics such as Homi Bhabha are suspicious that cosmopolitanism 'implies the denial of culture or, as with globalization, the imposition of a way of life on to vulnerable minority groups without the political or cultural resources to resist it' (2013: 42–3), ultimately argues that 'there is not a necessary conflict between the protection of cultural difference and cosmopolitanism' (43). Indeed, Clohesy's validation of empathy as a potentially ethical operation requires a cosmopolitan framework to function, but a new cosmopolitanism that is a condition for the protection of difference, not the capitalist effacement of it. Only in this model of culture, he argues, is the protection of difference, which is the desired consequence of an ethical empathetic operation, secured by 'a shared disposition of openness and finitude' (56). Cosmopolitanism is thus proposed as 'an inclusive form of community in which we recognize each other *in our difference* as equals'

(37, original emphasis). Conversely, a rejection of cosmopolitanism, as advanced by those who defend more communitarian models, 'prevents us from acknowledging our duty to recognize those in other communities and [...] engage critically with their political and ethical practices' (44).

Yet, Clohesy passes too quickly over the really thorny questions advanced by critics of cosmopolitanism, questions that I believe are getting more urgent the more dominant the cosmopolitan ideal becomes. When Clohesy does ask the crucial question 'What does this ... mean for disempowered subjects who live in societies in which a strong cultural identity provides the only source of hope for the future or where it provides an effective platform of resistance against oppression?' (43), his response is simply to call for ethical engagement with those others and understanding of, if not acceptance of, their differing moral codes of behaviour. This is framed by Clohesy within the historical binary discourse of postcolonialism: the call for the Western subject to empathize with the foreign other and for the two subjects to 'recognize each other *in our difference* as equals' (37).

But, as I have noted in relation to *Queens*, when notions of proximity are broadened as Clohesy, earlier in his study, proposes, those who seem distant and strange in one sense can elicit certain Western subjects' empathy and compassion much more easily via a shared political proximity than those 'other others' who might be physically much closer to home. In a world dominated by global cosmopolitan and vast social media networks, communities of identity and political affiliation may well have a far stronger pull on our instinctive empathy than geographical neighbours or fellow citizens whose political identities are rejected as abhorrent and ultimately threatening to our own sense of self and vision for the future. Indeed, I would argue that the spectators at *Queens* are easily able to empathize with the refugees *precisely because* they are so distant from their suffering and their demands. No action, in any real sense, is being asked of them other than to confirm their sense of subjecthood, defined by a demonstration of their capacity for compassion towards the other that underpins their cosmopolitan identity. It thus becomes a pleasure to empathize, to acknowledge shame; it is a shoring up of Clohesy's 'armour of unity' of the self, not a breaking apart of it.

Cosmopolitanism is not, moreover, all-inclusive, and it is within this context that the spectre of the 'other other' emerges. Because the fundamental ethical requirement of cosmopolitanism is the protection of difference, it inevitably excludes those whose mark of difference from the liberal consensus is the rejection of the protection of the difference of others in the name of their own survival. This is because the pluralist environment that has emerged following the Marxist and postcolonial eras no longer functions in a binary way: the proletariat against the bourgeoisie, the global South against the developed West. In today's pluralistic society, the protection of some differences – a fact that advocates of cosmopolitanism are sometimes reluctant to acknowledge – most often threatens the survival of other differences, as Mouffe's agonistic paradigm makes clear.

Mouffe herself is suspicious of advocates of cosmopolitanism, precisely because the end point is an illusory utopic 'pain free' society in which the political dynamic of 'them' and 'us' is extinguished. At this point, she argues, actual democracy can no longer be sustained, as the notion of 'the demos' relies on a commonality of those within a certain political community that is defined by the otherness of those outside of it, 'the establishment of frontiers, the determination of a space of inclusion/exclusion' (Mouffe 2013: 13). Conversely, cosmopolitanism, driven by liberal humanism, aspires towards a community of the whole of humanity. Mouffe writes that 'when democratic confrontation disappears, the political in its antagonistic dimension manifests itself through other channels. Antagonisms can take many forms and it is illusory to believe that they could ever be eliminated' (Mouffe 2005: 114).

Democracy can only be sustained, Mouffe insists, through structures which permit ongoing adversarial dispute or 'a vibrant clash of democratic political positions' (2005: 104). Such clashes, it has become commonplace to acknowledge, are no longer straightforwardly between nation states, different ethnicities or binary formulations of social class but between those who are 'at home' with a shared political identity and vision, and those who would threaten the legitimacy of such an identity and vision. The multiplicity of political identities and subsequent conflicts open to citizens in the West can be understood through innumerable lenses, but the particular adversarial conflict outlined by Rob Ford is highly pertinent to my examination of the emergence of the 'other other' in the contemporary European context. In his public lecture, delivered in the wake of the UK's 2016 referendum vote to leave the EU, Ford categorized the citizens of the UK using two distinctive groupings: confident cosmopolitans and left-behinds (Ford 2017). Recent demographic shifts, Ford argued, have shown divisions in society that are now producing new fault lines in a differently divided nation state between the young and the old, the graduates and the school leavers, and the immigrants/ descendants of immigrants and those with long-standing indigenous family histories. The 'left-behinds' are those in which the older generations are preponderant, generations in which the graduate contingent is much lower and the generational memory of family migration much less common. They are also dominated by the old industrial working class, with long-standing indigenous histories and low levels of educational, cultural and economic capital who rightly perceive that they are, numerically and politically, a constituency in decline, their political power waning as the demographics of increased migration, new generations of mixed-heritage citizens and rising levels of graduates among the general population point to a future in which the constituency defined by Ford as 'confident cosmopolitans' will inevitably become the dominant cultural and electoral force.

Despite the inevitable generalization that such categorization requires, Ford's categories do confirm a sense of newly emerging fault lines not only in the UK but across Europe and North America. This was manifested explicitly in the election victory of President Donald Trump in the United States (2016) and in the far-right contributions to government coalitions in Austria (2017) and Italy (2018) but is also evidenced in binary political divisions in recent elections in the UK, France and other European nations. In all cases, countries appear to be divided more or less precisely down the middle between those who consider themselves citizens of the world, cosmopolitan and liberal-minded towards difference, and those who consider themselves citizens of the nation state, communitarian and often (although not always) protectionist and wary of difference. For Mouffe, it is vital that this contestation is permitted and legitimated within democratic (i.e. not fascist or racist) parameters; and her prediction in *The Democratic Paradox* (2005) that the demise of the radical left and the rise of the centre left in European politics would threaten to establish a dangerous left–right consensus of global capitalist cosmopolitanism has been thoroughly borne out. Despite the horror by many on the liberal left, at UK Prime Minister Theresa May's pronouncement that if you were a citizen of the world you were a citizen of nowhere (May 2016), Mouffe's caution to those would-be 'citizens of the world' more than a decade previously might have been better heeded: 'such a cosmopolitan democracy, if it were ever to be realized, would be no more than an empty name disguising the actual disappearance of democratic forms of government and indicating the triumph of the liberal form of governmental rationality' (2005: 42). The danger that the cosmopolitan vision carries, Mouffe argues, is 'the crystallization of collective passions around issues which cannot be managed by the democratic process and an explosion of antagonisms that can tear up the very basis of civility' (2005: 104).

Those whose voices are not permitted legitimacy on the democratic stage are those who have nothing to gain from the cosmopolitan vision of increased mobility and opportunity; those whose only property of value is a communitarian identity that is being placed under threat; those whose sense of belonging and locality has become mocked and degraded by those who have privileged mobility and choice; those who are fighting to secure resources for their own communities in a context of prolonged deprivation. Such subjects are precisely those vulnerable to the call of fascist extremism, as can be seen by the rise of the far right in the United States, Austria, Italy, France and Germany in recent elections. These are also, I would speculate, the subjects least likely to be in attendance at productions such as *Queens of Syria* that toured mainstream theatre venues in the UK. Whereas the confident cosmopolitans, those I have termed compassionate or magnanimous spectators, were most likely to be present and most likely to feel politically 'at home' with those 'others' who were eliciting their empathy and compassion. The danger, as I proposed above, is that with the acceptance of shame by proxy, the spectre of the 'other other' emerges, the subject who is not compassionate towards the plight of the refugees and the subject who rejects the liberal cosmopolitan imperative to empathize with difference and is vilified for it by refugees (explicitly) and magnanimous spectators (implicitly) alike. There is a new brand of communalism at work here that remains unacknowledged by Clohesy in his critique, and this is the communalism that hides within an ostensibly open and diverse cosmopolitanism but enjoys its own communitarian identity of love of difference and otherness to which its subjects can be as emotively and unquestioningly protective as any of those 'other others' they decry for traditional communitarian stances consolidated by class, race, national or regional characteristics.

Sara Ahmed's discussion of multicultural love highlights such concerns with the cosmopolitan ethos defined by Kelly Oliver as 'love [as] an ethics of differences that thrives on the adventure of otherness' (Oliver 2001: 20 in Ahmed 2014: 140). Drawing on Renata Salecl, Ahmed argues that 'the pleasure of identifying with the multicultural nation means that one gets to see oneself as a good or tolerant subject' (Ahmed 2014: 133), yet the danger with such an attachment, like all identitarian attachments, is that it is defined by those 'others' who are perceived to threaten it, in this instance, those white working class and minority ethnic communities who are unwilling to assimilate and 'give it [their difference] back to the nation' (Ahmed 2014: 134). Not only does the ideology of love for difference (which underpins both Ahmed's conception of multiculturalism and wider notions of cosmopolitanism) do violence to the 'otherness' within communities that are so often framed as homogenous and without difference (e.g. the white working class), it also denies the narcissistic love it feels for its own ideal of difference, while castigating those as narcissistic who reject such an ideal in favour of a love of their own communitarian identity. While many 'others' are willingly 'loved' and assimilated into the plurality of the multicultural society, the 'other others' who refuse its predicates become 'the explanation for the failure of multiculturalism to deliver the national ideal' (Ahmed 2014: 139). Their vilification, or refusal to love difference, is thus necessary to rationalize the failure of, what Ahmed terms, the 'humanist fantasy', the 'idea of a world where we all love each other' (2014: 140).

Conclusion

In this chapter I have explored the implications of an empathy operation that has been reconfigured by the logic of autonomy for the contemporary moment. I argued that the political charge of such an operation lay in the attempt to engage dialogically with the other whom we could never know. By so doing, we would be confronted not only with the difference of the other but with the illusion of our own sovereign wholeness of selfhood that was rather revealed to be as contingent, fragmented and unknowable as that of the other. I have examined the ways in which *Queens of Syria* sought to employ this reconfigured empathy operation through, for example, its ironic playback to the audience of their potentially prurient interest in the sadness of refugees' stories. Through strategies such as these we were to understand that it was not sufficient to gratify our own sense of self with empathetic engagement but to acknowledge the impossibility of understanding, or owning, the refugees' experience.

Yet, the 'real people' model of theatre in this instance resulted in an absence of character that could provide the critical field on which agonistic, two-way dialogue could occur. Confronted with the reality of women who were Syrian refugees there was no ethical space for dissent, disagreement with or challenge to the narratives we were offered. Thus, the production's political logic was driven solely by the women's insistence, *pace* Rancière, on their equality in an unequal world order, taking the right to tell their own stories without challenge and enjoying affective release from so doing. Any further potential of the egalitarian logic was somewhat hampered by the disavowal of the logic of autonomy that would insist on a recognition of the pluralist antagonisms of the post-Marxist moment. In the drive to political consensus between egalitarian-leaning spectators and refugee performers and its charge of 'shame on you', the production risked raising a potentially dangerous antagonism between the consensus in the theatre and the spectres of those 'other others' who remained excluded from both theatre and consensus, who could be safely critiqued, or even vilified, in their absence from the debate.

8

Questions of Antagonism and Agency

In Chapter 4, I set up a framework of analysis that proposed that the political dramaturgies under examination in the second part of this study might be productively understood as operating across the field of tension between the two political logics of egalitarianism and autonomy. The spectator of practice in which the egalitarian logic dominates is offered an egalitarian (and so ideological) view of the world to which they are invited to subscribe and an egalitarian (and so ideological) collective project in which they are invited to participate. The spectator of practice in which the autonomous logic dominates is granted the autonomy of individual interpretation and invited to take precisely what they want from the experience. Throughout this study I argue that, since the poststructuralist moment, the logic of autonomy has been in the ascendency, and the challenge for contemporary political theatres has been how to best uphold the poststructuralist demands for pluralism and autonomy without necessitating the abandonment of the collective egalitarian imaginary of Marxism.

In Chapters 5 and 6, I argued that the logic of autonomy needed to be balanced by the logic of egalitarianism for theatre practice to be meaningfully aligned with the post-Marxist project of radical democracy. In the previous chapter, I conversely identified the potential dangers that arise when the logic of egalitarianism over-dominates to the detriment of the logic of autonomy that would seek to insist on the recognition of the plurality of political antagonisms in the contemporary moment. To this end, I drew on the theories of Chantal Mouffe, first introduced in Chapter 4, who insists that the post-Marxist terrain must acknowledge that 'antagonisms can take many forms and it is illusory to believe that they could ever be eliminated' (Mouffe 2005: 114). In the previous chapter's analysis of *Queens of Syria*, I highlighted the risk that, as refugee performer and egalitarian-leaning spectator were likely to share political aims, the production may rather have established a cosmopolitan consensus from which the 'other other' who was neither present in the theatre nor hospitable to refugees was 'othered', accused and excluded. In the first part of this final chapter, I will pursue the question of how we might think to extend the empathetic operation to those who explicitly reject the cosmopolitan consensus and who represent, in Mouffe's terms, the antagonistic enemy whose politics are indeed manifested through non-democratic channels of discourse.

I will thus develop further my examination of the ways in which the contemporary operation of empathy has been reconfigured through the logic of autonomy. In the previous chapter, I argued that the political charge of such an operation now lay in the attempt to engage dialogically with the other whom we could never know. By so doing, we would be confronted not only with the difference of the other but with the illusion of our own sovereign wholeness of selfhood that was rather revealed to be as contingent, fragmented and unknowable as that of the other. The analysis of Chris Thorpe and Rachel Chavkin's *Confirmation* (2014), with which this chapter opens, might, in light of the previous chapter, be seen as an exercise in pushing the demands of such dialogic empathy to its limits. Thorpe's solo performance draws predominantly on his encounters with an 'other' who is his ideological and antagonistic 'enemy', a white supremacist neo-Nazi he calls 'Glen'. Much of the theory I drew on in the previous chapter in relation to the reconfiguration of empathy, as is common across the field of theatre studies, locates empathy with the other as an ethical aim and tends to avoid the more difficult question of how this might continue to apply, or not, when confronted with an 'other' who is, himself, antithetical to the egalitarian, democratic project in its entirety. *Confirmation*, I will argue, thus extends, through its own fieldwork and reflection, the thorny questions of empathy and engagement addressed in the previous chapter, with Thorpe ultimately rejecting the ethical call for an endless, mutual dialogue of unknowable difference with his 'other'.

This conclusion sets up the second part of this final chapter which questions whether Thorpe's decision to relinquish his attempts to empathize with the other in order to hold onto his own sense of self might have traction as an alternative ethical or political position beyond its rationalization, in this instance, as a necessary defence against fascism. Through an analysis of Common Wealth Theatre's *The Deal Versus the People* (2015), and drawing on Slavoj Žižek, Judith Butler and Athena Athanasiou, I will argue that the affective *feeling* of the security of the illusion of selfhood, as clung to by Thorpe, may offer agency to those subjects who are most denied agency under neoliberalism, and thus might hold further political potential that is underexplored in a historical moment that remains dominated by poststructuralist discourses of contingency, fragmentation and difference that are driven by the logic of autonomy.

Empathizing with the enemy

Confirmation was written and performed by Chris Thorpe and developed with and directed by Rachel Chavkin.[1] The project had been inspired by the notion of confirmation bias: the psychological theory that confirms that in making our decisions about the world we listen only to the evidence that supports what we already think and refute otherwise rational evidence that might challenge that or force us to undo our existing prejudices. The specific challenge Thorpe set himself was to highlight and interrogate the confirmation bias that led him, a self-confessed liberal and, by proxy, his audience, who were assumed to broadly share his political affiliation, to acknowledge only the evidence that corroborated his/their existing ideological beliefs and to resist any challenge to the liberal convictions he/they held.

Such political convictions, as many theorists now evidence, are less rationally held conclusions that are open to debate than they are identitarian structures of ideological fantasy, mythical foundations which nonetheless support the subject's sense of identity and communitarian kinship which must be protected and defended at all cost. In *Democracy for Realists*, Christopher H. Achen and Larry M. Bartels (2016) demonstrate how the vast majority of people vote not for policies but in relation to their own constructed sense of identity and hard-wired ideological legacies of community and belonging. Drew Westen (2008) likewise concluded from cognitive experiments he conducted that when those who were politically partisan were shown evidence of contradictions that should have undermined their allegiance, their 'neural footprints' instead demonstrated the brain work that was undertaken 'to "reason" to emotionally biased conclusions' (xiii) that would enable their allegiance to remain intact. This was as Westen had predicted, but he discovered something more:

> The political brain also did something we didn't predict. Once partisans had found a way to reason to false conclusions, not only did neural circuits involved in negative emotions turn off, but circuits involved in positive emotions turned on. The partisan brain didn't seem satisfied in just feeling better. It worked overtime to feel good, activating reward circuits that give partisans a jolt of positive reinforcement for their biased reasoning. (xiv)

---

[1] The piece premiered at the Warwick Arts Centre on 21 May 2014 where I attended my first production and toured the UK during 2014, where I saw it a second time at Northern Stage at King's Hall during the Edinburgh Festival in August.

Rob Ford (2017), in his lecture discussed in the previous chapter, highlighted how predictably you could map a subject's views on any one of a whole range of topics onto another seemingly unrelated one. For example, a subject's views on gay marriage would enable you to predict with reasonable accuracy their views on immigration, on climate change, on the UK's 2016 referendum decision to leave the EU. Because these were not necessarily distinct positions that had been arrived at through accrued knowledge or rational debate, but most often via attachment to a particular identity to which a whole package of opinions and biases were tethered. Thus, confirmation bias is a protective mechanism that shores up our sense of identity, sometimes against all the evidence to the contrary, and defends from attack the illusions we hold about the infallibility of our subject-self. Our 'armour of unity', in Anthony M. Clohesy's words (2013: 5), is so often clung to because, as Weston's research evidences, it is neurologically distressing for our sense of self to accept anything that contradicts it.

Thorpe sets the bar as high as possible for his examination of confirmation bias by challenging his own sense of self – defined by a left-wing liberalism – through a sustained dialogue during the research process with someone who is as far from him as he could conceive: a white supremacist he calls 'Glen'. Glen, as performed by Thorpe, is thus here the character that occupies the emotional field identified, in the previous chapter, by Maria Grazia Turri, on which the actor's and spectator's critical engagement and analysis can meet. Thorpe's own attempts to empathize with the real 'Glen' during the research period of the play are presented to the audience who are implicitly requested to make the same journey through the re-presentation of the dialogue Thorpe has undertaken, in addition to engaging with Thorpe's own analysis of it. Clearly, the challenge here, set up by Thorpe, is not for the audience to counter with critical judgement, an otherwise over-emotional engagement with the character of Glen, a self-confessed Nazi, racist and Holocaust-denier. The challenge is rather to attempt, through the reconfigured empathetic operation explored in the previous chapter, to confront a seemingly unknowable otherness that might shake the foundations of their own certainty and cause them to reflect on their own contingent preferences and fallible, ideological positions. As critic Lyn Gardner observed, 'Amid so much theatre that simply confirms its audience's liberal sympathies, *Confirmation* is that rare and valuable thing: a piece that makes you alert to your own selective use of evidence' (Gardner 2014).

In his choice of a white supremacist, as opposed to, for example, a Conservative, Thorpe provisionally extends and further complicates the agonistic arena of contestation proposed by Mouffe, who is clear that this arena cannot contain those positions, such as fascism, that reject the fundamental predicates of democratic debate, categorized by a shared commitment to 'liberty and equality for all' (2005: 113). The dialogue between Thorpe and Glen cannot be agonistic, but only antagonistic, as the racist character of Glen's position excludes him from the adversarial structures of democratic agonism. Glen is precisely the manifestation of the enemy that Mouffe fears emerging when opportunities for agonistic debate are suppressed. For some audience members, this rendered *Confirmation* deeply problematic, and there were those who felt that to voice racist views through the character of Glen and his characterization by Thorpe was giving a dangerous credence and legitimacy to them. While I will argue to the contrary, it is important to note that my engagement with the piece was, as indeed was Thorpe's, undertaken from the perspective of a white, left-wing liberal to whom, I would argue, the piece was implicitly addressed. The experience of a black, Asian or Jewish spectator would certainly have been a more difficult one, and one I cannot speak for, although Thorpe did note, in a conversation with me, that there had been differing responses on the question of legitimacy within all ethnicities of spectatorship. Notwithstanding the responses of individual spectators, the very fact that the dialogue could only take place because of Thorpe's racial identity (a black, Asian or Jewish actor would clearly have been an unacceptable dialogue partner on Glen's terms) is a clear sign that such a dialogue lies outside of any democratic framework of agonistic debate.

Yet despite such legitimate reservations, Thorpe's extension of the stage to accommodate the views of a right-wing extremist offers its spectators the opportunity to ask some really difficult questions that are often sidestepped by those theorists on the left with whom this study has been engaged in sustained dialogue. Clohesy, for example, is clear that 'where the pragmatists declare a bedrock position marking the limits of our responsibility to continue our dialogue with others, is exactly the place where (following Arendt) we have to *bring into being* that which could not have been imagined before' (Clohesy 2013: 39). Yet, the paradoxical and dangerous imperative to extend that dialogue to those who would, if they were able, eliminate others from the debate is not specifically addressed, nor is the role, or ethics, of empathy when dealing with an enemy, rather than an adversary. *Confirmation* explicitly meets this challenge head-on through Thorpe's attempts to overcome his own confirmation bias to enable him to see the reality around him through the eyes of the unknowable other.

During this process Thorpe locates some uncomfortable, and perhaps unanticipated, parallels between himself and Glen. The example given of the 'thought experiment' where he tries to find a coffee shop where he would be safe from Glen is relatively humorous and light touch. But Thorpe's acknowledgement that Glen is also 'a socialist, and a localist, so given the choice he'd probably go for an independent coffee shop, like I would' (Thorpe 2014: 33) is far-reaching in its highlighting of the shared ground of anti-capitalism between those to the left and far right that is rarely explored as the potential for engagement with the enemy that it might (notwithstanding all the obvious caveats) constitute. As Thorpe's thought-experiment continues, he evokes the image of him carrying a 'pocket version of Glen around in my head' to 'compare how I'm discovering his biases work to how I *think* mine do' (2014: 32, original emphasis). At the close of the performance, Thorpe sits opposite an empty chair on the stage and describes, very gently and calmly, how each will take the eyes of the other, without pain, and slip them into their own sockets:

> and we will walk through a city.
> Your mind, my eyes, your eyes, my mind. Holding hands.
> And I will see what you see everywhere, with your eyes and my mind.
> And I will see your sense of rightness feels the same as mine.
> Because your world is the right world.
> And my world is the right world. (2014: 56)

Yet ultimately, Thorpe concludes, if the piece has been about an empathy exchange, an experiment in getting to know the 'other', then it has probably failed. 'I don't know which of us moved most towards the other', he concludes, 'I don't even know if that happened' (2014: 59). Yet, the failure of empathy, as discussed at length in the previous chapter, is precisely what might constitute the ethical possibility of empathetic engagement: the confrontation with difference, the acknowledgement of the unknowable and the subsequent realization of the fallibility of the subject-self's convictions and identity. There is a significant moment when Thorpe admits, during his research into the Holocaust, his absolute resistance to the possibility that there had not been six million Jews massacred, but perhaps fewer. Even when lower figures are provided by legitimate historians, Thorpe confesses that to admit to anything less than six million feels like agreeing with Glen, and a step closer to that situation is so intolerable to him that he actually requires the number of Jews killed to be as high as possible (2014: 53–4). If Clohesy, echoing Richard Rorty's observation, holds that 'there are groups to which we cannot be disloyal and still like ourselves' (Clohesy 2013: 39), in *Confirmation* Thorpe acknowledges the precise flip side that there are groups with whom we cannot agree and still like ourselves. Both of these acknowledgements challenge us to realize that the conviction of being right is an emotional, identitarian commitment as much as, if not much more than, a rational conclusion. Thorpe spells this out literally in letters on the stage: 'What you see is all there is. Everybody thinks they're right. In our minds, we're reasonable. Everybody thinks they're right' (2014: 44–5). He concludes, in implied dialogue with Glen, that 'our sense of rightness is just as deeply rooted. And the only way I can think of to shake that – It would require us to mutilate ourselves' (2014: 57).

This is the revelation of *Confirmation*: not that it is possible to find points of contact with a white supremacist (such as Glen's campaigning on behalf of disability rights and keeping the local fire station open) or that they can also be complex individuals that are more than the sum total of their political beliefs. If this were the point, as Thorpe decisively asserts, it would have been a waste of his time (2014: 31). The revelation for Thorpe is precisely that Glen's conviction of rightness, identity and belonging is a mirror image of its liberal counterpart and does indeed, as Clohesy proposes, threaten to pierce Thorpe's 'armour of unity' in showing it to be equivalently rigid and unshakeable (and so equivalently illusory) to that which is impenetrably and oppositionally 'other'. Both positions cannot be right, and yet both are absolutely felt as such, and both are shored up by the same mechanisms of confirmation bias and identity attachment. Thorpe's fear of self-mutilation is significant in light of the contemporary reconfiguration of empathy; he is aware that engagement with his recognition of the other's difference would result in real violence to his own narrative of subjecthood, but such violence is difficult to read, in the context of the fascist other, as unquestionably ethical or political in the way that Clohesy suggests, as I will return to below.

The failure of the attempt at empathetic engagement undertaken by Thorpe is likely to be echoed by the spectator, on whose behalf Thorpe is standing in, and the dramaturgical decisions taken by Thorpe and Chavkin ensure that the spectator's potential failure to empathize likewise holds critical potential. Although on reading the published playtext it is always clear whether it is Thorpe or Glen who is speaking, in performance, at one critical moment, there was an intentional blurring of personae. Both the manner of performance, choice of words and emotive delivery in the following exchange required the spectator to follow the actual content carefully before they could be clear which antagonist was accusing the other. The content is intentionally held back requiring the spectator to listen to the emotional attack before they know whether they are on side with it or not:

> I am going to hold my hand up and say it. No dog-whistle. No coded language. I am going to hold up my hand and say that I believe you're fucking stupid
>
> […]

The problem with you is, you're a fucking child. And I'll explain that. I know you think I'm too stupid to explain myself, so I'm happy to prove you wrong. (2014: 42–3)

In the stage directions of the printed text, it states that Glen should never be characterized, or 'acted', but should always be delivered in the voice of the performer (2014: 3). Thorpe has chosen to work with someone as distant from him politically as possible but, in performance, the two men are required to sound the same, look the same and speak in precisely the same kind of diction. The aggressive exchange drawn on above had the deliberate effect of watching Thorpe shouting at the audience twice. Not only did this deliberate fusion of the two characters emphasize Thorpe's conclusion that each felt his absolute rightness with the same level of passion and conviction as the other, but it also served to destabilize the 'character' of Glen, who often became a shadowy figure that morphed in and out of Thorpe's own 'characterized' persona. Returning to Grazia Turri, if character here was indeed the emotional field on which the actor's analysis and the audience's critical reception could meet, then Thorpe was explicitly offering the characterization of his own subject-self up for scrutiny alongside that of the characterization of Glen. Thorpe's professional technique, and his intentional crafting of a persona whose opinions are open to question, offers an emotional field that, unlike that discussed in the previous chapter, is able to invite critical consideration, alongside empathy, from the spectator.

Given the likely shared political affiliation of the audience with Thorpe, over Glen, and the indisputable fact that the portrayal of Glen is entirely in the gift of Thorpe's authorship, from the text he speaks to the manner in which he is presented, it might be predicted that empathetic engagement with the persona of Thorpe would not be too much of a challenge for the audience. Yet, his very attempt to empathize with a white supremacist, to 'know what that feels like' (2014: 48), may well have been greeted with suspicion or outright hostility by those spectators who believed, with Mouffe among others, that there could be no dialogue with fascism. For this reason, the activities that Thorpe directly engaged the audience in were vital to draw each spectator into the equation, rather than the piece existing simply as a replayed dialogue and commentary between two antagonists for the audience to witness.

These activities included a numbers exercise in which spectators were given a series of numbers and had to speculate on the rule before offering three more as a way of testing their hypothesis. This was a way of demonstrating that all spectators (in the shows I attended and reportedly in the majority of shows) chose three numbers to *confirm* their hypothesis, rather than to disprove it. Thorpe also left spectators with the lyric sheet to the song 'Guilty of Being White' by Minor Threat, while he played the song and changed costume. The audience then have the opportunity to come to their own conclusions before the staged argument between Thorpe and Glen as to whether the lyrics support the white supremacy cause or whether they are against racism in all guises: the point, again, being that Thorpe and Glen both interpret the song (which they like) to confirm their own political stance. These activities further draw the audience into contemplation about their own confirmation bias, a contemplation which is then placed in dialogue with their responses to the show and the two characters throughout. Selected spectators were also asked to read out sections of the text, at one point providing Glen's voice in dialogue with Thorpe and at another point reading Thorpe's own lines while Thorpe responded with Glen's. In this way, you might argue that each of these spectators was engaging with the emotional field of character the piece offered, as both actor and spectator.

All of these dramaturgical structures offer the spectator the opportunity to undertake on their own part the journey that Thorpe had undertaken, an attempt to empathize with the 'other' that is inevitably blocked and a consequent critical appraisal of their attempt, their failure, the increased fallibility of their own certainties and the ethics of the entire enterprise. The 'armour of unity' of each spectator is thus potentially exposed and made vulnerable. It is highly significant, then, in the context of this study that at the close of the piece, Thorpe essentially rejects the conclusions of Clohesy, refusing to weaken his own sense of self through continued attempts to engage in dialogue with Glen. Thorpe has undertaken this very journey in search of the cosmopolitan utopia that Andy Smith's *Summit*, discussed in Chapter 6, envisioned, admitting to Glen that 'I really want to be your friend. I want us all to be friends. I want a world in which it is possible for us all to be friends' (2014: 57), but he ultimately acknowledges the impossibility of such a 'humanist fantasy', in Sara Ahmed's terms (2014: 140), and pulls back from Clohesy's ethical imperative, opting instead to protect his own sense of self from the exposure of its vulnerability:

> I don't think I can talk to you again
> ...
> I am diluting myself, talking to you.
> I am losing myself and I can't fight if I lose myself.
> If I am reasonable enough.
> If I listen enough.
> If I feel I am being listened to enough.
> It will seduce me.

And I need to guard my own certainty now because I've realised it helps me defend my tolerance. There is only so much understanding in the world.
And if I am wasting that making myself more tolerant of *you*. Maybe I don't want it. (2014: 58)

This could be read, of course, as falling into line with those who would define the agonistic arena and its imperatives of empathy and dialogue precisely by its necessary exclusion of fascism. Yet, the need to guard one's own certainty against a weakening of its foundations, I will now propose, may not only be a necessary defence against those extremist positions that lie beyond democratic debate but may be a tactic that could be employed more productively than the discourse underpinning the logic of autonomy, examined throughout this study, might commonly suggest.

Ideological fantasies and precarious spectators

In the remainder of this chapter, I will examine whether the political currency of the preservation of the subject's 'armour of unity' can be extended beyond instances in which the 'other' holds fascist views that necessitate his exclusion from the parameters of agonistic debate and empathic engagement. To this end, I will first turn to Slavoj Žižek's analysis of the psychoanalytical processes that underpin the attractions of such an armour, as introduced in Chapter 2. Here, I will develop the argument that Žižek's reading of the power of ideological fantasy offers a ground from which the ethics of contingency and difference that underpin the logic of autonomy under investigation throughout this study can be productively contested and somewhat qualified. My reading of Žižek's analysis will present this study with the opportunity to return to the mode of counter-hegemonic interpellation, as seen operating in Andy Smith's *Summit* explored in Chapter 6, to examine the further potential of such a strategy. In Smith's work, I argued that the egalitarian logic of such interpellation was counterbalanced by the strong presence of the logic of autonomy that maintained a narrative framework full of open and contingent spaces which each spectator-subject was invited to take in their own chosen direction. In my following analysis of Common Wealth Theatre's *The Deal Versus the People*, I will ask if a significant suppression of the logic of autonomy through a more closely determined mode of interpellation than that adopted by Smith might strengthen, rather than weaken, the political currency of the strategy in certain material contexts of performance. This will then lead, in conclusion, to a modest realignment of some underlying imperatives of poststructuralism that remain mostly unchallenged in discourses of 'the political' in which the post-Marxist trajectory from egalitarian and collectivist ideological steer to autonomy, contingency and indeterminacy has tended to dominate.

There isn't space here to unpick the full implications of Žižek's dialogue with Laclau and Mouffe's notions of antagonism, but a particular aspect of his reading of *Hegemony* offers a vital insight into how a more determined, and less contingent, counter-hegemonic interpellation might be adopted for progressive, radical ends. Žižek (2005) argues that the inevitability of antagonism within social reality, and the subsequent impossibility of closure, as proposed by Laclau and Mouffe, can also be understood through the psychoanalytical lens of Lacan. *Social* antagonism, Žižek proposes, provides each subject with the illusion that it is their antagonist who is preventing the subject from achieving 'full identity with themselves' (2005: 274), an illusion that is preferable to being forced to confront the traumatic experience of, what Žižek terms, '"pure" antagonism' (276) which is the 'internal limit' of the subject in Lacanian theory: that which prevents the subject from ever being 'fully realized' to his or her self. This correlates with Clohesy's conception of the 'armour of unity': the illusion of wholeness that protects the subject from acknowledging the Difference that is a constituent part of their divided, fallible and contingent selfhood. The refusal to engage with the difference of the other, and the consequent denomination of them as the 'enemy', is thus a tactic to shore up the completeness and infallibility of the self, a move to hold off the inevitable realization that we can never be complete or infallible. Žižek explains that

> it is not the external enemy who is preventing me from achieving identity with myself, but every identity is already in itself blocked, marked by an impossibility, and the external enemy is simply the small piece, the rest of reality upon which we 'project' or 'externalize' this intrinsic, immanent impossibility [...] That is why we could say that it is precisely in the moment when we achieve victory over the enemy in the antagonistic struggle in social reality that we experience antagonism in its most radical dimension, as a self-hindrance: far from enabling us finally to achieve full identity with ourselves, the moment of victory is the moment of greatest loss. (2005: 274)

For Žižek, the impossibility of closure, or full identity, within the individual subject is homologous to the impossibility of closure, or consensus, within the social real, as identified by Laclau and Mouffe, due to the ongoing and necessary existence of antagonistic forces in both instances. To ground this argument Žižek argues, as noted in Chapter 2, that there is an 'inherent impossibility of isolating a reality whose consistency is not maintained by ideological mechanisms, a reality that does not disintegrate the moment we subtract from it its ideological component' (1994: 15–16). Therefore, if the social reality we all experience is more accurately understood as a symbolic fiction, then what we experience today as the ideological goal of cosmopolitan global capitalism is one that has been ideologically configured to appear non-contingent, without contradiction, and without alternative. Žižek terms this fantasy1, 'the dream of a state without disturbances' (2005: 265), yet such an ideological fantasy could be exposed as such by the continuous eruption of, in Žižek's terms, the traumatic kernel of the Real that it cannot cover over and seeks to repress: that of antagonism, be that class struggle, the rise of the far right or the more complex configurations proposed by Laclau and Mouffe.

For those who are unable, or who do not wish, to confront the fact that their social reality is a symbolic fiction or ideological fantasy1, the gap must be filled by what Žižek terms a 'spectral apparition', or fantasy2 (2005: 265). This is conjured up as an essential part of the symbolic fiction to cover over the gap that would otherwise expose the 'seemingly real' as fictional and ideological, and dispel the myth of wholeness, leaving the interminable antagonistic nature of the political exposed. Thus, the failure of the fantasy1 of 'the Nazi harmonious *Volksgemeinschaft*' was explained by the evocation of the spectral apparition of the Jew (2005: 266). Likewise, today we see the failure of the fantasy1 of harmonious global cosmopolitanism explained, for those on the right, by fantasy2, the evocation of the spectral apparition of the 'Foreigner', 'Immigrant' or 'Muslim', or, for those on the liberal left, as argued in the previous chapter, by the evocation of the 'other other' – the subject who rejects the cosmopolitan ideal of multiculturalism or the tolerance of difference more broadly.

Thus, in both cases outlined above, the individual subject is seen to *require* a fantasy antagonist: on the psychoanalytical level to have a spectre on which the subject's own failure for self-realization can be projected; and on the social level, to have a spectre on which the failure of the harmony or consensus of the social real can be projected. What is critical about Žižek's theory for this study is the fact that he makes it crystal clear that the subject – in our case the spectator-subject – is never a blank page to be ideologically interpellated by a piece of theatre (or anything else) but an already ideological subject, who is already primed for a fantasy1 and has at their disposal the offer of a spectral apparition, or fantasy2, through which a confirming and conforming sense of self and subjecthood can be fabricated:

Fantasy is then to be conceived as an imaginary scenario the function of which is to provide a kind of positive support filling out the subject's constitutive void. And the same goes, *mutatis mutandis*, for social fantasy: it is a necessary counterpart to the concept of antagonism, a scenario filling out the voids of the social structure, masking its constitutive antagonism by the fullness of enjoyment (racist enjoyment, for example). (2005: 277)

This argument is most commonly made in contexts aligned to the one Žižek describes, whereby the subject under question is set against a 'foreign other' – be that the Jew in Nazi Germany or the Muslim in the contemporary West. The need for a fantasy2 is thus most often attached to a racist or intolerant subject as a way of rationalizing the fear of difference that is also commonly afforded to such a subject. Sara Ahmed's multicultural subject, as discussed in the previous chapter, is rarely configured as requiring such a fantasy as they are assumed to embrace difference and to be better able to accept the contingency and incompleteness of their own subject-self and the social field of endless antagonism which they inhabit. Yet, *Confirmation* makes no such distinction. Thorpe, as a liberal, would-be cosmopolitan subject, is no less fearful of losing his 'armour of unity' than we presume Glen would be to lose his. Each, through the dramaturgy of *Confirmation*, is mirrored in the other and requires the enemy to remain absolutely their other: a race traitor (for Glen) or a fascist (for Thorpe). In both cases, the enemy constitutes a fantasy2 on which the endless antagonisms of the world and the failure of a utopian consensus can be blamed.

I will now suggest that the logic of autonomy that advocates confrontation with the vulnerability, contingency and incompleteness of the subject-self risks underestimating the attractions of fantasy2 that may offer the precarious neoliberal subject a reassuring 'armour of unity', however illusory, or potentially dangerous, such an armour may prove to be. Judith Butler, herself, acknowledges that 'where social categories guarantee a recognizable and enduring social existence, the embrace of such categories, even as they were in the service of subjection, is often preferred to no social existence at all' (Butler 1997b: 20). For those who risk particular exclusion from the distribution of the sensible – in Butler's terms, the dispossessed – their grip on whatever ideological fantasy can sustain a desired social identity and meaningful sense of self might prove particularly difficult to prise open when they are offered nothing conclusive in its place. Whereas Rancière is clear that the political task of the subject is precisely to reject the illusions of the singular, coherent identity that society would bind them to, he nonetheless concludes that 'the place of a political subject ... an interval or gap ... is, to be sure, an uncomfortable position' (1992: 62). Simon Bayly further contends of Rancière's proposition that

> it is a short step from a salutary insistence on our relational liminality to a potentially crippling emphasis on the indeterminate or in-between as such ... it is far from clear that the resources of the interval as such can give effective analytical purchase on the forms of relation – oppression, exploitation, representation, but also solidarity, co-operation, empowerment – that shape any particular situation. (2009: 125)

This returns us to the question, first addressed in Chapter 5, and developed in Chapter 6, as to whether the precarious spectator-subject, rather than being set adrift and charged with constructing their own modes of response and survival (as in the case under neoliberalism), might not rather benefit from the offer of a determinist, counter-hegemonic interpellation that is precisely ideological and foregrounds the egalitarian aim of Laclau and Mouffe's project of radical democracy. Such an ideologically determined counter-hegemonic interpellation, I will now argue, has the capacity to induce a concrete *sense* of agency that can combat the impotence induced by neoliberalism and potentially replace the subject's existing ideological structures of subjecthood or fantasy support. This strategy may, in particular material contexts, offer greater political potential than the offer to the precarious spectator-subject, made by the logic of autonomy, that goes no further than the invitation to throw away their existing ideological crutch and choose their own direction in which to fall.

Acts of resistance

The Deal Versus the People was a co-production of Bradford-based company Common Wealth and the West Yorkshire Playhouse in Leeds.[2] Directed by Evie Manning, it was devised and performed by non-professional performers with experience of unemployment who attended auditions that were held throughout Bradford in community centres, advice surgeries and children's centres. The cast, and many of the spectators who were mostly connected in some way to the project or performers, could thus broadly be described as those who lived at the sharpest and most precarious edge

---

[2]   It was performed in Bradford City Hall from 21 to 24 October 2015, and I attended the matinee performance on 24 October from which this analysis is taken. All citations are taken from an unpublished script, kindly provided by Common Wealth.

of neoliberalism; many would constitute those who were 'excluded' from the count, in Rancière's terms, and be defined by Judith Butler and Athena Athanasiou as the 'dispossessed', those whose 'proper place is non-being' (2013: 19).

The political aims and impact of the piece in relation to the performing participants and the efficacy of the extended activist components of the project, although central to the company's own vision for the work, will not be the focus of this analysis. Rather, in line with the subject of my study, I will focus specifically on the invitation for specific political action that was offered to the spectators of the theatre performance, and the way in which this invitation can be seen to explicitly determine the counter-hegemonic interpellation that was more cautiously and contingently extended in Andy Smith's *Summit*, discussed in Chapter 6.

The performance took place in the council chamber of Bradford City Hall, a Grade I listed building dating back to the nineteenth century and a landmark of civic pride from Bradford's great industrial history. Set within the beautiful and austere debating chamber, the performance located itself explicitly as an occupation to protest against the pending ratification of the Transatlantic Trade and Investment Partnership (TTIP). TTIP was a series of trade negotiations underway at the time of the performance between the European Union and the United States that were widely perceived to be designed to empower global corporations in ways that held significant dangers for the future democratic accountability of national governments. The invitation of the piece was for the spectators to join the actors in their protest, and the interpellation was designed for those spectators who, like the actors, recognized themselves as those who have been, in the terminologies adopted thus far in this study, excluded or dispossessed, both materially and as subjects who hold agency. By aligning the performers and spectators in this way, a political consensus was proposed, but unlike the evasion of agonistic debate noted in the previous chapter, the agonistic 'Them' to the proposed 'Us' of the audience and performers was here implicitly defined and invited into the theatre space, global capital as represented by the character of the European Commissioner.

The counter-hegemonic interpellation at play in *The Deal Versus the People* was much more explicit than that extended in Smith's work. Here, the spectators encountered a specific political scenario and were invited to play a designated role in a performative piece of activist politics. To this end *The Deal* made use of many traditional strategies associated with historical agitprop practices, thus permitting the egalitarian logic to dominate the dramaturgies of the piece. The spectator-subjects were not only left with an invitation to act on leaving the chambers but were incorporated into an act of resistance that was constructed in the time and space of the performance from the bodies of the actors and spectators. Spectators were asked to put on balaclavas and make a noise as one of the actors filmed a video letter to send to the European Commissioner in Brussels 'to show you that we've taken over Bradford City Hall because we don't agree with TTIP'. The actors then removed their balaclavas to speak to the video, in their own words, the audiences framed as witnesses and accomplices in the background. Some spectators also chose to participate and delivered a speech to the camera. On the video footage of this letter on Common Wealth's website, from a different performance to the one I attended, a young boy is filmed, instructing the adults who are watching him, that it is their votes who have placed the people in power where they are and so it is their votes that can remove them.

The strong egalitarian steer and activist components of this performance clearly make it vulnerable to Rancière's charge of mastery, that the spectators were being taught about TTIP by the actors and instructed in the course of action they were required to undertake. Yet here I would agree wholeheartedly with Simon Bayly's challenge to Rancière, that political action seeking to interrupt an inegalitarian distribution of the sensible surely requires knowledge and understanding of the complex ways in which exploitation is organized and sustained through the operations of governments and multinational corporations (2009: 127). As Bayly also contends, this knowledge, or lack of knowledge, is, itself, a product of the unequal distribution of capacity in the contemporary context of neoliberal capitalism, and the discrediting of dramaturgical structures that seek to rebalance such a context, through offering knowledge to those from whom it is most often withheld, would seem counterproductive to Rancière's political project as a whole.

Significantly, the overriding refrain of the performance, also serving as a title for the related activist website, was 'we're not stupid'. This refrain referenced the positioning of the actors by and within the dominant hegemony at the same time as comprehensively rejecting the absence of intelligence and agency that characterized their allocated 'no-place' in society. Rather than accepting their 'proper place as non-being', the actors *took place* as political subjects with agency to occupy the institutional space usually reserved for political dignitaries in whose place the actors were now granted the voice to speak and to share the knowledge which they had accrued over the course of the project to further extend such agency to others. In place of the debate of the authorized dignitaries, there was noise: chanting, banging, shouting, a young man dances on the debating table, the audience puts on balaclavas; a girl sings and plays the guitar.

Such displays of agency contrasted with the actions the performance opened with which were borne of despair rather than empowerment: the young man standing on the table threatening to set himself alight or the mother making a bomb out of the food she's received from the food bank. These representations haunted the performance even after they'd been disavowed as 'real' by the actors, manifestations of the violence that is always waiting to erupt when subjects are dispossessed of all other modes of agency and excluded from the parameters of agonistic debate. Yet the invitation of the performance was ultimately to reject the 'no place' of despair, self-harm or the solace offered by the proactive violence fostered by extremists and to accept the offer of political subjectivation and a role in the advancement of radical democracy.

Similar to the strategies operating in *Summit*, the actors and spectators here were aligned as 'we': a community prefigured as already subjectivized, already wanting change, already capable of individual agency, but individual agency that could only be realized through collective action.

Text is spoken by everyone in any order, there is urgency, we can't wait to speak
It's not just us.
It's all round the world
In Mexico indigenous people have taken back their land.
In London people are resisting eviction from social housing that's been sold off.
In Spain there's a town that owns all its industry and shares the money equally.
It's not just us.
It's last night's audience
And tomorrow's audience
It's not just us.
But even if it is.
If everyone here fights for an hour, between us we've fought for a month.
If everyone here fights for a month, between us we've fought for a decade.
If everyone here fights for a year, between us we've fought for a lifetime.
There are more people than there are governments.
There are more people than there are corporations.
It's not just us.
It's not just us.
It's not just us.
It's not just us.
It's not just us.

It's not just us.
The audience leave City Hall out of the main doors to find the square full of people. The audience have sparklers.

In this way, as in Smith's work, the performance explicitly targeted the dangers of precarity identified in Chapter 3 of this study as most damaging to Mouffe's project of radical democracy: the individualism that arises out of destroyed communities and competing interests, and the powerlessness to hope for better futures in the face of the complexity, pervasiveness and seeming omnipotence of late global capitalism. In a mounted challenge to the nihilism of individualism, each spectator was invited to understand that their only individual agency lay in the power of the collective and that collective agency was only possible through individual agency.

The dialogue between Judith Butler and Athena Athanasiou in *Dispossession: The Performative in the Political* focuses precisely on establishing subjectivity as relational rather than individualized, to refuse the violence to the other that has historically underpinned the sovereignty of the bourgeois subject (2013). Butler and Athanasiou instead seek to establish 'that the limits of the sovereign subject constitute the precondition of its agency' (Butler and Athanasiou 2013: 155), thus making political agency contingent on the subject's relation with others rather than 'a property of an originating self' (2013: 155). Athanasiou's call for subjects to be 'crafted and re-crafted as intelligible, vulnerable, and relational beings' (Butler and Athanasiou 2013: 155) echoes Rancière's insistence that the individual subject can be defined only in relation to others and substantiates Clohesy's identification of the ethics of the empathy operation lying in the subject's necessary confrontation of their own Difference, contingency of identity and the inevitable violence that their insistence on wholeness commits to the difference of others.

The emphasis Butler and Athanasiou place on the necessity of the vulnerability and incompleteness of the subject throughout their dialogue is on account of their commitment to reinstating the full human subjecthood, visibility and agency of those who have been dispossessed without merely re-inscribing the norms of the sovereign individual that have led to the inequality of such dispossession in the first instance. Both theorists are driven by the poststructuralist imperatives to which they adhere, most pertinently the critique of a 'metaphysics of presence' (Butler and Athanasiou 2013: 19), the myth of full presence of selfhood and sovereign individual subjectivity, that substantiated the 'colonially and postcolonially embedded notions of the self-contained, proper(tied), liberal subject' (2013: 27). The particular modes of subjectivity legitimated and capacitated by neoliberal power are sustained, Athanasiou argues, by 'normative fantasies … of the "good life"' in self-owned subjects (a life defined, for instance, by property ownership, commodity fetishism, consumer excitement, securitarian regimes, national belonging, bourgeois self-fashioning, and biopolitical normalcy)' (Butler and Athanasiou 2013: 30–1). It is those very norms, they argue, that are also responsible for 'shattering and economically depleting certain livelihoods, foreclosing them, rendering them disposable and perishable' (31). Butler and Athanasiou ask how, given the violent history of the proper(tied), liberal subject, can the dispossessed (of land, of property, of subjecthood) be *re*-possessed of those things that have been forcibly withheld from them in ways 'that do not depend upon a valorization of possessive individualism' (7), the mode of the subject that underpinned their dispossession and exclusion in the first instance. Where and how, they ask, 'do the lives of those whose "proper place is non-being" take place after the critique of the metaphysics of substance? How is the "substance" of these lives produced?' (20)

Butler and Athanasiou thus raise the question of *what kind* of subjectivity should be aspired to by those who are currently dispossessed of full subjecthood, those who are currently excluded from being 'a part', in Rancière's terms, of the social and political sphere. For both Butler and Athanasiou, the notion of a selfhood that remains tied to the 'myth of full presence' would merely reiterate the norms of bourgeois sovereign subjectivity and so sustain the structures of oppressive identity categories and inequality that led to dispossession in the first instance. In this particular historical moment where the rise of the far right across Europe and North America is stoking fundamentalism and tribal modes of identity on all sides, it is easy to understand the urgent political currency of the 'post-identity' subjects that Butler and Athanasiou seek to reconfigure. Such subjects are characterized in the same terms as Rancière's political subject as 'fractured, dispersed, heterogenous and provisional' (Butler and Athanasiou 2013: 154), and Athanasiou proposes detaching the notion of freedom from the wholeness of the sovereign subject by arguing that 'freedom with others' is 'freedom from the violence inherent in the freedom of individual will' (183).

However, the characteristics of this new relational concept of the 'post-identity' subject as fractured and provisional raise warning bells when attached to those who are rendered most precarious in the neoliberal distribution of the sensible. As Athanasiou cautions, vulnerability is a double-edged sword. On the one hand it offers the 'post-identity' subject the 'vital potentiality of being affected by others and of owing ourselves to others', but it is also the characteristic of those who have experienced 'injuries of injustice' that are 'unevenly distributed' (158). For those subjects who have historically been excluded from claiming full presence, and who have never been afforded the status of 'viable actors' within the public sphere (Butler 2004: xvii), the idea that the only subjectivity on offer in an agonistic democracy is a fractured, provisional and partial one might well seem more like a threat than a promise.

The philosophical aims of Butler and Athanasiou for an ethics of relationality are compelling but they also both, at different points, raise important questions that might moderate an unqualified celebration of the vulnerability of the incomplete and contingent subject that I would like to interrogate further. For the most precarious spectator-subjects, such as many of those attending *The Deal Versus the People*, who might most urgently need alternatives to their 'perennial occupation as non-being and non-having' (Butler and Athanasiou 2013: 19), the vision held out for them by Athanasiou 'to take part by not being exactly a part' (155) might not feel satisfactory, and one justifiable retort might well be that they would quite like to experience the privilege (that scholars like Butler, Athanasiou and myself have been granted) of occupying the illusion of feeling 'exactly a part' before being asked to abrogate a sovereignty of individual agency they have never enjoyed to a collective care for 'the lives and actions of others' (155). Relational subjectivity as it is evoked through dialogic empathy, or collective responsibility, for the other, may be precisely what is most vital in an age of precarity but the very conditions of precarity make it less easy than ever to achieve. I am speculating, as I move towards the conclusion of this study, as to whether the poststructuralist insistence, underpinned by the logic of autonomy, on the contingency, relationality and incompleteness of each human subject is always the best strategy for the project of radical democracy to harness.

In his discussion of Spinoza's belief that 'there is no longer a subject, but only individuating affective states of an anonymous force' (in Thrift 2008: 13), affect theorist Nigel Thrift asserts the value, nonetheless, of holding 'to a sense of *personal authorship* .... Because how things seem is often more important than what they are' (Thrift 2008: 13, original emphasis). He offers a vital insight from D. M. Wegner who argues that 'the fact is that it seems to each of us that we have conscious will. It seems we have selves. It seems we have minds. It seems we are agents. It seems we cause what we do. Although it is sobering and ultimately accurate to call this an illusion, it is a mistake to think the illusory is trivial' (Wegner 2002: 341–2 in Thrift 2008: 13). Although the philosophical detail of Butler and Athanasiou's argument is not precisely aligned with the Spinozan theories of Thrift, they share a desire to conceptualize the subject-self primarily in relation and difference to otherness, and to reconceptualize what might be seen as limits to the agency of the sovereign self as the very potential for agency which is borne of an inescapable relationality and co-dependency for survival. The irony, it seems to me, is that for those of us for whom the illusion of agency is most convincing, those of us who do, in Thrift's words, *seem* to have real agency in the social world of which we are a recognized part, the philosophical move proposed by Butler and Athanasiou is much less threatening, as the appearance of individual agency will remain regardless of what we understand to be the reality. Conversely, however, for those who do not even *seem* to hold agency, the excluded, the dispossessed, those not afforded even the bourgeois illusion of subjecthood, the attempted withdrawal of such an illusion from their sights might propel them to seek such an illusion elsewhere. To return to Žižek, if ideological fantasy primarily serves as a comforting support for the illusion of full subjecthood, perhaps it is worth considering whether a *sense* of full subjecthood underpinned by radical political agency might offer a more persuasive invitation than the mere demolition of existing fantasy structures. The latter will reveal only the reality of a fragmented, fallible and vulnerable subjectivity, a move that might, as Mouffe cautions, leave 'the door open for attempts at re-articulation by non-progressive forces' (2013: 73). Mouffe identifies such a deconstructive move in isolation from any subsequent reconstruction of oppositional identities as a 'problematic' conviction which assumes that 'the negative moment would be sufficient on its own to bring about something positive, as if new subjectivities were previously available, ready to emerge when the weight of the dominant ideology has been lifted' (Mouffe 2013: 93).

The political subject called forth by the actors of *The Deal Versus the People* was indisputably relational, called to embrace 'freedom with', as opposed to the free will of the bourgeois individual, yet the *feeling* of individual agency was paramount to those who participated in the production and highlighted as the ground from which 'a "commons" was mobilized by the theatrical landscapes of the production' (Hughes 2017: 77):

I'm.
A Person.
We're. People. Living. Breathing
And **we're** here. Hurting. Bleeding

I want **my** child to grow up in a world that isn't against him.
I want people to listen to **us** and appreciate what **we're** saying

If every**one** here fights for a year, between **us we've** fought for a lifetime.

The 'I's at play here are not the individualized voices satirized in the ironic dramaturgies explored in Chapter 5, but the individuals who are called up to speak on behalf of a commons, as a full *part* of a collective 'we', to *take their place* in the resistance to a global capitalism that would render them faceless, nameless and stupid.

In the previous chapter, I argued that *Queens of Syria* had adopted a strategy of re-facement by affording names, faces and individual histories to refugees whose faces were most commonly obliterated by media representations of 'swarms' and 'hordes'. Butler herself argues that 'those who remain faceless' without individual names or public representation are not fully constituted as humans who are permitted to die grievable deaths (Butler 2004: xviii). Thus, the claiming of individuality in such contexts is a radical act that must appropriate the guise of the sovereign individual in order to challenge the limitations that neoliberalism would tie such a subject into, to challenge the near-total hold the neoliberal subject has on the rights to a name, a face and a voice and the subsequent means of production and communication.

The importance of this sense of individual agency to those who have been denied a 'proper place' of being is made clear in the refrain of the song that is sung by one of the participants of *The Deal Versus the People* as her contribution to the video letter to the European Commissioner. 'This voice is mine', she sings, something that neither 'they' nor 'you' can take away from her. Without the *feeling* of individual agency, the *feeling* that one has the capacity to act on and change the environment for better or worse, precarious individuals will remain disempowered and vulnerable to the affective manipulation of right-wing extremists who will indeed offer them the feeling of individual agency they crave, but at a great cost to the project of radical democracy.

None of the above analysis seeks to discredit or contest the radical potential of the political discourses that have sought to counterbalance the egalitarian logic of Marxism with the values of the libertarian logic: contingency, relationality and incompleteness. Yet it does propose that in certain material contexts, the ideological steer that comes with determined counter-hegemonic interpellation of the spectator-subject can also be a powerful tool in political dramaturgies aligned to the project of radical democracy. The spectator-subjects of *The Deal Versus the People* are interpellated with precision, and this precision offers a *feeling* of complete identity and complete community that might support political change quite as well as the more open, contingent invitations made to the spectator-subjects of Smith's *Summit*.

Conclusion

Drawing on my analysis of *Confirmation*, this chapter has proposed that the fear Thorpe expressed of acknowledging his own contingency of subjecthood, in the face of the fascist other, might well be replicated in spectator-subjects, such as the audience of *The Deal Versus the People*, whose material context locates them as dispossessed subjects who are often excluded from the existing parameters of debate. Such spectator-subjects, and many beyond such communities, may prefer to avoid a traumatic confrontation with the endless antagonisms of both subjecthood and social reality and seek the solace and substantiation of the *feeling* of a more determined subjecthood, the hope of a utopian future and the security offered by being handed a specific ideological task to undertake. If this is rejected wholesale by political dramaturgies on the left that are too uncritically bound to the poststructuralist imperative of autonomy, then the indeterminacy, contingency and fallibility of the post-Marxist project might not always be sufficient to counter the affective satisfaction of the illusion of such a subjecthood or the promise of a utopic society that is always on offer from the far right.

This danger with the contemporary democratic imaginary is foregrounded by Laclau and Mouffe: it opens up a constellation of endlessly deferred and disparate antagonisms that cannot be relied on to necessarily drive forward the 'struggle for equality' in a broader egalitarian sense and, furthermore, uncovers a site of indeterminacy 'that leaves the door wide open for totalitarian projects, such as fascism, to fill the ideological space that has been left vacant by the departure of Marxist certainty from the site of struggle' (170–2). This is a caution that I don't believe is always sufficiently heeded in the subsequent discourses of contemporary political dramaturgies, where the embrace of the dominance of Rancière's logic of autonomy has served to constrain the political potential of ideological, counter-hegemonic interpellation that I have argued remains highly potent in certain contexts.

Not least, I would argue, the poststructuralist conviction, shared by Butler and Rancière, that no mode of interpellation can be secured, nor any artist's desired response to their invitation be determined, will always safeguard the ultimate autonomy of the spectator-subject regardless of any ideological steer that may be offered. Even when the invitation is accepted, or the interpellation turned to, Butler is clear that a 'full recognition, that is, of ever fully inhabiting the name by which one's social identity is inaugurated and mobilised' is impossible (Butler 1993: 226); the subject will always exceed their interpellated identity, and the same can be argued in the context of counter-hegemonic interpellation. Given this, I would propose that there is nothing to fear from a strategic, counter-hegemonic hail to the spectator that may, on the contrary, hold significant potential to counteract the neoliberal imbrication of the precarious spectator-subject and offer specific means by which the neoliberal project can be discredited or derailed. In an age of precarity, an invitation to step onto firmer ground in which subjecthood and future actions take on concrete form may, in certain dramaturgies and in certain material contexts, be precisely what is most needed.

Epilogue

This research project began with my reflections on a series of experiences as a spectator in which I felt I had been 'badly written', to cite the character of 'Adrian' speaking in Tim Crouch's *The Author*, which happened to be one of the shows in question (Crouch 2009). I had been, in the terms of this study, ironically interpellated as a complicit spectator-subject of particular manifestations of neoliberalism, but my feeling was not one of self-reflection, but of irritation at having been misrecognized as guilty by association and at having my agency to explicitly resist such an interpellation constrained by the dramaturgies of the work. Turning my attention to the invitations offered to the spectator of contemporary political dramaturgies, I became intrigued by the increasingly political direction of theatre that nonetheless continued to operate in tension with notions of emancipated, or autonomous, spectatorship, and from these starting points this study began to evolve.

What I hope to have achieved in this book is a modest corrective to the direction of travel within the discourse of political theatres in Europe over recent decades that has tended to discredit notions of ideological steer, artistic intention and political effect. I hope to have demonstrated that there is no binary choice to be made between a respect for the spectator's autonomy and the intention to provoke political change, but rather a consideration of how the tension between the two might best be managed and manipulated in relation to specific material contexts of production. I believe that in discourses of political theatres, as in political discourses more broadly, a revaluation is critically and urgently required of the ideological egalitarianism of the Marxist project that was subsumed for many decades under the rise of poststructuralist theory and the demands for autonomy that were able to override all other considerations. None of this is to devalue the political achievements and potential of the poststructuralist project, but to seek a rebalancing of autonomy with concerns for egalitarian outcomes, a gentle pushback of the pendulum that might have swung too hard against the authoritarianism of State-Communism to operate at full efficacy against the current threat – coming now not only from the neoliberal mainstream but also from the rising currents of the far right.

Beyond this study's analysis of political dramaturgies that counterbalance the logics of autonomy and egalitarianism, I have suggested that dramaturgies driven solely by the logic of autonomy might better be categorized as libertarian in their politics or be productively removed from the discursive framework of political theatres altogether. This latter move would perhaps enable a clearer understanding and appreciation of the important philosophical, aesthetic or therapeutic work that is taking place in such practice. This would certainly be one benefit of this study's aim to narrow the field of what constitutes 'the political' and to more clearly distinguish work driven entirely by the logic of autonomy from political dramaturgies that are characterized by the tension between both logics and intent on challenging the inegalitarian injustices of the neoliberal context in which they exist.

As an epilogue to the study, I would like to conclude with a creative, rather than critically conclusive, response to the invitation this study has extended to others. *The Cassandra Commission* is a short piece of spoken-word performance that was conceived in the early stages of this research, and which formed part of a longer performance lecture that was delivered at the 2014 IFTR (International Federation of Theatre Research) conference at Warwick and subsequently at the Universities of Exeter, Manchester and Birmingham during 2014/15. In response to my scepticism of the deployment of ironic interpellation in work I had attended, *The Cassandra Commission* was designed to interpellate its spectators as paragons of political activism, in contrast to the speaker who herself takes on the guilt of the subject who has failed to sufficiently resist the hegemonic call of neoliberal individualism and apathy. Her failure has also, as foreseen through an apocalyptic vision of the future, sealed the ecological fate of humanity through her neglect to live up to the standards of the audience to whom she speaks. Juxtaposing the dramaturgical structure of the Truth and Reconciliation Commission reports from post-Apartheid South Africa with the mythical figure of the doomed prophet Cassandra, the speaker embodies the role of the academic, representing a modern-day Cassandra who has foreseen everything, and foretold everything, but has actually done very little, a charge I felt validated in taking on myself and which I suspected would be shared by many in the academic audiences to whom the piece was performed.

My gamble was that a sincere interpellation of this kind – overly generous and utopic in its call – would land on most spectators with a sense of unease: that most would know very well they were not as they were being interpellated; they had not been, as I had not, the most actively radical subject that they could have, and would like to have, been. For such spectators, there would be the opportunity to reflect on this and to opt internally to take their share of the blame for the future of humanity that was being foretold and, perhaps, to prevent its realization, be inspired to go beyond, in the words of the prophet Cassandra, 'knowing and speaking only'. Yet, I also wanted those spectators who were better placed to turn in recognition to such an interpellation to be excluded from a critique that I had no right or authority to level at the audience in general, but only to those spectators who self-selected to identify themselves with the character of Cassandra, rather than the spectator-subject that the piece alleged to recognize.

This performance lecture thus began my engagement with the practice of interpellation that has been at the heart of this study and seeded the thinking that followed on the tension between political intention and autonomous response in contemporary political dramaturgies. It seems fitting to end, then, where I began, by making the text of *The Cassandra Commission* available as my own creative, and necessarily inconclusive, contribution to the questions I have raised. I hope that this book as a whole has offered its readers, at the very least, the opportunity to consider if now is the time for a reconsideration of the too-often discredited ideological steer that underpins the logic of egalitarianism, and to ask what might be gained should it take a more prominent role in contemporary and future political dramaturgies that are operating at a time of acute and accelerating global crisis.

The Cassandra Commission

A performer steps forward. She holds an A–Z like a witness in a courtroom holds the holy book. She speaks to the audience. She may read from notes.

It is with some regret that I reflect on my past
It is with some sorrow that I acknowledge my complicity
It is with some degree of guilt that I assume a certain level of responsibility for what has happened and for what will happen next
For what will happen now, here, in this room, and for what will happen later.
Not later as in this evening, or next week. Not later as in next year, and probably not later as in the year after.
But later
For sure
Pause
I, on this inauspicious day in history, wish to say the following:
To everyone who suffered because my prophecies were not believed, I am truly sorry for upsetting the God Apollo.
To Apollo, I wish to express my deepest regret for rejecting your advances

To the Trojans, who it has to be said might have done well to take me more
seriously, I am still sorry for your humiliating defeat
To the Trojans who held me back, with my axe and my burning torch, as
I ran towards the wooden horse, I'm sorry I didn't fight you harder. More
brutality towards individuals who would not listen might have saved an
entire race.
To classical scholars I express my deepest regret for my unnecessary and self-
serving appearances in Smallville, Buffy, Red Dwarf and, of course, my wilful
self-parody in Walt Disney's version of Hercules
To classical music fans I am sorry for the part I have played in the rise of
Gothic rock
Pause
I cannot say 'I did not know', because I truly did know
I cannot say 'I did not speak out' because I did, at every opportunity, speak
out
So for knowing and for speaking only
For all that I have done and all that I have failed to do
Mea Culpa.

*The performer no longer reads from notes. She speaks as if she is describing
something that only she can see.*

You are the first to arrive for the last coach to leave the depot.
You thought you would be fighting for a seat. Elbowing through the weak
and the elderly and those unaccustomed to the brutality of public transport
like the old days when you took the train to work. The days when there were
trains. The days when there was work.
But the depot is as deserted as the city. The city where the light is slowly
dying, and everyone is trying to get used to the dark. Because the forest
has spread into the city and no-one can see the sky anymore. The street
signs have been stolen and no-one can find their way home. A city where
everyone is afraid of everyone else and no-one believes in the future.
Wherever the people of the city have fled, they have not fled here. Which
should perhaps tell you something. Which should perhaps warn you,
that you are either too late or too trusting of systems that have long since
stopped working.
You wait in your seat by the window near the back of the coach for others to
arrive. But no-one comes. The coach pulls out into the darkness of the city.
You take out your A–Z and follow the road that begins at the tear on page
83. No longer sure which city it refers to, it still comforts you to read it from
time to time, trying to match the place names and the angles of the lines on

the page with the tracings of your journey. But the occasional light from the occasional cracked streetlamp has now gone. And the rain drums invisibly on the black window. And you close the A–Z for the last time and put it in the pocket of the seat in front. As if it was a newspaper. As if anyone else would come along now, to read it. As if it any longer contained anything at all that could help.

The performer speaks to the audience. She may read from notes.

I didn't come before you all to make excuses
I expect no forgiveness, and little understanding, from any of you here today.
But I do think I should stress the extenuating circumstances
How difficult it increasingly became for all of us as the twentieth century in all its complexity rolled into action.
There was, from this point on, no more wooden horses which – however huge – could possibly contain the danger that we faced
Could be effectively targeted
Could be effectively torched
Could be effectively eliminated to leave a clean result, a lasting peace, or even provisional prosperity.
It was no longer those inside the horses
Or even those who built the horses
Who were the ones who needed torching for the future to be saved.
But I am making my excuses to the ones who least need to hear what they have always known.
Prophecy becomes cheap when any fool can see what will happen.
It is not enough to go on stating the obvious in ten different languages and 300,000 different turns of phrase.
So to Emily Davison, I am sorry that I did not jump with you, and I am also sorry that the democracy you died for has not always proved worthy of the sacrifice you made.
I cannot say 'I did not know', because I truly did know
I cannot say 'I did not speak out' because I did, at every opportunity, speak out
So for knowing and for speaking only
For all that I have done and all that I have failed to do
Mea Culpa.

The performer no longer reads from notes. She speaks as if she is describing something that only she can see.

The coach pulls up as the road runs out. The engine shudders and dies. No lights come on. You feel your way down the coach in darkness, the door is already open and as you step out into the gently lapping waves of the sea, the sea that is gathering momentum as it gathers together the detritus of the land, you turn to thank the driver but there is no-one there. There was no-one driving, only you, all along, no-one driving.

The water is rising in the gutters, spilling out onto the pavements, washing away the cars and signposts as if they are nothing more than plastic toys. As if they have poured out all the oceans. As if the world is going under. And the wind is howling in the distance as it blows the cities clean. And so you run down broken railway tracks to the city that the homeless once made their own. Through the old pavilion and crumbling grandeur, following the flames of the pier that is burning for the ninth time, lighting up the night sky.

You sense you are being followed as you turn down the narrow lane of empty shops where broken windows spill their rain-soaked stock of scented drawer liners and ethnic tat that no-one wants even at a time like this. Although perhaps it is a mark of times like this that no use can any longer be found for plastic pink flamingos on green sticks, or chiffon scarves, or faded Victorian photographs of anonymous and long-dead families. The wooden ducks have all been burned for firewood and the world seems to have passed the point where herbal remedies might be seen to offer any kind of answer. The vegetarian shoes have long gone, providing ethical protection to save your feet from being torn to shreds by the glass underfoot or the sharp, jagged pebbles that were washing up like lorryloads dumped from the beach onto the city streets. The animals had more to worry about in the end, it seemed, than being made into footwear that could withstand the increasingly harsh climate; and neither the cattle nor the badgers could fly like the guillemots from the rising waves of panic; for them, like for us, you think, there is no escape.

The performer speaks directly to the audience. She may read from notes.

I didn't come before you to defend myself
I deserve no concessions from any of you here today
But I do think it is important that you are reminded of the small things
That I did, in all fairness, hope would make a difference.
A few examples should suffice.
In 1984 I gave tinned peaches and corned beef to the striking miners and their families
I boycotted oranges from South Africa and marched against the BNP.

In 2003 I marched against the invasion of Iraq
I boycotted BP and Shell and set up a direct debit to save the orangutans, and
Sumatran tigers, and provide clean water for a few people, somewhere in the
world where there was none.
I think I should perhaps stop there.
And say to the miners who I hope enjoyed their tins of peaches
I am sorry that I did not stand beside you when the horses charged.
And to the people who marched against austerity
I am sorry I was too busy to make it
There was a good reason but I can't remember what it was
Something to do with work I think I was at the university then.
Some of you might not remember –
What we did there seemed important at the time
But for all the wrong reasons, perhaps.

*The performer no longer reads from notes. She speaks as if she is describing
something that only she can see.*

The seagulls shriek like the souls of the dead, and circle above the scraps
of humanity that litter the beaches rising over the promenade and over the
bandstand and up to the entrance to the grand hotel, the road no longer
visible under the seaweed and driftwood, the lampposts stunted and their
lanterns hanging by a thread. Where the sea starts and the city stops is no
longer clear. How high the waters will come is yet to be seen. You settle
yourself on the top stair of the grand staircase, underneath a chandelier
that flickers a little light over the debris as it sways gently in the breeze.
Looking out over the vast blue ocean you can see the different shades of the
land below, and on the horizon familiar landmarks are still visible above
the swell. You imagine, but cannot see, that pigeons and seagulls are now
settled side by side on the window ledges of the shard, and you see, but
cannot imagine, how the little plastic bubbles that once took people high
over the river, now bob like boats on the crests of the waves. You look for a
clue amongst the birds that are hovering overhead, but you have never been
sure what the difference between a dove and a pigeon is, the seagulls you
can easily identify and discount. None of the pigeons, cleft footed, starving,
scraggy and bedraggled in the never-ending rain, look like the dove you
had imagined as a child. You wonder if we've blown our second chance. You
wonder if our second chance was our last one.

The performer speaks directly to the audience. She may read from notes.

For knowing and for speaking only
For all that I have done and all that I have failed to do
To those of you here today who fight so hard against the future I foresee and will let happen
Not later as in this evening, or next week. Not later as in next year, and probably not later as in the year after.
But later
For sure
Mea maxima culpa.

References

Achen, C. H. and L. M. Bartels (2016), *Democracy for Realists: Why Elections Do Not Produce Responsive Government*, Princeton: Princeton University Press.

Adiseshiah, S. (2016), 'Spectatorship and the New (Critical) Sincerity: The Case of Forced Entertainment's *Tomorrow's Parties*', *Journal of Contemporary Drama in English*, 4 (1): 1–16.

Ahmed, S. (2010), 'Happy Objects', in M. Gregg and G. J. Seigworth (eds), *The Affect Theory Reader*, 29–51, Durham and London: Duke University Press.

Ahmed, S. (2012), *On Being Included: Racism and Diversity in Institutional Life*, Durham and London: Duke University Press.

Ahmed, S. (2014), *The Cultural Politics of Emotion*, 2nd edn, Edinburgh: Edinburgh University Press.

Alston, A. (2016), *Beyond Immersive Theatre: Aesthetics, Politics and Productive Participation*, Basingstoke: Palgrave Macmillan.

Althusser, L. ([1971] 2008), *On Ideology*, London: Verso.

Anderson, B. (2010), 'Modulating the Excess of Affect: Morale in a State of "Total War"', in M. Gregg and G. J. Seigworth (eds), *The Affect Theory Reader*, 161–85, Durham and London: Duke University Press.

Angel-Perez, E. (2014), 'Martin Crimp's Nomadic Voices', *Contemporary Theatre Review*, 24 (3): 353–62.

Angelaki, V. (2012), *The Plays of Martin Crimp: Making Theatre Strange*, Basingstoke: Palgrave Macmillan.

Angelaki, V. (2017), *Social and Political Theatre in 21st-Century Britain: Staging Crisis*, London: Bloomsbury Methuen.

Balme, C. (2008), *The Cambridge Introduction to Theatre Studies*, Cambridge: Cambridge University Press.

Barker, M. (2012), 'Crossing Out the Audience', in I. Christie (ed.), *Audiences: Defining and Researching Screen Entertainment Reception*, 188–206, Amsterdam: Amsterdam University Press.

Barnett, D. (2013), 'Performing Dialectics in an Age of Uncertainty, or: Why Post-Brechtian Postdramatic', in K. Jürs-Munby, J. Carroll and S. Giles (eds), *Postdramatic Theatre and the Political: International Perspectives on Contemporary Performance*, 47–66, London: Bloomsbury Methuen.

Barthes, R. (1977), 'The Death of the Author', in R. Barthes (ed.), *Image – Music – Text*, trans. S. Heath, 142–8, London: Fontana.

Bauman, Z. (2001), *The Individualized Society*, Cambridge: Polity Press.

Bayly, S. (2009), 'Theatre and the Public: Badiou, Rancière, Virno', *Radical Philosophy*, 157: 20–9.

Beck, U. (1992), *The Risk Society*, trans. M. Ritter, London: Sage.

Beck, U. and E. Beck-Gernsheim (1995), *The Normal Chaos of Love*, trans. M. Ritter and J. Wiebel, Cambridge: Polity Press.

Ben Chaim, D. (1984), *Distance in the Theatre: The Aesthetics of Audience Response*, Ann Arbor: UMI Research Press.

Bennett, S. (1990), *Theatre Audiences: A Theory of Production and Reception*, London and New York: Routledge.

Biggin, R. (2017), *Immersive Theatre and Audience Experience: Space, Game and Story in the Work of Punchdrunk*, Basingstoke: Palgrave Macmillan.

Blau, H. (1990), *The Audience*, Baltimore: Johns Hopkins.

Boal, A. ([1979] 2008), *Theatre of the Oppressed*, trans. C. McBride, M. Leal McBride and E. Fryer, London: Pluto Press.

Boll, J. (2013), *The New War Plays: From Kane to Harris*, Basingstoke: Palgrave Macmillan.

Boltanski, L. and E. Chiapello (2005), *The New Spirit of Capitalism*, trans. G. Elliott, London: Verso.

Booth, W. C. (1974), *A Rhetoric of Irony*, Chicago and London: The University of Chicago Press.

Bone, J. (2010), 'Irrational Capitalism: The Social Map, Neoliberalism and the Demodernization of the West', *Critical Sociology*, 36 (5): 717–40.

Bourdieu, P. (1993), *The Field of Cultural Production*, trans. R. Johnson, Cambridge: Polity Press.

Bourdieu, P. (1996), *The Rules of Art: Genesis and Structure of the Literary Field*, trans. S. Emanuel, Stanford: Stanford University Press.

Bourdieu, P. (1997), 'La précarité est aujourd'hui partout', Intervention lors des Rencontres européennes contre la précarité, Grenoble, 12–13 December. https://www.scribd.com/document/235153665/La-Precarite-Est-Aujourdhui-Partout.

Bourdieu, P. (1998), *Acts of Resistance: Against the New Myths of Our Time*, trans. R. Nice, Cambridge: Polity Press.

Bourriaud, N. (2002), *Relational Aesthetics*, trans. S. Pleasance and F. Woods, Dijon: Les Presses du Réel.

Brecht, B. (1964), *Brecht on Theatre*, trans. J. Willett, London: Shenval Press.

Brecht, B. (2015), *Brecht on Theatre*, ed. M. Silberman, S. Giles and T. Kuhn, London: Methuen Drama.

Brecht, B. and C. R. Mueller (1964), 'Notes on Stanislavski', *TDR*, 9 (2): 155–66.

Butler, J. (1993), *Bodies That Matter: On the Discursive Limits of 'Sex'*, London: Routledge.

Butler, J. (1997a), *Excitable Speech: A Politics of the Performative*, London: Routledge.

Butler, J. (1997b), *The Psychic Life of Power: Theories in Subjection*, Stanford: Stanford University Press.

Butler, J. (2004), *Precarious Life: The Powers of Mourning and Violence*, London and New York: Verso.

Butler, J. (2009), *Frames of War: When Is Life Grievable?*, London and New York: Verso.

Butler, J. (2015a), *Notes toward a Performance Theory of Assembly*, Cambridge, MA and London: Harvard University Press.

Butler, J. (2015b), *Senses of the Subject*, New York: Fordham University Press.

Butler, J. (2016), 'Rethinking Vulnerability and Resistance', in J. Butler, Z. Gambetti and L. Sabsay (eds), *Vulnerability in Resistance*, 12–27, Durham and London: Duke University Press.

Butler, J. and A. Athanasiou (2013), *Dispossession: The Performative in the Political: Conversations with Athena Athanasiou*, Cambridge: Polity Press.

Butler, J., Z. Gambetti and L. Sabsay (2016), 'Introduction', in J. Butler, Z. Gambetti and L. Sabsay (eds), *Vulnerability in Resistance*, 1–11, Durham and London: Duke University Press.

Chouliaraki, L. (2012), *The Ironic Spectator: Solidarity in the Age of Post-Humanitarianism*, Cambridge: Polity Press.

Clohesy, A. M. (2013), *Politics of Empathy: Ethics, Solidarity, Recognition*, London and New York: Routledge.

Cooke, D. (2014), 'Bringing In the Republic of Happiness to the Royal Court Stage', *Contemporary Theatre Review*, 24 (3): 410–11.

Crimp, M. (2012), *In the Republic of Happiness*, London: Faber and Faber.

Crouch, T. (2009), *The Author*, London: Oberon.

Cummings, L. B. (2016), *Empathy as Dialogue in Theatre and Performance*, Basingstoke: Palgrave Macmillan.

Day, G. (2009), 'The Fear of Heteronomy', *Third Text*, 23 (4): 393–406.

Delgado-García, C. (2015), *Rethinking Character in Contemporary British Theatre*, Berlin: De Gruyter.

Derrida, J. (1973), *Speech and Phenomena*, trans. D. A. Allison and Evanston, Illinois: Northwestern University Press.

Diamond, E., D. Varney and C. Amich, eds (2017), *Performance, Feminism and Affect in Neoliberal Times*, Basingstoke: Palgrave Macmillan.

Dolan, J. (1988), *The Feminist Spectator as Critic*, Ann Arbor: UMI Research Press.

Dolan, J. (2005), *Utopia in Performance: Finding Hope at the Theater*, Michigan: University of Michigan Press.

Dolan, J. (2013), *The Feminist Spectator in Action: Feminist Criticism for the Stage and Screen*, Basingstoke: Palgrave Macmillan.

Esslin, M. (1987), *The Field of Drama*, London: Methuen.

Finburgh, C. (2017), *Watching War on the Twenty-First Century Stage: Spectacles of Conflict*, London: Bloomsbury Methuen.

Fisher, T. (2017), 'Introduction: Performance and the Tragic Politics of the Agon', in T. Fisher and E. Katsouraki (eds), *Performing Antagonism: Theatre, Performance and Radical Democracy*, 1–24, Basingstoke: Palgrave Macmillan.

Fisher, T. and E. Katsouraki, eds (2017), *Performing Antagonism: Theatre, Performance and Radical Democracy*, Basingstoke: Palgrave Macmillan.

Ford, R. (2017), 'Nationalism, Referendums and Political Choice in England and Scotland: The Rise of Identity Politics and the Decline of Labour', The 2017 Mackenzie Lecture in Politics, University of Glasgow, 25 May. https://www.youtube.com/watch?v=nBU78xhnuZ8&feature=youtu.be.

Fragkou, M. (2018), *Ecologies of Precarity in Twenty-First Century Theatre: Politics, Affect, Responsibility*, London: Bloomsbury Methuen.

Freshwater, H. (2009), *theatre & audience*, Basingstoke: Palgrave Macmillan.

Frieze, J., ed. (2016), *Reframing Immersive Theatre: The Politics and Pragmatics of Participatory Performance*, Basingstoke: Palgrave Macmillan.

Gale, M. B. (2016), 'Introduction' to 'The Historical Avant-Garde: Performance and Innovation', in M. B. Gale and J. F. Deeney (eds), *The Routledge Drama Anthology: From Modernism to Contemporary Performance*, 2nd edn, 168–88, London and New York: Routledge.

Garde, U. and M. Mumford (2016), *Theatre of Real People: Diverse Encounters at Berlin's Hebbel am Ufer and Beyond*, London: Bloomsbury Methuen.

Gardner, L. (2013), 'Gym Party Review: Edinburgh Festival 2013', *Guardian*, 15 August. https://www.theguardian.com/stage/2013/aug/15/gym-party-edinburgh-2013-review.

Gardner, L. (2014), 'Edinburgh Festival 2014 Review: Confirmation – Chris Thorpe's Electrifying Monologue', *Guardian*, 1 August. https://www.theguardian.com/stage/2014/aug/01/edinburgh-festival-2014-confirmation-review-chris-thorpe.

Gauss, C. E. (1973), 'Empathy', in P. P. Wiener (ed.), *Dictionary of the History of Ideas: Studies of Selected Pivotal Ideas*, Vol. II, 85–9, New York: Charles Scribner's Sons.

Goffman, E. (1959), *The Presentation of Self in Everyday Life*, New York: Anchor Books.

Goode, C. (2011), 'The Audience Is Listening', *Contemporary Theatre Review*, 21 (4): 464–71.

Goode, C. (2014), *Men in the Cities*, London: Oberon.

Grazia Turri, M. (2017), *Acting, Spectating, and the Unconscious: A Psychoanalytic Perspective on Unconscious Processes of Identification in the Theatre*, London and New York: Routledge.

Grehan, H. (2009), *Performance, Ethics and Spectatorship in a Global Age*, Basingstoke: Palgrave Macmillan.

Grochala, S. (2017), *The Contemporary Political Play: Rethinking Dramaturgical Structure*, London: Bloomsbury Methuen.

Hall, S. (1980), 'Encoding/Decoding', in S. Hall, D. Hobson, A. Lowe and P. Willis (eds), *Culture, Media, Language*, 117–27, London: Hutchinson & Co.

Hallward, P. (2005), 'Jacques Rancière and the Subversion of Mastery', in M. Robson (ed.), *Jacques Rancière: Aesthetics, Politics, Philosophy*, 26–45, Edinburgh: Edinburgh University Press.

Hardt, M. and A. Negri (2000), *Empire*, Cambridge, MA: Harvard University Press.

Harvie, J. (2013), *Fair Play: Art, Performance and Neoliberalism*, Basingstoke: Palgrave Macmillan.

Heim, C. (2015), *Audience as Performer: The Changing Role of Theatre Audiences in the Twenty-First Century*, London and New York: Routledge.

Hill, L. (2018), 'Quality Metrics to Go Ahead under New Name', *Arts Professional*. https://www.artsprofessional.co.uk/news/quality-metrics-go-ahead-under-new-name.

Hill, L. and H. Paris (2014), *Performing Proximity: Curious Intimacies*, Basingstoke: Palgrave Macmillan.

Hillman, R. (2015), '(Re)constructing Political Theatre: Discursive and Practical Frameworks for Theatre as an Agent for Change', *New Theatre Quarterly*, 31 (4): 380–96.

Hoffman, M. (1990), 'The Contribution of Empathy to Justice and Moral Judgement', in N. Eisenberg and J. Strayer (eds), *Empathy and Its Development*, New York: Cambridge University Press.

Holland, G. S. (2000), *Divine Irony*, Pennsylvania: Susquehanna University Press.

Horkheimer, M. and T. Adorno (1997), *Dialectic of Enlightenment*, London: Verso Classics.

Hughes, J. (2011), *Performance in a Time of Terror: Critical Mimesis and the Age of Uncertainty*, Manchester: Manchester University Press.

Hughes, J. (2017), 'Notes on a Theatre Commons: Common Wealth's The Deal Versus the People (2015)', *Research in Drama Education: The Journal of Applied Theatre and Performance*, 22 (1): 76–91.

Hurley, E. (2010), *theatre & feeling*, Basingstoke: Palgrave Macmillan.

Hurley, K. (2016), *Heads Up*, Kindle Edition, London: Oberon books.

Hutcheon, L. (1994), *Irony's Edge: The Theory and Politics of Irony*, London and New York: Routledge.

Jameson, F. (2005), *Archaeologies of the Future: The Desire Called Utopia and Other Science Fictions*, London and New York: Verso.

Jeffers, A. (2012), *Refugees, Theatre and Crisis: Performing Global Identities*, Basingstoke: Palgrave Macmillan.

Jestrovic, S. (2015), 'Theatricality vs. Bare Life: Performance as a Vernacular of Resistance', in S. M. Rai and J. Reinelt (eds), *The Grammar of Politics and Performance*, 80–92, London and New York: Routledge.

Jürs-Munby, K., J. Carroll and S. Giles, eds (2013), *Postdramatic Theatre and the Political: International Perspectives on Contemporary Performance*, London: Bloomsbury Methuen.

Kelleher, J. (2009), *theatre & politics*, Basingstoke: Palgrave Macmillan.

Kelly, A. (2010), 'David Foster Wallace and the New Sincerity in American Fiction', in D. Hering (ed.), *Consider David Foster Wallace: Critical Essays*, 131–46, Los Angeles and Austin: Sideshow Media Group.

Kennedy, D. (2011), *The Spectator and the Spectacle: Audiences in Modernity and Postmodernity*, Cambridge: Cambridge University Press.

Kershaw, B. (1992), *The Politics of Performance: Radical Theatre as Cultural Intervention*, London and New York: Routledge.

Kester, G. H. (2004), *Conversation Pieces: Community + Communication in Modern Art*, Berkeley and London: University of California Press.

Laclau, E. and C. Mouffe ([1985] 2014), *Hegemony and Socialist Strategy: Towards a Radical Democratic Politics*, 2nd edn, London: Verso.

Latour, B. (2005), *Reassembling the Social: An Introduction to Actor-Network-Theory*, Oxford: Oxford University Press.

Lavender, A. (2016), *Performance in the Twenty-First Century: Theatres of Engagement*, London and New York: Routledge.

Lavery, C. (2016a), 'Introduction' to 'Late Modernism', in M. B. Gale and J. F. Deeney (eds), *The Routledge Drama Anthology: From Modernism to Contemporary Performance*, 2nd edn, 546–66, London and New York: Routledge.

Lavery, C. (2016b), 'Introduction: Performance and Ecology – What Can Theatre Do?', *Green Letters: Studies in Ecocriticism*, 20 (3): 229–36.

Lehmann, H. T. (2006), *Postdramatic Theatre*, trans. K. Jürs-Munby, London and New York: Routledge.

Lehmann, H. T. (2013), 'A Future for Tragedy? Remarks on the Political and the Postdramatic', in K. Jürs-Munby, K. J. Carroll and S. Giles (eds), *Postdramatic Theatre and the Political: International Perspectives on Contemporary Performance*, 87–110, London: Bloomsbury Methuen.

Lehmann, H. T. (2016), *Tragedy and Dramatic Theatre*, trans. E. Butler, London and New York: Routledge.

Lewis, J., S. Inthorn and K. Wahl-Jorgensen (2005), *Citizens or Consumers? What the Media Tell Us about Political Participation*, Maidenhead: Open University Press.

Lichtenfels, P. and J. Rouse, eds (2013), *Performance, Politics and Activism*, Basingstoke: Palgrave Macmillan.

Machamer, J., ed. (2018), *Immersive Theatre: Engaging the Audience*, Location: Common Ground Publishing.

Machon, J. (2009), *(Syn)aesthetics: Redefining Visceral Performance*, Basingstoke: Palgrave Macmillan.

Machon, J. (2013), *Immersive Theatres: Intimacy and Immediacy in Contemporary Performance*, Basingstoke: Palgrave Macmillan.

Malzacher, F. (2004), 'There Is a Word for People Like You: Audience: The Spectator as Bad Witness and Bad Voyeur', in J. Helmer and F. Malzacher (eds), *Not Even a Game Anymore*, 121–38, Berlin: Alexander Verlag.

Mason, P. (2015), *Postcapitalism: A Guide to Our Future*, Milton Keynes: Allen Lane.

May, T. (2016), Conference Speech, Conservative Party Conference, 5 October, Birmingham.

McConachie, B. (2008), *Engaging Audiences: A Cognitive Approach to Spectating in the Theatre*, Basingstoke: Palgrave Macmillan.

McConachie, B. (2013), 'Introduction: Spectating as Sandbox Play', in
   N. Shaughnessy (ed.), *Affective Performance and Cognitive Science*, 183–98,
   London: Bloomsbury Methuen.

McIvor, C. (2016), *Migration and Performance in Contemporary Ireland: Towards
   a New Interculturalism*, Basingstoke: Palgrave Macmillan.

McMillan, J. (2013), 'Gym Party/Holes', 24 August. https://joycemcmillan.
   wordpress.com/2013/08/24/page/2/

Meikle, G. (2016), *Social Media: Communication, Sharing and Visibility*, Kindle
   version, New York and London: Routledge.

Milling, J., ed. (2012), *Modern British Playwriting: The 1980s: Voices, Documents,
   New Interpretations*, London: Bloomsbury Methuen.

Mitter, S. (1992), *Systems of Rehearsal: Stanislavski, Brecht, Grotowski and Brook*,
   London: Routledge.

Mouffe, C. (2005), *The Democratic Paradox*, London and New York: Verso.

Mouffe, C. (2013), *Agonistics: Thinking the World Politically*, London and New
   York: Verso.

Moyn, S. (2006), 'Empathy in History, Empathizing with Humanity', *History and
   Theory*, 45 (3): 397–415.

Oliver, K. (2001), *Witnessing: Beyond Recognition*, Minneapolis: University of
   Minnesota Press.

Olson, G. (2013), *Empathy Imperiled: Capitalism, Culture and the Brain*, New
   York: Springer.

Orr, J. (2013), 'Edinburgh Fringe Review: Gym Party', *A Younger Theatre*,
   14 August. https://www.ayoungertheatre.com/edinburgh-fringe-review-
   gym-party/

Radbourne, J., K. Johanson and H. Glow, eds (2013), *The Audience Experience*,
   Bristol: Intellect.

Rai, S. M. and J. Reinelt, eds (2016), *The Grammar of Politics and Performance*,
   London and New York: Routledge.

Rancière, J. (1992), 'Politics, Identification and Subjectivization', *October*, 61:
   58–64.

Rancière, J. (2004), *The Politics of Aesthetics*, ed. and trans. G. Rockhill, London:
   Bloomsbury.

Rancière, J. (2009), *The Emancipated Spectator*, trans. G. Elliot, London: Verso.

Read, A. (2008), *Theatre, Intimacy and Engagement: The Last Human Venue*,
   Basingstoke: Palgrave Macmillan.

Reinelt, J. (2015), '"What I Came to Say": Raymond Williams, the Sociology
   of Culture and the Politics of (Performance) Scholarship', *Theatre Research
   International*, 40 (3): 235–49.

Reinelt, J., D. Edgar, C. Megson, D. Rebellato, J. Wilkinson and J. Woddis (2014),
   Critical Mass: Theatre Spectatorship and Value Attribution, London: The
   British Theatre Consortium.

Ridout, N. (2013), *Passionate Amateurs: Theatre, Communism, and Love*, Ann
   Arbor: University of Michigan Press.

Riff, D. and D. Vilensky (2009), 'From Communism to Commons?', *Third Text*, 23 (4): 465–80.

Roberts, J. (2009), 'Introduction: Art, "Enclave Theory" and the Communist Imaginary', *Third Text*, 23 (4): 353–67.

Rockhill, G. (2004a), 'Editor's Introduction: Jacques Rancière's Politics of Perception', in J. Rancière, *The Politics of Aesthetics*, ed. and trans. G. Rockhill, xii–xvii, London: Bloomsbury.

Rockhill, G. (2004b), 'Appendix I: Glossary of Technical Terms', in J. Rancière, *The Politics of Aesthetics*, ed. and trans. G. Rockhill, 83–98, London: Bloomsbury.

Rousseau, A. (2014), '"Didn't See Anything, Love. Sorry": Martin Crimp's Theatre of Denial', *Contemporary Theatre Review*, 24 (3): 342–52.

Saunders, G., ed. (2015), *British Theatre Companies 1980–1994*, London: Bloomsbury Methuen.

Schröder, K., K. Drotner, S. Kline and C. Murray, eds (2003), *Researching Audiences: A Practical Guide to Methods in Media Audience*, London: Bloomsbury Academic.

Sedgman, K. (2016), *Locating the Audience: How People Found Value in National Theatre Wales*, Bristol: Intellect.

Smith, A. (2014), 'What We Can Do with What We Have Got: A Dematerialised Theatre and Social and Political Change', unpublished PhD thesis, University of Lancaster.

Smith, A. (2015), *The Preston Bill*, London: Oberon.

Smith, A. (2018), *Summit*, London: Oberon.

Solnit, R. (2005), *Hope in the Dark*, Edinburgh: Canongate.

Spelman, E. V. (1997), *Fruits of Sorrow: Framing Our Attention to Suffering*, Boston: Beacon Press.

Staiger, J. (2005), *Media Reception Studies*, London and New York: New York University Press.

Stalpaert, C., K. Pewny, J. Coppens and P. Vermeulen, eds (2018), *Unfolding Spectatorship: Shifting Political, Ethical and Intermedial Positions*, Gent: Academia Press.

Standing, G. (2011), *The Precariat: The New Dangerous Class*, London: Bloomsbury Academic.

Staten, H. (1985), *Wittgenstein and Derrida*, Oxford: Basil Blackwell.

Svitch, C., ed. (2016), *Audience Revolution: Dispatches from the Field*, New York: Theatre Communications Group Inc.

Thompson, J. (2009), *Performance Affects: Applied Theatre and the End of Effect*, Basingstoke: Palgrave Macmillan.

Thorpe, C. (2014), *Confirmation*, London: Oberon.

Thrift, N. (2004), 'Intensities of Feeling: Towards a Spatial Politics of Affect', *Human Geography*, 86 (1): 57–78.

Thrift, N. (2008), *Non-Representational Theory: Space, Politics, Affect*, London: Routledge.

Tomlin, L. (2013), *Acts and Apparitions: Discourses on the Real in Performance Practice and Theory 1990–2010*, Manchester: Manchester University Press.

Tomlin, L. (2015), 'The Academy and the Marketplace: Avant-Garde Performance in Neoliberal Times', in K. Jannarone (ed.), *Vanguard Performance: Beyond Left and Right*, Ann Arbor: University of Michigan Press.

Van Oosten, R. (2014), 'Writing Music for *In the Republic of Happiness*', *Contemporary Theatre Review*, 24 (3): 411–12.

Villa, D. (1999), *Politics, Philosophy, Terror: Essays on the Thought of Hannah Arendt*, New York: Princeton University Press.

Wegner, D. M. (2002), *The Illusion of Conscious Will*, Cambridge, MA: MIT Press.

Westen, D. (2008), *The Political Brain: The Role of Emotion in Deciding the Fate of the Nation*, New York: Public Affairs.

Whalley, J. and L. Miller (2017), *Between Us: Audiences, Affect and the In-Between*, Basingstoke: Palgrave Macmillan.

White, G. (2013), *Audience Participation in Theatre: Aesthetics of the Invitation*, Basingstoke: Palgrave Macmillan.

Wickstrom, M. (2006), *Performing Consumers: Global Capital and Its Theatrical Seductions*, London and New York: Routledge.

Wickstrom, M. (2012), *Performance in the Blockades of Neoliberalism: Thinking the Political Anew*, Basingstoke: Palgrave Macmillan.

Wilmer, S. E. (2018), *Performing Statelessness in Europe*, Basingstoke: Palgrave Macmillan.

Zaroulia, M. and P. Hager, eds (2015), *Performances of Capitalism, Crises and Resistance: Inside/Outside Europe*, Basingstoke: Palgrave Macmillan.

Žižek, S. (1994), 'The Spectre of Ideology', in S. Žižek (ed.), *Mapping Ideology*, London and New York: Verso.

Žižek, S. (2004), 'The Lesson of Rancière', in *The Politics of Aesthetics*, ed. and trans. G. Rockhill, 65–75, London: Bloomsbury.

Žižek, S. (2005), *Interrogating the Real*, ed. and trans. R. Butler and S. Stephens, London and New York: Continuum.

Index

Note: Locators with the letter 'n' refer to notes.